ADVANCE PRAISE

"I anticipate *Going on Offense: A Leader's Playbook for Perpetual Innovation* will quickly become required reading in boardrooms and classrooms around the world."

—RON JOHNSON, Senior Vice President of Apple and pioneer of
Apple store under Steve Jobs, 2000–2011; CEO of JCPenney, 2011–
2013; Board Member of Ermenegildo Zegna Group, 2019–Present

"Behnam Tabrizi and I both started our careers at IBM, and it's been exciting to see him become an expert on organizational and leadership transformation and trusted advisor to more than 100 companies. *Going on Offense* is full of practical and actionable solutions for unlocking game-changing innovation. It should be required reading for companies of all sizes."

—MAYNARD WEBB, Former Chief Operating Officer
of eBay, Director at Salesforce and Visa, Founder of the
Webb Investment Network, and bestselling author

"Based on practical lessons from the most innovative companies, Behnam Tabrizi provides a well-researched playbook for organizations looking to enhance their culture while adapting to new challenges and expanding into new markets. *Going on Offense: A Leader's Playbook for Perpetual Innovation* is rich with actionable insights to help you drive innovation in your organization."

—HAMID MOGHADAM, Cofounder, CEO, and Chairman
of Prologis, the world's largest industrial landlord

"As a former student and researcher for Professor Tabrizi at Stanford, I have applied many of the practical toolkits of his earlier books, especially *Rapid Transformation*, throughout my career. In his latest book, *Going on Offense*, his keen game-changing insights outline critical frameworks and blueprints for any manager or executive that wants to keep their company ahead in a rapidly accelerating world."

—DREW BENNETT, Tesla Head of Global Charging reporting
to Elon Musk, 2018–2020; Executive Vice President of Network
Operations, Volta Charging, recently sold to Shell Global

"I have known Behnam for the better part of a decade from since I introduced the "Strategic Execution Framework" I had studied at Stanford as the key management system into the European Parliament. Behnam is a prolific thinker and writer. *Going on Offense* will give you the best of his in-depth knowledge about very successful companies and leaders making agility their reality."

—KLAUS WELLE, Secretary General of the European Parliament, 2009–2022

"Behnam Tabrizi offers us a comprehensive playbook for how people and organizations must work in the modern economy. Unlike the many management books that focus on a single important topic like purpose, *Going on Offense* brings it all together—purpose, agility, leadership, ambidexterity, radical collaboration, and more—presenting a treasure chest of practical insights for companies that are serious about thriving in a turbulent future."

—AMY EDMONDSON, Professor at Harvard Business School and author of *Right Kind of Wrong: The Science of Failing Well*

"I expect *Going on Offense: A Leader's Playbook for Perpetual Innovation* to quickly become required reading for entrepreneurs, CEOs, and boardrooms."

—ARASH FERDOWSI, Cofounder of Dropbox

"Behnam Tabrizi knows the key to some of the most successful companies in the world is unleashing human magic to inspire innovation. Companies like Apple, Starbucks, and Microsoft have done so successfully, and in *Going on Offense*, you'll hear the lessons that helped them stay agile and tap into the power of their teams. These lessons gained from years of Tabrizi's own research at Stanford, through his teaching and consulting with various companies, can be applied to organizations of all sizes and used by leaders at all levels. This book is a must-read for creating the right innovative culture."

—HUBERT JOLY, Senior Lecturer at Harvard Business School, former Chairman and CEO of Best Buy, and bestselling author of *The Heart of Business: Leadership Principles for the Next Era of Capitalism*

"Behnam Tabrizi is a guru of transformation and innovation. *Going on Offense* brings it to the next level with detailed actions companies can take to achieve perpetual innovation, which is becoming a necessity since new and faster competitors are showing up every day."

—SPENCER FUNG, Group Executive Chairman of Li & Fung

"Behnam Tabrizi has written a must-read primer for anyone considering transforming their organization into a perpetual innovator. . . . Read this book and learn from the best."

—DAN WALKER, Chief Talent Officer at Apple, under Steve Jobs, 2000–2005; Chief Talent Officer at JCPenney, 2011–2013

"A rich and actionable compendium on sustaining innovation in large enterprises, *Going on Offense* fills a critical gap in the literature on leadership and organizational management."

—LILY SARAFAN, Cofounder and Executive Chair of TheKey, Board Member at Stanford University, Instacart, and Thumbtack

"After reading Professor Behnam's book, I can relate my experience observing the author's work with our commercial bank in Thailand to his belief that culture drives transformation and innovation. We have hired many renowned consultants to help us transform our bank to cope with rapidly changing industry forces. Professor Behnam's approach and his commitment to implementation set him apart from our other advisors. By the end of his transformation coaching, he had us all believing that empowerment is a critical success factor in creating an agile culture that puts clients' needs at the center of every innovation. This book is the definite innovation playbook."

—KATTIYA INDARAVIJAYA, CEO of Kasikornbank, Thailand's second largest commercial lender and ranked #1 in digital banking services

"When it comes to transformation, Behnam Tabrizi is the best of guides. His work is based on deep research, powerful human connections, and insights gathered from the world's leading organizations. *Going on Offense* is required and inspiring reading."

—STUART CRAINER, Cofounder of Thinkers50

"Behnam Tabrizi has written a well-researched book that provides a practical playbook on how to turn your organization and employees into perpetual innovators. I highly recommend this book."

"*Going on Offense* provides a practical blueprint and timely shift to the winning mindset and practices that enable best-in-class organizational innovation and transformation. I'm done playing not to lose, and I'm grateful for Dr. Tabrizi's playbook guiding my improvement journey."

Going On Offense

Going On Offense

A Leader's Playbook for Perpetual Innovation

Behnam Tabrizi

IDEAPRESS
PUBLISHING

WASHINGTON, DC

IDEAPRESS
PUBLISHING

Printed in the United States

Ideapress Publishing | www.ideapresspublishing.com

All trademarks are the property of their respective companies.

Cover Design: Pete Garceau
Interior Design: Jessica Angerstein

Cataloging-in-Publication Data is on file with the Library of Congress.

Hardcover ISBN: 978-1-64687-137-7

Special Sales
Ideapress Books are available at a special discount for bulk purchases for sales promotions and premiums, or for use in corporate training programs. Special editions, including personalized covers, a custom foreword, corporate imprints, and bonus content, are also available.

1 2 3 4 5 6 7 8 9 10

Contents

Preface i

Chapter 1 Introduction: Seeing the Challenge 1

PART ONE
Generous

Chapter 2 Setting an Existential Purpose: Why Does
Your Company Matter? 21

Chapter 3 Customer Obsession 43

Chapter 4 Pygmalion 61

PART TWO
Ferocious

Chapter 5 The Start-Up Mindset 83

Chapter 6 Managing the Tempo of Change 103

Chapter 7 Bimodal 123

PART THREE
Courageous

Chapter 8 Go Boldly 147

Chapter 9 Radical Collaboration 167

Chapter 10 Putting It All Together 189

About the Author 213

Endnotes 215

Index 229

To my mom, Nahid, my perpetual cheerleader

Preface

How do you transform a typical organization into one that is *perpetually* agile, innovative, and fast-paced, and crackles with heightened expectations and intensity?

I thought I already had the complete answer to that question.

After all, for over twenty-five years I've taught organizational transformation at Stanford University in its Executive Program, which I direct. I teach a popular course on leading organizational transformation, and I have a busy consulting practice, having advised over one hundred companies in planning, mobilizing, and implementing major changes. I've studied over one thousand organizational transformations. Moreover, I've written nine books, including the popular book *Rapid Transformation* (HBR Press, 2007), with an action plan to quickly overhaul organizations into agile innovative ones. I'm also a coauthor of the international bestseller *The Inside-Out Effect* (Evolve, 2013), which guides business leaders in personal transformation so they can direct organizational change. When used together, these two books become a winning "secret sauce" that enables companies to become more agile, innovative, and entrepreneurial.

However, it took a random business dinner to make me realize that I was missing a critical piece.

In the winter of 2014, I was sitting across the table from Hans Vestberg, then CEO of telecommunications giant Ericsson. (Today he is CEO of Verizon.) We knew each other because I planned and directed a customized Stanford Executive Program and taught its classes in organizational leadership and transformation, and Hans had sent 70 of his top executives to our program and was planning to send another 150. After a couple of glasses of wine, I asked him why he had chosen Stanford. He replied that he wanted his people to learn from the most innovative and agile companies in the world, and most of them were based in Silicon Valley. He wanted his executives immersed in the business culture that had produced Apple, Tesla, Amazon, Cisco, and others.

He confided that he hoped his people would return with the lessons they had learned at Stanford and transform Ericsson's culture into a more innovative corporation that could pivot rapidly to new opportunities.

I left the dinner struck by Hans's comment that he wanted his executives to "learn from the best." It sent my mind spinning. What, I wondered, would you find if you took a deep dive into the most innovative companies, the ones with what I call the *winning mindset*: a dedication to perpetual innovation and relentless experimentation that runs through the entire organization, top to bottom? Could I discover, through analysis, the key ingredients that enable these types of firms to pull this off?

I couldn't stop thinking about this line of inquiry. I was not satisfied with the previous studies on agility and innovation. I also realized that the results of this research would fill in what was missing from my first two books on the subject.

Rapid Transformation offers a blueprint to boost an organization's agility and innovation. It's a practical methodology to quickly pivot large organizations and their key leaders across ranks, like a tanker ship, toward a new North Star. But the book lacks a way to spread the new mindset throughout the organization and permanently shift the culture. *The Inside-Out Effect* improves upon its predecessor by laying out the means for imbuing change to culture by personally transforming its people. And it focuses on the leaders and employees. Nevertheless, even the combined effect of these two books does not guarantee that the organization stays agile and innovates perpetually beyond a couple of years—it also needs a strong foundation.

Going on Offense is the third leg of the stool, completing my efforts to provide practical, actionable advice on how an organization can attain and *sustain* what was once known as the Silicon Valley mindset, and thus lock in perpetual agility and innovation. With this book, a company will be able to go on offense, continually adapting to new environments and expanding into new territories—and perhaps minimizing the need for another radical transformation.

Starting in 2015, I enlisted a dozen talented students at Stanford as well as three who had graduated from the school to help me conduct a comprehensive study of some of the most innovative and agile companies around the world.

Based on a survey of 6,873 global executives, academics, and consumers, we took a deep dive into twenty-six companies, including Amazon, Apple, Tesla, Microsoft, AMD, Bumble, Etsy, Unilever, Netflix, Haier, Intel, DBS Bank, KBank (Thailand), Starbucks, Zara, SpaceX, Nike, Next, Barnes & Noble, and California's Santa Clara County (our lone public institution). Some were failures; we examined Blockbuster, Borders, Kodak, and Nokia to determine the characteristics those firms lacked that could explain their inability to transform. We also addressed companies that are struggling lately, such as Peloton and Facebook. Stories from all twenty-six companies are sprinkled throughout this book.

The framework, however, ended up drawing heavily on just five of those organizations. The book highlights the similarities and differences among their five cultures, which, interestingly, mirror the five icons of industry who are leading or led them: Steve Jobs (Apple), Elon Musk (Tesla), Jeff Bezos (Amazon), Howard Schultz (Starbucks), and Satya Nadella (Microsoft).

We selected the five centerpiece companies based on our global survey ranking the most perpetually innovative organizations in the world. Incidentally, these five companies have also significantly outperformed the S&P 500 in the past twenty years. While their leaders are hardly perfect (both Elon Musk and Steve Jobs can/could be highly erratic and abrasive to colleagues), nevertheless, I hope you walk away with actionable lessons from each company example.

It's important to note that most of the selected companies are far from Silicon Valley, and some are not tech firms. They simply share a mentality that prioritizes agility and innovation. And being in Silicon Valley doesn't guarantee that mentality, as firms that once epitomized the place, such as Facebook and Google, are discovering in their current struggles. Further, the successful companies we studied differ substantially from each other. We focused on what was similar while still discussing those differences. We found that perpetually innovative organizations were always on offense—on the lookout for innovation and opportunities to improve. They had developed a culture of agility.

You may be skeptical that this book can offer you methods that can vault your organization to the heights of the ultra-successful companies described herein. I want to say emphatically that is not the point of *Going on Offense*. The point is improvement, not copycat performance. In truth, 99 percent of firms around the world don't fit into the category of achievement that Apple, Starbucks, Tesla, Microsoft, or Amazon have attained. And that's OK. Whether you're a frontline employee, a middle manager, an executive, or a CEO, this book is designed to show you the key characteristics and give you practical steps so that you and your organization, or the area you control, can reach your full potential. And remember, even a 10 percent or 20 percent improvement in agility and innovation will improve your bottom line and set you toward a culture that will benefit everyone in your organization.

When I was twenty-two years old, I had finished my masters in computer science and taken a position at IBM's Research Center. I was working on improving the manufacturing process at IBM, and I came up with a related idea. It wasn't directly tied to my job, but it was something that the company could easily implement, and it could save millions of dollars. My manager declined to pass on my idea, sat me down, and said, "Behnam, IBM is like a big log, if you will, going down a slow-moving river. You and I are a couple of small ants on this log, and we're barely trying to survive."

As you can imagine, this twenty-two-year-old just shrank and shrank as he heard about what this organization was all about. That became the defining moment of my life. I wanted to spend the rest of my life helping people connect to their power. I decided to help transform organizations with a total of one hundred million people so they could connect to their power. Too often big ideas require big people; small companies are organizations with figuratively big people, but as they grow, people feel less visible and less heard. They lose interest in the company's challenges unless they are directly accountable. This book is a kind of culminating effort to help change that dynamic.

Before you turn the page (and I hope that you are eager to do so), I would like to thank all the people who made *Going on Offense* possible. First and foremost, I thank my wife, Nazanin, for her unflagging support and encouragement from the moment I came up with the idea for this book, through the years of research, and up through publication. Nazanin, this book would not be here without you.

I also thank the Brightline Initiative (part of the Project Management Institute) and all the PMI leaders—especially Ricardo Vargas and Tahirou Assane—who helped me combine the essence of *Rapid Transformation* and *The Inside-Out Effect* into a streamlined booklet, "The Transformation Compass." These two former students of mine generously shared this booklet with their two million members and had it covered in *The Economist*. They have been longtime cheerleaders of my ideas and have been instrumental in spreading my approaches throughout the world.

I would have been in trouble from the beginning if not for Nadia Mufti, a graduate of the Stanford School of Design. She helped me enormously in the early research and coding of *Going on Offense*. Also, it was her idea to add the start-up mindset as a category, so thank you for that as well. And much thanks to Benny Banerjee, who introduced Nadia to me.

I can't say enough about my phenomenal Stanford research team, led by Callie McKenna Rosenthal, who demonstrated exceptional leadership skills throughout the project. Thanks to the other members of the team: Parker Thomas Kasiewicz, Parthav Shergill, Matthew Macario Yekell, Vivian Urness-Galindo, and Lauren Taylor, who are all absolutely brilliant and made excellent contributions to this book. Further, Andrew LaForge, Alex Avery, Tara Viswanathan, Toby Espinoza, and Michael Terrell also contributed to this research and earlier works. I'd also like to thank Bonnie Chan, who not only assisted me with my previous work but also helped keep me and the research team focused.

A huge thank-you to the brilliant Stuart Crainer, cofounder of Thinkers50 (considered the Oscars for management), who initially interviewed me on this research. His incisive questions deepened the book's content. I'm also grateful to Karen Christensen, chief editor of *Rotman Management Magazine,* for her follow-up to Stuart's Q&A.[1]

Many thanks to my magnificent editor John Landry (formerly of *Harvard Business Review*), who dived into my early drafts and initiated numerous inspiring conversations with me about both content and direction. I'd also like to thank my publisher, Rohit Bhargava, cofounder of Ideapress, for always being there for insightful advice and for sharing my enthusiasm for this book.

I am extremely grateful for the business leaders with whom I have had the privilege of working closely; they have made a profound impact on my life. First and foremost, the late Andy Grove, CEO of Intel, who took a chance on an energetic and curious graduate who had just been awarded his doctorate; his faith in me helped lay the foundation for both design thinking and agile development. He hired me to train seven thousand Intel executives and mid-level managers around the globe on product development innovation and agility. From that experience, I learned what it's like to run a fast-paced organization that embraces many of Silicon Valley's cultural values, such as effective meeting practices, the decision-making process, and a culture of constructive conflict that encourages the airing of all ideas. I stopped working with Intel in the late 1990s; after Grove's death in 2016, Intel slowly reverted to a bureaucratic organization in need of transformation back to its roots.

The leader who has perhaps had the biggest impact on me is David House, executive vice president of Intel, who left in 1996 to become chairman and CEO of Bay Networks. There, he presided over one of the most successful organizational transformations in Silicon Valley's history: profits increased twentyfold and market value by fivefold to nearly $10 billion. He brought me in, and I basically slept in a sleeping bag in my office while I assisted in that transformation. He was a master of cultural change, and many subsequent leaders in Silicon Valley were his protégés: Maynard Webb, a former chief operating officer of eBay, and Lloyd Carney, CEO at a number of high-profile networking and telecom firms. Working with executives and senior managers from global organizations with market caps above a trillion dollars has been a highlight of my career. Through these experiences, I have gained a deep understanding of their transformation and rapid growth. In my book, I discuss several of these organizations and the valuable lessons I learned. I am grateful for the opportunity to contribute to their success.

I'd also like to thank Khun Suphachai Chearavanont, CEO of C.P. Group, and the top leaders at Kasikornbank (Kbank), including Khun Banthoon Lamsam, chairman emeritus; Khun Kattiya Indaravijaya, CEO; and Khun Patchara Samalapa, president, for teaching me to balance the Silicon Valley culture with one that commits to all its full-time employees. My proudest experience was working with Khun Patchara in transforming a twelve-thousand-employee traditional retail organization into a nimble Silicon Valley digital culture that met or surpassed all its objectives and has won many awards.

I would also like to thank Spencer Fung, group executive chairman of Li & Fung, who has been a great supporter of my transformation work within Li & Fung's manufacturing, retail, and finance divisions. Special thanks to Ed Lam, former CFO of Li & Fung, headquartered in Hong Kong, who in 2017 won the Asset CFO of the Year award for our successful efforts in applying the Rapid Transformation and Inside-Out methodologies to the finance organization of this $18-billion company with operations in 40 countries. Ed is currently the founder and CEO of LFX and is digitally transforming the retail industry. Dr. Peter Bertke, a nephrologist who attended my executive class at Stanford, also applied these concepts in 2018 to transform the most prestigious private Swiss hospital group, Hirslanden, into the most efficient acute care hospital group in Switzerland. He is currently working his magic at several public hospitals. Professor Oriol Amat, former dean of UPF Barcelona School of Management, also applied these methodologies in transforming the school in 2020 and was subsequently promoted; since then, he has been successfully employing the same techniques as the rector, president, of UPF. We have published several cases on this that can be accessed through European Case Clearing House.

Many thanks to Vernon Irvin, a serial star CEO and a friend with whom I have enjoyed several transformation project collaborations. It was a great pleasure to work with Irvin to transform the largest division within Verisign from a $380-million failing organization into a nimble, thriving, $1-billion division in two years. My close friend and former client, Faraj Aalaei, who has led two successful Silicon Valley IPOs, has also been a kindred spirit and intellectual partner during my entire journey, including this book. Finally, I wish to express my gratitude to the people who lead Santa Clara County, especially CEO Dr. Jeff Smith, Leslie Crowell, Megan Doyle, James Williams, Greta Hansen, Rene Santiago, Paul Lorenz, Dr. Sanjay Kurani, Dr. Cliff Wang, and all the great leaders and individual contributors I had the privilege of working with. They and countless others gave me the opportunity to apply my expertise to the public sector. Since our work together, I am proud to say that Santa Clara County has become the model for major transformation, saving tens of thousands of lives during the COVID-19 pandemic and reducing costs by more than $450 million across various departments while improving employee and customer satisfaction. It is deeply humbling to see that many leaders who worked with me earlier on various transformation efforts are currently the top executives of Santa Clara County.

Now you can turn the page . . .

CHAPTER ONE

Introduction:
Seeing the Challenge

Have you ever watched the television series *See* on Apple TV+? It takes place in the distant future, long after a deadly virus has decimated humankind. Those who survived became blind. Now, centuries later, the idea of sight is considered a myth. But then twins are born who can see just as their ancestors did. They become targets of members of the tribe who fear what "seeing" will bring.

Likewise, many leaders treat the idea that large organizations can transform into perpetually innovative firms as a myth, a fanciful story from a distant past. Even tech companies that used to be nimble in the 2000s, such as Facebook and Google, are now a shadow of their former, stunningly innovative, selves. JD Ross, cofounder of Opendoor, tweeted that "Google's greatest evil is grooming brilliant twenty-two-year-olds into becoming complacent careerists instead of ambitious founders who might one day compete with them." In response, Tesla chief Elon Musk tweeted that "most big companies in tech have turned into places where talent goes to die."[2]

Likewise, in 2013, soon after Microsoft acquired his company, Nokia's CEO Stephen Elop ended his speech saying, "We didn't do anything wrong, but somehow, we lost."[3] It was a devastating end to a company that had a major share of mobile phones before Apple's entry in 2007. Nokia's laser focus on operational metrics, combined with its failure to cultivate a cultural transformation, and a lack of courageous and innovative products that customers would love, led to its downfall. In other words, the world changed, and Nokia failed to change accordingly. That was a decade ago. As I was completing this book in 2023, impressive advances in artificial intelligence were adding yet another disruption to many markets. Agile innovation is becoming more important than ever—and further out of reach for complacent giants.

This begs the question: Can any sizable firm see a way to course correct and make the myth real again?

Few executives would object to their companies becoming agile innovators—which I define as always being on the lookout to reimagine and implement new processes, partnerships, products, markets, and services and improve existing ones. Innovation is essential in order to thrive in our increasingly disruptive markets. Agility is necessary to move quickly to address opportunities and threats. Agility in this book does not refer to software methodology—as Steve Denning has pointed out, "Agile has sometimes become a pretext for the creation of sweatshops."[4] Instead, I'm focusing on agile as a mindset first and a critical element of a perpetually innovative culture that responds quickly to change. Thus, I use agile innovation and perpetual innovation interchangeably in this book.

The impediments are daunting. First, bureaucratic companies must contend with the legacy of the twentieth-century definition of success. Back then, they were rewarded for making quality goods at scale at an affordable price. They quite understandably hired bureaucrats to fulfill this goal. Innovation fell victim to predictable marketing and incremental improvements, both of which produced the steady growth that management and Wall Street craved. Companies jettisoned agility in favor of a massive, complex structure that, like an ocean liner, can't turn on a dime.

Besides the inertia of size and complexity, human nature is the main obstacle to change. First off, people are conditioned to give away their own power. From being entirely dependent as infants, to partially dependent as we grow into adulthood, we are tempted to continue that pattern. We often abdicate our own thinking to the books we read and the lectures we hear; we leave the dictates of morality to religious leaders and our diet to doctors.[5] Essentially, we're too afraid to think for ourselves. In the workplace, we're comfortable ceding our power to the bureaucratic hierarchy so we can settle into a predictable, stable set of routines and tasks.

Second, it is human nature to be self-interested and proud. Most managers in large companies have a touch of that, making them embrace command and control, and care about maintaining their fiefdoms and perquisites.

Third, people tend to commit themselves and resist change when they have invested significant resources in a project or strategic direction. They persist in the sunk cost fallacy even if abandoning that course of action makes long-term financial sense.

Finally, the sort of change that can break through the inertia of tradition takes tremendous resolve. Agility and innovation require a kind of alertness and flexibility that demands enormous mental and physical effort. It's exhausting just talking about it. And it definitely requires more energy than most people want to devote to their work.

What Perpetual Innovation Really Takes

From the above, you might conclude that transforming big companies is a nearly impossible task. Some books in circulation insist that human nature can change. In their view, people can simply set aside their pettiness, dismantle their command-and-control structures and dedicate themselves to work for the good of investors and consumers.

I've been hearing this argument for decades, ever since I began teaching and consulting in the mid-1990s. I live in Silicon Valley, where the rallying cries have been the worst, full of techno-optimism and gleeful ignorance of how big companies actually work. Command and control still reigns, yet evangelists keep agitating for a fully decentralized utopia of autonomous organizations. And now those same people believe that the pandemic, the

Great Resignation, and quiet quitting will act as a turning point and deliver their utopian vision.

It's not going to happen. Not that way.

But I assure you, transforming big companies is not an impossible dream. It's definitely hard—and it takes a lot more than a CEO's inspiring speech or other company rhetoric to get people to transform their organizations. They need a holistic approach that instills the discipline and generates the emotional energy necessary to thrive in a time of disruption. Leaders have to put aside personal wishes and transform for a larger purpose. In other words, they must open their eyes and "see" that they can't continue with business as usual.

Ironically, one excellent example of a driver for change comes from way back in 1977. Rob Strasser, Nike's first head of marketing, issued an internal memo entitled "Principles."[6] On one page, he laid out all of the principles. They didn't come from current operations. Rather, it reflected Strasser's gut feeling that these principles should guide the perspective of the Nike organization.

1. Our business is change.

2. We're on offense. All the time.

3. Perfect results count -- not a perfect process.
   Break the rules: fight the law.

4. This is as much about battle as about business.

5. Assume nothing.
   Make sure people keep their promises.
   Push yourselves push others.
   Stretch the possible.

6. Live off the land.

7. Your job isn't done until <u>the</u> job is done.

8. <u>Dangers</u>
   Bureaucracy
   Personal ambition
   Energy takers vs. energy givers
   Knowing our weaknesses
   Don't get too many things on the platter

9. It won't be pretty.

10. If we do the right things we'll make money damn
    near automatic.

These principles resonate on a visceral level, and they underscore the role emotions play in the process of change. Too many authors think we can do away with human nature, that companies can expect employees to drop their petty self-interest and collaborate in service to consumers and society. But if you're going to do away with one emotion, you have to replace it with another. Otherwise people will rationally decide to just work for bureaucracies.

Just look at the history of most great companies, including in Silicon Valley. You'll discover that the founder, and often the subsequent leaders, were hardly the super-rational creators they often portrayed themselves to be. They would like you to think that they approached a particular market, saw how to solve its problems, and then overcame the challenges standing in the way of that solution. There's some truth in that description, but their emotional commitments, along with a variety of odd quirks and even sometimes their extreme behavior, were crucial to their success.

Take Steve Jobs as a shining example, especially in his second reign at Apple. In his first reign, he was the opposite of the prevailing model of a successful CEO. He was rude, obnoxious, arrogant, narcissistic, and paranoid. Even in a largely sympathetic account, his biographer Walter Isaacson asserted that "driven by demons, he could push those around him to fury and despair . . . his personality and passions and products were all interrelated."

The company Jobs cofounded and the directors he picked eventually fired him because they believed his obsessions were running Apple into the ground. Yet the experienced corporate bureaucrats who succeeded him failed to revive operations, and in desperation, Apple's board hired him back.

It turned out the pain and hardship he suffered during his post-Apple stint at Next transformed Jobs's personality. He became more empathic while retaining his passion and ambition. This "new" Jobs was also much clearer about where he wanted to steer Apple.

When he returned as CEO in 1997, the company was nearly bankrupt, and Jobs had to make decisions that would determine Apple's survival. He proceeded to transform the company along many dimensions, completely revamping the board of directors and canceling products and projects in which his predecessors had invested millions of dollars. This time, the changes worked, and the company came up with breathtaking innovations that gave customers what they didn't realize they wanted. When Jobs stepped down as CEO in 2011, Apple had become the most valuable company in the world—which it remains twelve years later.

That emotions such as passion, energy, obsession, and ambition were vital ingredients in Apple's success is no accident. Building an innovative organization, whether from a transformed bureaucracy or from scratch, takes enormous work. It's also quite risky; many of these efforts go nowhere. If you're merely a capable, highly rational person interested in a stable business, you're better off joining an established company and dealing with the hierarchy. But if you feel a deep-seated drive to create an enterprise for unmet needs in the marketplace and to realize your vision free from the dictates of superiors, you should choose an agile innovator. And that's important because, in addition to being hyper-rational, you're going to need all the emotion you can muster to sustain yourself and your organization in the tough beginnings.

Coming Up with the Key Elements

From my experience and the interviews and surveys I've conducted using my large professional network, I came up with thirty-seven qualities that a large company needs, in both its leaders and its employees, to become perpetually innovative. To confirm that my hunches held up in the real world, I assembled a team of a dozen researchers comprised of current and former Stanford graduate students, researchers with doctorates, and a former editor of the *Harvard Business Review*. We chose fifty-two companies that experienced either high growth, average growth, or major decline sometime between 2006 and 2022. This period deliberately included multiple eras: prerecession, the great financial crisis, the post-crisis period of growth, prepandemic, pandemic, and shortly after the pandemic.

The team—based on a survey of 6,873 global executives, academics, and consumers—narrowed the list to twenty-six firms, grouped into high, medium, and low degrees of agility and innovation. Then we gathered credible accounts of those companies from published articles and books. In addition, we interviewed dozens of managers and other employees from each company. Finally, we coded all this data, several thousand pages worth, according to those criteria.

We then performed regression, pairwise analysis, and cluster analysis to determine what separated the best from the worst-performing organizations. In order to verify the results derived from our regression, pairwise and cluster analyses, a separate team used another research approach created by my PhD advisor, Kathleen Eisenhardt. It's called *multi-case theory building*, which starts by picking a driver you're studying, such as fast decision-making in an organization. First, you do a deep dive into one case to come up with an explanation for what drives fast decision-making. Then you dive into a second case, and then a third, and so on. We examined a case study for each of our companies. Once you derive these explanations, you need to find the commonality among them. Perhaps several cases have substantial overlap. You still must arrive at an explanation that satisfies *each* case. To do that, you must increase the level of abstraction, which means you simplify the complex elements of your explanations iteratively until you arrive at a unified answer.

As with any research, distinctions across some categories can be fuzzy. We road-tested the integrity of these categories with managers in eight companies. The results held up, but we adjusted the wording of the categories to make sure our descriptions reflected their distinctiveness.

Going on Offense lays out those drivers and how they propel an organization to transform. It starts with *existentialism*, not as philosophy but as a commitment to a meaningful purpose that gives the organization and its employees both its reason for existing and its North Star for decisions. Such employees' passion usually leads to *customer obsession*, which entails sometimes following their customers' wishes and other times empathetically imagining what those customers would value. This type of obsession is the best way to realize the company's purpose.

Those two elements in turn create a *Pygmalion effect*, in the sense that the leaders influence most people in the organization to adopt that purpose and mindset. That's essential because one leader can't directly influence enough people to move an organization to overcome the challenges of achieving innovation. You need to create a culture that promotes your ideal employee, just as the sculptor Pygmalion did when he created his future spouse.

Then I add the *start-up mindset*, which impels companies—especially their leaders—to put aside normal calculations of profitability and work zealously for the purpose described above. The actual founder may have retired or died long ago, but the current leaders behave like missionaries, not mercenaries, in pursuit of their goal.

However, organizations need to conserve energy for that start-up mindset. That means *managing tempo*, preparing slowly and deliberately for their next move, then proceeding quickly to seize the opportunity as it emerges. Conserving energy also means *working bimodally*, with one part of the organization producing incremental improvements while the other chases experimental possibilities; both modes are essential to sustained success. Here as well, organizations need to disrupt the normal human tendency to approach all tasks with the same speed and creativity.

With this purpose, mindset, and culture—as opposed to rational directives—the company creates the passion to *move boldly*. That passion generates a restless striving that pushes people to overcome the ever-present temptation to value sunk costs or to seek growth that may be easy and profitable but weakens quality.

That boldness also leads to *radical collaboration*, in which people are so crazed with passion that they dare to work with others outside their own silos. Ordinary, rational people would rather stick with the people they know, but companies that are perpetually innovative transcend that impulse.

To achieve agility and innovation, a company cannot rely on creating a sense of urgency or communicating its goals repeatedly; leaders must dig deep and commit themselves, and the organization, to a rigorous process. The transformation they need requires relentless discipline, powered by the courage and resilience that only come from deep emotional commitment.

The eight elements mentioned above explain most, but not all, of what drove the impressive success of the highly innovative firms we studied. Underscoring the importance of these eight elements, as some or all fell away, the corresponding companies struggled.

Six Other Characteristics for Perpetual Innovation

Nevertheless, our research and analysis unearthed six other interesting characteristics that also contribute to perpetual innovation within an organization. These six are sprinkled in varying degrees throughout the following eight chapters.

The first of these is to be *meta-agile*, which is the ability to change your perspective from big picture to close attention to detail, and to do it quickly as needed. In her *Harvard Business Review* article, Rosabeth Moss Kanter labels these two distinct viewpoints "zooming out" and "zooming in."[7] *Meta* refers to the company's leaders and employees all having the ability to see the big picture on any given issue. That implies that the firm empowers and encourages all its members, regardless of their place in the hierarchy, to get out of the weeds and know the business thoroughly. Such an environment gives everyone a stake in the firm's mission, and the incentive to accomplish it. In contrast, a company that compartmentalizes the big picture perspective ends up with leaders who become controlling and tactical, and employees who become nothing more than cogs in a wheel.

The *agile* part of meta-agile refers to the ability to switch easily from the big picture to close detail. That ensures a comprehensive view of the current opportunity or threat, which leads to better adaptation in the face of uncertainty. For example, such a company can adapt to changing modes of work, such as remote versus in-office, in response to a pandemic. In contrast, a firm that doesn't value agility discourages people from taking initiative, even when they see solutions. Instead, leaders play politics, saying the right things but avoiding doing anything that will get them in trouble.

Another characteristic is *first principles*, a way of thinking that challenges your assumptions until you reach the fundamental truths about a situation. The questions that you keep asking include (1) Why do I believe this assumption? (2) What is the counterargument to this belief? (3) How can I prove my belief? and (4) What are the consequences of holding on to this belief if I'm wrong? Eventually, you strip away the assumptions that are standing in the way of innovation.

In one of his articles on this characteristic, author James Clear gives the potent example of Elon Musk pursuing his goal of sending the first rocket to Mars: "He ran into a major challenge right off the bat . . . [when he] discovered that the cost of purchasing a rocket was astronomical—up to $65 million." Musk decided to rethink the problem using first principles. Why did he have to buy a rocket? Could he make one instead? He broke down all the raw materials that go into a rocket and discovered that he could buy them "for around 2 percent of the typical price [of a rocket]." Then he challenged his assumptions about the feasibility of constructing his own rocket, and the result was the creation of SpaceX. Through innovation, the company, in a few years, "cut the cost of launching a rocket by 10x while still making a profit."[8]

The next characteristic is *unlearning and reconfiguring* the mental constructs you use to make sense of your world. An article by the team at Causeit, Inc. and Mark Bonchek entitled "Unlearning Mental Models" cautions that "mental models can be hard to identify and shift because they are usually unconscious and deeply embedded into how we are used to doing things." Their solution is a threefold process. First, you have to "know when your mental models are growing outdated." Second, you must distinguish between your old mental model and the new one you hope to adopt. Third, "it's not enough to show the new [mental model] is better," you have to make it accessible to the rest of your company. The authors suggest using "a familiar image to build a bridge between the old and the new." Their example is Henry Ford originally calling his product a *horseless carriage* to help consumers transition to the unfamiliar term *automobile*.[9] Columbia Business School professor Rita Gunther McGrath adds that unlearning and reconfiguring need to be employed constantly to remain competitive in today's world.[10]

For the next characteristic, I use the shorthand term *subtraction*. It is the antidote to the human tendency to add more layers of bureaucracy to an enterprise as it grows in size. More people require more coordination, increasing the possibility of error just as the stakes have increased. In response, management adds standardized processes and procedures, rules and restrictions, oversight from gatekeepers and auditors, and more and larger meetings to keep everyone on the same page.

These additions can sap the energy of your workforce up and down the line. To demonstrate how that might work, Stanford professor Baba Shiv conducted a fascinating experiment: He chose two random groups and asked the first to remember a two-digit number and the second group to remember a seven-digit number. In essence, the cognitive load was greater for the second group than the first. Then everyone was sent down a hallway to a table containing snacks: chocolate cake or fruit salad. Surprisingly, the second group was twice as likely to choose the cake than the first group. These snacks were proxies for right (healthy) and wrong (unhealthy) decisions. Professor Shiv concluded that when the cognitive load was high, a person didn't have the reserve of energy to make the right decision. Simply put, brainpower knocked out willpower.[11]

To reduce the cognitive load and thus improve decision-making, the best leaders actively fight "addition sickness." Subtraction is their mantra as they continually ask, what's essential? What can be eliminated? Can thirty reports be reduced to four? If a meeting is large, can the team assigned to the project be shrunk? Does the team have to meet weekly? Can meetings be cut from an hour to thirty minutes? This paring down frees up brainpower and thus boosts efficiency.

Ironically, the next characteristic is *controlled chaos*. Its opposite, *conformity*, chokes off dissenting views so that everyone marches to the same tune. And that leads to an autocratic culture. In contrast, a company in controlled chaos can seem out of whack because it is taking bold risks, assessing them quickly, jettisoning failures, and plowing forward in new and better directions.

In a December 2021 interview, Ken Griffin, CEO of major hedge fund Citadel, recalled how Jack Welch, the legendary leader of General Electric in its heyday who was acquiring several dozen companies, described buying both a successful venture and a failing one. Welch asserted that running a great company was like driving a Formula One car as it flies down the straightaway of the track at 220 miles per hour, and then brakes to take a curve, spinning out and nearly hitting the wall, but swerving at the last minute to hug the curve and hit the accelerator once again. It's a marvelously visual image of controlled chaos. In contrast, Welch used another driving metaphor to describe what it was like to operate a failing company: "Picture a beautiful day in Texas and you're in a Cadillac going down the highway at 55 miles an hour, playing John Denver music."[12]

The final characteristic we discovered springs from the dissent that flourishes in controlled chaos. Developed at Intel and embraced at Amazon, it is known as *disagree and commit*. It requires a psychologically safe space in which dissent is encouraged. If your company has that, then your people can argue all sides of a particular issue. Suppose your superior vetoes your proposal right off the bat. That veto isn't the last word—it's the trigger to start disagreeing, respectfully. As Amazon executive Mark Schwartz notes, "Disagreeing doesn't mean acting like a jerk. It means making a cogent case, using data where possible to support your arguments." Disagreeing also involves empathetically considering the proponent's concerns and responsibilities. Moreover, if a company supports the airing of different viewpoints, then "if you disagree with something, it's your *responsibility* to argue."[13]

Having made your argument, your superior may agree, arrive at a compromise, or reject your proposal outright. Whatever the result, you have been an active part of the process. You've committed to your argument and to presenting it to others. The second part of *disagree and commit* is as important as the first: As Schwartz points out, "You're committed to the decision [no matter the outcome]. You can't be passive-aggressive or later say, 'I told you so.' You own the final decision, even though it may not be what you originally wanted." This element has two important functions: it enables the best solution to come to the surface, and it ensures that everyone will support it.

Navigating the Book

To make your time spent on *Going on Offense* as productive as possible, I am summarizing the next nine chapters in this first one. You can read selectively by jumping to the elements that interest you, or read through the book from start to finish.

Each of the next eight chapters addresses the eight elements described above, but in a different order that I believe will resonate best with readers. I've divided *Going on Offense* into three overarching parts based on my research: Generous, Ferocious, and Courageous. After this introductory chapter, we take up the Generous section (chapters 2 to 4). Chapter 2 addresses existentialism as an authentic way of making work matter. Corporate purpose is trendy these days, but too often the idea is bandied about in a soft way, like public relations, to give employees an easy sense of meaning in their day-to-day work. There's nothing wrong with that, but I use the term *existentialism* to convey the seriousness of the commitment required for change. Companies are not people, but they need a powerful reason for being in order to call forth the extra effort required to become perpetually innovative. They must generously commit to making the world better in a specific way.

Chapter 3 focuses on generosity through an obsession with customers, but perhaps not as you anticipate. Yes, some companies are so committed to their customers' desires that they rely on the marketplace to determine most of their products and services. That reliance requires close listening to customer feedback and quick reaction, generating a kind of cocreation that drives successful products. But this obsession can also play out as empathetic imagination. This approach doesn't involve feedback, or even consulting with customers, who may suggest only an improved version of what they currently have. Instead, it requires the company to imagine intensely what customers will want in the future and then work rigorously to deliver it, as Apple did with the iPhone and Henry Ford did with the Model T automobile.

Chapter 4 applies the Pygmalion effect to companies. Like the mythological sculptor, leaders must project their generous commitments onto the rest of the organization through a strong culture. Most companies are too large to expect employees to share top management's existential commitment. But contrary to what other writers say, the Pygmalion process isn't about communication or propaganda. It's about selection and trust: finding people disposed to the purpose, trusting them to advance it, and graciously ushering out those who decline to embrace the purpose. One-on-one mentoring and performance reviews reinforce this process. The Pygmalion effect comes from creating a community of like-minded individuals ready to collaborate toward shared goals.

Next up is the Ferocious section (chapters 5 to 7), where companies aggressively apply these generous commitments to the real world. It begins with chapter 5 on the start-up mindset. To drive those commitments forward, companies need to convert at least some of their employees, who originally joined as money-focused mercenaries, into missionaries. It needs a core of people, most likely in management, who take responsibility for making progress on that purpose. They act as though they were in a start-up, so passionate about their purpose that they suppress the need for conventional profitability and a life of comfort in favor of pursuing what's right for the purpose. In their minds, they are choosing truth and speed over convenience. They assume—with the right focus and intensity—the profits will come in time, and they're usually right. This mindset imposes concrete discipline on the rest of the organization.

That doesn't mean driving hard all the time. Chapter 6 describes how to manage tempo, an essential method for applying energy when you need it most. Most companies move, automatically or passively, at the same speed pretty much all the time. But some opportunities or threats are so urgent that only firms ready to pick up their pace immediately can meet them. As with lions in the wild, which move slowly much of the time, that readiness depends on more than a guiding purpose and discipline that make people intentional all the time. It also requires varying the tempo so people can store up energy at other times.

Chapter 7 continues this point by laying out how companies operate bimodally. Even in disruptive times, success requires more than just stunning innovation. Companies also have to commercialize those new ideas and keep improving their existing offerings. Similar to managing tempo, companies need to operate in two modes: a steady state of improvement and a special state of agility with rapid, iterative gains. Usually one area of the company emphasizes compression to reduce costs on familiar, stable tasks, while another emphasizes creativity to generate new products and services. Intentions are key here; leaders need to keep the creative area, with dedicated, multifunctional teams, shielded from the pressures of business as usual.

The third and final section, Courageous (chapters 8 and 9), recognizes that all these activities require audacity, not just a willingness to act. Chapter 8 advocates for boldness and taking big steps, using all the restless energy from those commitments and aggressiveness. Leaders need to encourage that restlessness while also guiding it toward productive ends. Sometimes that means investing in major innovations even when existing products are thriving, as Amazon did with Amazon Web Services (AWS). Alternatively, it can mean taking a chance on a risky initiative but doing so in a way that matches the company's existential commitment, as Bumble did in India. It could even mean scaling back an initiative to ensure quality. Boldness becomes a force that overcomes the worries that stymie the efforts of cautious, conventional companies. But to unleash that bold energy from employees, management must provide an environment that is psychologically safe.[14]

Chapter 9 delves into a familiar challenge, *radical collaboration*, in which companies must figuratively break up the hierarchy to give projects the help they need. How do you encourage people to courageously go beyond their comfortable groups and teams? It's easy to tell companies not to allow silos, but silos are a fact of organizational life. What matters is in what areas you permit the silos, because that determines the possibilities for collaboration. Furthermore, choosing where to allow silos depends on your strategy, whether you emphasize responsiveness to customers or fundamental innovation itself.

A final chapter brings all three sections together with an extended case study. Most of the examples in *Going on Offense* are technology-oriented companies in Silicon Valley and their analogs in other high-tech environments. But chapter 10 presents an extended case study of a low-tech company, Starbucks. It also explores practical steps that established companies can take to transform themselves using the energy generated by these elements.

I've coached over a hundred private and public organizations in their transformations, and I've seen ordinary companies in conventional industries fundamentally change their operations. They come up with a powerful movement that drives passion throughout the hierarchy, which over time leads to a level of agility and innovation that few thought possible. Most of them were mature, established companies, not start-ups, and they didn't transform overnight. But by approaching change in a systematic way, which I lay out in this book, they shed their old habits and built the mindset of success.

You, dear reader, are about to embark on the same journey of transformation. But as I've noted, it isn't easy. You may find yourself alone, parsing through the sections, wondering how closely to adhere to them if you want to achieve success. Jeff Bezos of Amazon offers some sage advice that buoyed him on the tenth anniversary of the 1999 *Barron's* cover that caricatured him as a businessman doomed to fail.

He tweeted the following: "Listen and be open, but don't let anybody tell you who you are. This was just one of the many stories telling us all the ways we were going to fail."[15] Because of its perpetual innovation, Amazon today is one of the most successful companies in the world, having revolutionized two entirely different services: shopping and web services.

If you keep an open mind and an open heart, you will gain much from what follows.

PART ONE

Generous

CHAPTER TWO

Setting an Existential Purpose: Why Does Your Company Matter?

For small creatures such as we, the vastness is bearable only through love.
—CARL SAGAN

He who has a why to live can bear almost any how.
—FRIEDRICH NIETZSCHE

Microsoft was stuck. It was 2014, and the world was passing by the once-dominant technology company. Back in the 1990s, it had achieved astounding profits and market share with its Windows operating system and Office products for personal computers. That dominance soon extended to corporate servers. But now it was losing out to younger aggressive tech firms such as Amazon and Google, as well as the newly revived Apple.

Windows and Office were still delivering profits, but Microsoft's market capitalization, a sign of investors' belief that the company could rise ever higher, had barely moved since 2001. The organization had a mentality of "too big to fail," which meant it shrugged off failed investments in Bing Search and the Windows Phone. Instead of agile innovation, it focused on milking its cash cows and defending fiefdoms, squandering its huge advantage in resources and market presence.

Back in 1997, for example, Microsoft managers got interested in a device that stored and presented written media—what we now know as e-readers. But the higher-ups vetoed the product because it didn't promise the kind of market success of Office or Windows. Instead they put the development team into the larger Microsoft Office business group. Rather than deliver a revolutionary product, the developers had to concentrate on profit and loss for the group. The result was just simple e-reading software for Office, which soon faded into obscurity. A decade later, Amazon released the Kindle, which quickly dominated the e-reader market.

In the absence of a compelling vision for the entire company, Microsoft's divisions worked on maintaining their existing products and profitability—discouraging talented developers from pursuing game-changing opportunities. When the company did enter a new business, as with the me-too Windows Phone, it failed to come out with distinctive innovation.

Facing the threat of slow but permanent decline, Microsoft's board in 2014 promoted Satya Nadella to succeed the retiring Steve Ballmer. He had a simple solution: to "rediscover the soul of Microsoft, our reason for being."

At that point, the closest the company had to an animating purpose was its long-standing goal of "a PC on every desk and in every home, running Microsoft software." Nadella and his colleagues reoriented the company to "empowering every person and every organization on the planet to achieve more." After all, the company had built up pioneering capabilities in harmonizing the needs of both individuals and organizations, on a global scale. The old statement concentrated on making branded products and gaining market share. The new statement was an elevated vision, where the company's offerings became a vehicle for individuals and organizations to make the world a better place.

As Nadella pointed out, the company had a "unique capability in harmonizing the needs of both individuals and organizations. This is in our DNA." But he added, "We also deeply care about taking things global and *making a difference* in lives and organizations in all corners of the planet."

The old statement concentrated on Microsoft products and how popular the company wanted them to be. The new statement was about how those products *contributed* to improvement. The shift to a greater meaning was undeniable.

But Nadella had a larger vision than just corporate strategy. He saw the coming of "the most transformative wave of technology yet," with artificial intelligence, virtual reality, and quantum computing. He saw that people, organizations, and societies would have to transform, to "hit refresh," and he wanted Microsoft to play a role in that process. He quoted the mystical Austrian poet Rainer Maria Rilke: "The future enters into us, in order to transform itself in us, long before it happens." He was driven by an empathetic desire to empower others.

By moving away from product-oriented thinking, Nadella unlocked new avenues for innovation. Once-discouraged opportunities for collaboration and new projects now made sense. The organization developed apps for Apple products, embraced rival operating systems such as Linux, and threw its weight behind groundbreaking technology such as virtual reality and artificial intelligence. In eight years, Microsoft's market capitalization jumped from $372 billion to nearly $2 trillion.[16] By reorienting its existential vision, the company quintupled its value.[17]

Making Purpose Existential

This chapter begins the foundational section on becoming a perpetual innovator. Perpetual innovation is hard work, and only positive motivation can bring out the energy and enthusiasm necessary to sustain it over time. So the work has to start with a spirit of generosity.

Like many big organizations, Microsoft had become a victim of its own success. Responding aggressively to initial opportunities, it had brilliantly exploited a new and fast-growing market, but once it got there, it lacked an existential vision to stay dynamic. Due to this, people in the now-dominant company fell back on personal imperatives such as protecting existing products and structures. The company dominated the market for personal computing software—just as that market was saturated and growth shifted elsewhere. Without a new goal, it stuck to the old one.

Nadella was an exception—he led the server and tools group and, following Amazon's trailblazing, successfully moved much of this business to the cloud. Doing so was a major break from the PC-based world, and a big reason for his promotion. But the bulk of the organization remained in the old perspective.

This is a powerful example of a main point of this book: that large, successful companies inevitably resist the effort necessary to remain perpetual innovators. They've built up structures to scale up their business and deliver reliable profits, something to be proud of, so now they naturally resist bold, disruptive experiments. To change, they need something more than outside criticism or even seeing other companies win the accolades they garnered in the past. Transformation is especially difficult when the company is still quite profitable.

The usual solution in this case is to rally the organization around a compelling purpose. Leaders need to deliver an inspiring speech or ambitious strategy that fits with a current social or economic concern. But purpose by itself isn't enough to get large organizations to change their fundamental outlook. It's too easily manipulated into "purpose washing." Companies need to go deeper.

Here they can learn from a general predicament in Western society, starting back in the nineteenth century. Traditional approaches were losing their hold on people, and European philosophers sought a more reliable source of motivation and direction. They looked for a secular foundation for faith and meaning.

One of the first was Søren Kierkegaard, who emphasized an individual's desire to explore purpose through a free journey of introspection and reflection. In an edgier vein, Friedrich Nietzsche praised the "will to power" over traditional norms that favored communities, religion, and social expectations. By looking inward, people could now develop an individual purpose to live by. Traditions that had guided people were no longer sufficient to motivate people, as the old problems of life were being solved by economic progress.

In the twentieth century, Martin Heidegger centered the world on each individual person's frame of reference, rather than seeing a person as a subjective spectator of external activities. Jean-Paul Sartre focused on authenticity: people were the sole drivers behind their actions and had to develop an action-oriented philosophy unique to themselves.

By the 1950s, psychologists had taken up this approach, led by those who had escaped places of death. Viktor Frankl, who survived Nazi concentration camps in the Holocaust, centered "man's search for meaning" on reaching goals important to each individual. Instead of the prevailing "depth psychology," focused on unconscious desires or conflicts, he emphasized "height psychology," which activates a person's meaning in order to achieve new possibilities despite those unconscious troubles. Rather than trying to solve those troubles, he wanted to energize people around their dormant strengths.

Rollo May, who recovered from tuberculosis in a sanitarium, urged patients to self-actualize and go beyond simple egocentrism. He found that many people were overwhelmed by anxiety, and that discovering innate value for their lives could help overcome those fears. Both he and Frankl saw that people who chose to live for an authentic purpose could summon the energy to overcome terrible conditions.

Irvin Yalom extended these ideas to groups, having found that many people express and engage around a purpose better with other people than by themselves. Working in groups helped them overcome meaninglessness. But to work well, the groups depended on facilitators who nudged people to truly listen to others talking about their here-and-now reality.

For our purposes, what matters is the fundamental point that people need a deep-seated conviction in order to summon the energy to live effectively. Rather than take up a meaning dictated by tradition, these thinkers wanted each individual to develop or recognize a powerful purpose to animate his or her life, based on his or her specific personality and context.

How Existential Purpose Motivates Organizations

Companies are not people, but they need a similar reason for being in order to call forth the motivation required to be innovative. An existential commitment provides direction as well as motivation. Even in a commodity business, a company has too many avenues to explore for agile innovation. It needs a fundamental purpose both to dictate certain areas of innovation over others and to rally people around driving or at least supporting those experiments.

"Who am I and what is my calling?" is central at the organizational as well as individual level. The answer to this question grounds and directs all activity. It inspires members to imagine what the organization could become. It also embeds and energizes everyone in the transformation to get there.

Otherwise any transformation will stall, which I've learned from several failed projects. *No one wants to change*—and now companies must adopt a new approach to succeed in the twenty-first century. Companies need a compelling vision to shake people up. Only a hard purpose will make employees sacrifice some of those personal privileges or benefits. Before 2014, Microsoft's leaders might have voiced support for the pieties of the day, but what they really cared about was maintaining their division's profitability, budget, and prestige.

Hence the need for an existential, deep-seated, emotionally laden commitment. It goes beyond the usual talk about purpose nowadays, which is shallow and feel-good. Companies adopt a purpose to boost their reputation with customers or recruits, or to inspire employees to greater engagement, but it's little more than window dressing.

Existential purpose is hard and deep; it gets to the company's identity and reason for existence. It has real trade-offs; it closes off attractive opportunities and strategies. It should make some people leave. But only a hard, existential commitment to that purpose will force companies out of settled structures and toward perpetual innovation. Only an existential purpose inspires people to do the hard work of transforming an organization.

The harder the commitment, the greater the importance of sticking with the wording once it's set. Otherwise people will see the vision as adjustable to whatever they need in the moment.

As Nadella remembers, setting down the company's mission, worldview, ambitions, and culture on a single page was actually the easier part. The more challenging part was resisting the urge to tweak the language. "I'd want to edit a word here or there, add a row, just tinker with it before each speech. Then I'd be reminded, consistency is better than perfection."

Only a hard commitment, Nadella saw, could overcome Microsoft's confrontational culture of "us versus them" and "take no prisoners." So he made a point of emphasizing collaborating across internal and external boundaries to find mutually profitable solutions: "us with them."

Cynics saw the announcements as fluff, but Nadella kept to the direction. He invited managers who agreed with the vision to his leadership team. He didn't fire those who disagreed, but they soon saw that their future lay elsewhere. The result was little time lost on culture wars.

Making the Existential Purpose Operational

Let's get practical. A company's existential purpose has to be significant enough to motivate progress at scale, serve a realistic business model, and inspire engagement from a large employee base.

Here are examples from companies we'll cite throughout the book. Apple aims to make powerful technology accessible to ordinary people to improve their lives. Amazon overcomes traditional retailing trade-offs by making shopping as convenient as possible. The nonprofit Santa Clara Valley Medical Center, which serves high-risk and vulnerable populations in the San Francisco Bay Area, seeks a world-class patient care and flow process that patients and families love and makes staff proud.

These are all inspiring visions, but not so clear in directing action. An *existential vision* is usually a conceptual ideal—an end state or reality that serves as the ultimate achievement for the organization. It can serve as a kind of North Star.

An *existential goal*, on the other hand, is a concrete objective that describes the path to the vision—something to work toward in order to make the vision a reality. *Core values* are enduring ideas that fuel both the existential vision and existential goals. They have an intrinsic quality that transcends any external state or fleeting desires.

	Existential Vision (or North Star)	Existential Goals	Core Values
Definition	An end state that serves as the ultimate achievement for the organization.	Concrete objectives that describe the path to the existential vision— go after these areas and not those.	Enduring ideas that fuel existential vision and existential goals. Core values have an intrinsic quality that transcends any external state or fleeting desire.
Examples	Amazon: overcoming retailing trade-offs; Earth's most customer-centric company; building a place where people can discover anything they might want to buy online.	• Increase revenue in certain areas by X%. • Increase market share in these areas by Y%. • Increase employee satisfaction in these areas by Z%.	Focus on customers rather than competitors; passion for invention; operational excellence; and long-term thinking.[18]

As we saw with Microsoft, all of these elements can change, even the existential vision. As the company develops and its markets evolve, a new vision might well be in order. When Microsoft adopted its original existential goal, it was only a few years from starting up and was so eager to realize the opportunities unfolding in the PC market that it never bothered to develop a vision. Having achieved that impressive goal, the company couldn't find any similar goal equally compelling. So it needed not just a new goal, but a foundational vision that could apply the company's abundant expertise and resources to new challenges. With that new vision, it has developed existential goals around cloud-based software, sustainability, data analytics, and artificial intelligence.

In less extreme situations, companies will still need to refine their vision, goals, and values over time. Changes in economic conditions or the company's ecosystem can force refinement even if the basic markets don't. Goals are the practical translation of the vision and will need more frequent and greater revision than will visions or values.

Haier: Change the Goals as Markets Change

Those dynamics affected how Haier translated its existential vision into goals and values. Haier, the world's largest major appliances brand for most of the last decade, makes home appliances and consumer electronics.[19] Despite its challenging industry—appliance markets are often saturated as multiple products compete to provide similar functions—Haier has consistently grown and innovated.

The company began as the Qingdao Refrigerator Company in 1984 when Zhang Ruimin took over a failing state-owned factory. With help from a joint venture with a German company, which upgraded the factory's technology (and led to the renamed Haier), Zhang laid out a bold vision of making premium, innovative, modern products. The initial goal was "Make Quality Products, Compete for Gold Medals," referring to China's National Quality Product Award, which Haier won in 1988. Reliability and other measures of quality became core values.

To drive home this dedication to quality, Zhang invited some theatrics. He assembled the employees and gave them sledgehammers to smash seventy-six defective refrigerators. It sent a shocking but clear message that Haier was going to be a different kind of company.[20]

That was the first of what has become five stages of development, each with its own specific goals. In that first stage, as Haier was building a brand, its zero-tolerance policy on defects differentiated the company from competitors that favored quantity over quality. The underlying vision of insisting on quality refrigerators, rather than volume and low cost for the enormous emerging domestic market, kept people from the temptation to chase quantity.

The strategy worked, but keeping such an expensive brand in a single category was unsustainable. In 1991 the company diversified into other household appliances. It did so mostly by acquiring failing competitors with adequate products but poor leadership and turning them around with Haier management. In the third stage, after China joined the World Trade Organization in 2001, Haier looked overseas and developed a global brand. Thanks to its premium position, it could penetrate markets with strict entry standards.

The fourth stage came with the rise of e-commerce in appliances around 2005. With the internet empowering consumers as never before, Haier moved beyond mass production to working with personal preferences—the new existential goal. The company adjusted the factories it had built up globally to create localized products customized to the needs of individual markets.

The pressures of that challenge led to the fifth stage, with microenterprises. The company was simply too big to manage the complexity required to match consumer preferences. Starting in 2012, the company decentralized into a network of businesses, with a new goal of inculcating entrepreneurship. People were no longer employees, but members of strategic business units that functioned as independent businesses within the Haier ecosystem. These teams gained the agility of autonomous enterprises, but with access to the global resources of Haier. This shift, described in detail in the chapter on collaboration, may be the most difficult of all, but fueling it is Haier's existential vision of making premium, innovative, modern products.

Indeed, Haier's organizational structure today would have been unimaginable in 1984. But the vision of premium, modern products, with the core value of quality, has largely remained. The path to achieving it shifted in response to technological advancements and market opportunities, and Haier transformed its existential goal accordingly. Even highly successful organizations require a strong sense of awareness in order to change the vision or goal to set them up for success.

Setting the Existential Vision: What Problem Does the World Need Us to Solve?

How should organizations without an existential vision go about creating one? Start with scale: The most effective visions are large in ambition and scope. Your vision should be broad to inspire effort in many areas of operations. Even seemingly mundane products and services, such as cars and books, can come to embody solutions to global problems.

The clearest example of this phenomenon is Tesla. It went from start-up to the most valuable car company in the world in only twenty years—in an industry with notoriously high entry barriers and operational challenges. Fundamental to its success has been a daring vision to accelerate the move to sustainable energy. CEO Elon Musk wanted to create "the most compelling car company of the twenty-first century by driving the world's transition to electric vehicles."

That vision motivated Tesla managers and staff to develop some of the most innovative transport technologies, while diversifying into solar power and batteries. It continues to inspire employees and suppliers to help reduce our reliance on fossil fuels, the key contributor to climate change.

Tesla's vision guided the direction in which the firm grew. Its initial products, the Roadster and Model S, were priced above the mass market range, because only that way could Tesla offer its innovative technology. An affordable version would have compromised those emotional commitments.

Once it achieved success in the luxury market, it moved quickly to serving the mass market. If Tesla had focused on high-income customers, it still would have been profitable, but it would not drive *the world's* transition to sustainable energy. Had it opted for quantity at the expense of quality, it would not have delivered a car attractive enough to persuade many customers to give up the familiarity and reliability of fossil fuel vehicles. A clear vision helps firms settle tough questions and move ahead. It pushes organizations to innovate and overcome seemingly insurmountable obstacles.

That vision also led to a limited degree of diversification. Tesla Energy offers power generation and storage, including low-cost solar energy.[21] Its subsidiary, Gambit Energy Storage, built a one hundred-megawatt project in Angleton, Texas, that holds enough energy to supply twenty thousand homes on a hot summer day.[22] As the storage facility comes into operation, it will help Texas's ailing power grid avoid failures similar to the close call it experienced in early 2021. All of these moves fit the company's reason for being.

Most existential visions can't be as grandiose as Tesla's. Instead they'll focus on bettering the everyday lives of people, as Apple and Amazon have done. These visions must do far more than develop useful consumer electronics or sell attractive products. They aim to smooth out the friction of day-to-day life so customers have time for big personal goals.

When Steve Jobs conceptualized Apple in the 1980s, when it was still three people in his parents' garage, he envisioned "making a contribution to the world by making tools for the mind that advance humankind." During Apple's early years, this meant an unprecedented focus on user interface and accessibility. Later it meant revolutionizing mobile devices with the iPod, iPhone, and iPad. In his second stint as CEO, when the company had opportunities in a great many areas, he asked, "Who is Apple and where do we fit in this world?" That question helped focus the company's efforts on improving life for its main customers rather than competing on the nitty-gritty, such as technical benchmarks or hardware capabilities.

Jobs relentlessly told employees and others that the company had to "stand for something." He felt personally connected to the vision: "What we have is something that I'm very moved by. It honors those people who have changed the world."

Indeed, Apple's vision was hardly prosaic. Jobs himself looked high: "What we are about is not making boxes for people to get their jobs done—although we do that well. Apple is about something more than that. Its core value is that we believe people with passion can change the world for the better. Those people who are crazy enough to think they can change the world are the ones who actually do." Already in 1997 Apple announced that it would no longer advertise its products' "speeds and feeds." Instead it would communicate how the products would benefit the core customers—the crazy ones, the square pegs in the round holes.[23]

That continuing commitment to the vision at the top is essential to keeping it as an existential North Star in the organization. Even in 2010, when Apple had become a powerhouse valued at $300 billion,[24] Jobs said, "We come into work wanting to do the same thing today as we did five or ten years ago, which is to build the best products for people."[25] Nothing "makes my day more than getting an email from some random person in the universe who just bought an iPad and told me a story about how it's the coolest product they've ever brought home."

The vision both guides people and keeps them motivated. Jobs again:

> There needs to be someone who is the keeper and reiterator of the vision. . . . A lot of times, when you have to walk a thousand miles and you take the first step, it looks like a long way, and it really helps if there's someone there saying, "Well we're one step closer. . . . The goal definitely exists; it's not just a mirage out there."

When Tim Cook took over for Jobs, he reiterated, "We believe that we're on the face of the earth to make great products and that's not changing . . . And I think regardless of who is in what job, those values are so embedded in this company that Apple will do extremely well."[26]

Amazon is even more obsessed with its customers, an aspect we'll explore in the next chapter. The company aims to be "Earth's most customer-centric company, where customers find the lowest possible prices, the best available selection, and the utmost convenience." Jeff Bezos launched "Earth's Biggest Book Store" in 1994, disrupting the industry by offering a wider selection of books at lower prices by eliminating the need for physical retail space. But the company's vision makes no reference to books in particular. So it was a natural move into music and then a great many other products. By 1997, it was selling toys, home appliances, and clothing.

Even so, the vision says nothing about becoming an online department store. It focuses on convenience, selection, and prices, and Amazon has innovated accordingly. In 1997 it filed a patent for the "1-Click" purchase button.[27] Then in 2000 it introduced Marketplace, which brought in a wide range of third-party retailers to the online store. Amazon undoubtedly lost some sales from its own holdings, but its existential vision to serve customers overrode internal objections. The move enormously expanded the selection to customers without increasing Amazon's warehousing costs.

In 2005, Amazon pioneered Prime, with free unlimited two-day shipping for subscribers, making online shopping almost as fast as shopping in person. Twelve years later, Amazon acquired Whole Foods and thus extended the convenience of Prime to grocery shopping. All of these innovations arose from the reason for the company's existence: to overcome the limitations traditional retailers place on consumer choice.

Like the leaders of Microsoft and Apple, Bezos continued his hard commitment to the existential vision even as the company became a trillion-dollar giant. He was famous for being "stubborn on vision, flexible on execution." That's how he continued to focus on growth over profitability for decades, including the Prime offer of free shipping. The vision also freed the organization to innovate relentlessly—at lower risk than might appear because the vision gave coherence to the effort and market information along the way. As he pointed out, "If you invent frequently and are willing to fail, then you never get to the point of needing to bet the whole company."[28]

Those seemingly mundane existential visions have made Apple and Amazon both among the most revolutionary companies ever, changing how most of us go about our daily lives.

Aligning the Organizational Vision with Individual North Stars

An existential vision works only if embraced by many people in the organization—to the point where it becomes a personal calling.[29] It is only when individuals internalize the vision, the North Star, as personal motivation, that the vision overcomes the usual tendencies of big companies to resist change. Personal satisfaction becomes tied to the organization's success. Some employees may resist internalizing the existentialist vision, but the leadership and a large critical mass throughout the organization need to take it on to sustain a broad transformation. (See chapters 3 and 4 on extending the vision to the customers and the entire workforce and beyond.)

To get advocates throughout the organization, companies need to involve their members at all levels in setting the vision and translating it into values and goals. Leaders must resist the temptation to work alone or with external consultants and then announce the vision, goals, and values and expect employees to make these their own. For the organization to change, people need to change too. I learned that especially from one of my clients, the Santa Clara Valley Medical Center (SCVMC) in California.

SCVMC, serving most of Silicon Valley, is one of the biggest health care systems in the United States.[30] Its nine thousand employees serve a diverse population, operating on a $2.5 billion budget with some public funding. Rapid population growth in the 1980s and '90s brought the hospital to the breaking point. It struggled with problems at multiple stages of the patient cycle, from admission to discharge. With the county's population continuing to grow, these difficulties were likely to intensify. The hospital engaged an external consulting firm, but after spending $20 million, and fifteen months later, no long-term fixes were in sight.

The widespread nature of the problems pointed to trouble at the core: the absence of an existential vision to engage employees to meet the challenge. But what should that vision be? Led by Drs. Sanjay Kurani and Cliff Wang, the hospital started by collecting data from employees, customers, and other stakeholders about what needed to change. Cross-functional teams emerged from previously discrete departments, including administrators, nurses, doctors, physical therapists, and social workers. The input led to the existential vision: "To build a world-class patient flow process that patients and families love and makes staff proud."

That process across the hospital helped give people a sense of ownership, where they worked to make the hospital into a place employees wanted it to be—which would further that sense of ownership. But how could we be sure the hospital's vision lined up with the staff's individual aspirations?

Getting there involved a group of eighty to one hundred influencers in the organization, including doctors, nurses, and physical therapists. They engaged in multiple exercises to develop their personal vision statements as related to a larger vision. They used the SEE (Strengths-Evokes-Elates) framework from one of my previous books, *The Inside-Out Effect*.[31]

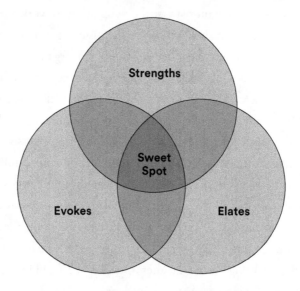

The framework helps participants discover their individual calling, the sweet spot at the intersection of their *strengths,* the things that *evoke* personal meaning, and what makes them feel *elated.* An individual calling should be what gives immediate joy and a sustained sense of purpose while matching what the individual already does well (or is willing to become good at).

Participants had to reflect on moments in their work when they were in the "flow"—when they felt totally involved, with their skills fully used.[32] Some participants were moved to tears as they recounted these moments of immersion and satisfaction. After those reflections, they created personal vision statements that described their ideal state, with their ultimate achievement.

To keep the exercises relevant to the larger challenge, the group frequently revisited the hospital's vision statement. They needed to develop their personal vision in the context of organizational change, to ensure alignment between each staff member's personal North Star and the organization's.

From there, the hope was that these influencers would spread this alignment throughout the organization—thus cementing the sense of ownership. The organizational transformation had to be as much about advancing their vision as it was about advancing the organization's vision. I cannot overstate the amount of energy and momentum that this process creates. In the history of the world, many people have devoted extraordinary effort to causes they believed in. But you cannot hand a cause to someone and ask them to sacrifice for it. The cause must be *from them*.

With this alignment, the hospital staff delved into improving the flow of patients. The cross-functional teams continued and took charge of different aspects of the transformation—including not just surveys of patients being discharged but "mystery shopping" exercises where they posed as patients to identify gridlocks and inefficiencies. The staff went the extra mile, and their initiative yielded findings that might have gone unnoticed otherwise. For example, they found delays frequently caused by patients who lacked transportation to leave or accommodation once they left. By bringing these unexpected issues to light, the teams helped administrators understand how the hospital's perspective needed to evolve. They also helped locate alternate housing for such patients.

Those insights weren't enough because hospitals are complex operations with many constraints. As the teams identified opportunities for improvement, they implemented different approaches in an experimental manner, measuring the success of one method against the other. This comparative, data-driven approach had a better chance of yielding effective improvements.

Even committed staff can falter as they tackle complex challenges. To sustain their momentum, the hospital implemented simple measures that visibly and regularly demonstrated progress. Little incentives, such as a weekly prize for the best-performing physician team, might seem negligible in the overall scheme but kept the transformation on employees' minds. By making the progress salient, these measures encouraged staff with concrete improvements that *they created*. People developed hope in further improvements they could contribute.

All of this change happened as the hospital's public funding fell 70 percent. Yet key indicators, such as percentage of ambulances turned away and patients' avoidable days in the hospital, saw significant decreases. Patients were spending less time in medical care with faster discharges and quicker bed assignments. Not only could they spend more time at home with their families, but 30 percent more patients were also admitted as a result of the transformation.

Effective companies such as KBank, one of the largest banks in Thailand, as well as several departments within Amazon, are engaged in similar efforts. After developing Microsoft's vision statement with his leaders, Satya Nadella asked all employees to create personal vision statements to determine whether their current positions lined up with their personal calling. The answers led to a number of people adjusting their roles.

At Amazon's many fulfillment centers, managers' performance reviews have them select three company values they feel they achieved and explain how they did so. They must also select three company values to work on and draw up plans to achieve improvement there. The company thus keeps the alignment with organizational values salient and recurrent.

After all, if existential visions, including goals and values, are to have ongoing power, companies must regularly bring them to the attention of employees. In group communication, for instance, leaders can refer to the vision and frame the output of the organization in terms of progress toward the vision. When teams set goals, the goals should bring them closer to achieving the vision.

Facebook: When Organizations Veer from Their Existential Vision

The best way to see the benefits of existentialism in action is to see what happens in its absence. Without an energizing vision, companies struggle to inspire high-performance work. They can't provide employees with a sense of continuity through changing circumstances.

The evolution of Facebook (now Meta) follows that of Microsoft, but without the new vision. The company actually started off with a powerful vision: "To give people the power to share and to make the world more open and connected." Its leaders and employees aggressively and successfully pursued this vision. The trouble is that Facebook failed to develop a new vision once it had realized its founding directive.

The company had done so well that almost half of Americans got their news mainly from the site. But the company's vision said nothing about the quality of information that people were sharing. What happens when this generally praiseworthy connectedness conflicts with the welfare of users or the societies where Facebook operates? Having built up a supremely popular platform, would the company aim to serve its users, or exploit them as eyeballs for advertisers?

Even beyond advertising, recurrent scandals have revealed how unmoderated connectedness could hurt individuals and groups. In 2018, we learned that the Cambridge Analytica political intelligence firm had collected data on tens of millions of unsuspecting Facebook users. Political advertisements were targeted based on comprehensive user psychological profiles obtained from Facebook, which did nothing to stop it.[33] In the same year, human rights investigators ascertained that Facebook had a "determining role" in the spread of Islamophobic content in Myanmar.[34] Over seven hundred thousand Rohingya people fled their homes after being threatened with killings and abuse.

The following year, the US Federal Trade Commission fined Facebook a whopping $5 billion for its failure to protect privacy.[35] Soon thereafter the company announced that it would not fact-check political ads.[36] In 2021, whistleblowers Sophie Zhang and Frances Haugen showed that Facebook knew the negative social effect of its policies but sought profit over safety.[37]

The company's behavior over the years followed a pattern: A scandal breaks out, the company does little to course correct, and then another scandal arises. The company's existential vision never changes in a substantial way, nor does the organization commit to values it would defend at the expense of short-term profitability.

Because Facebook is a social networking company, we could expect privacy, transparency, and accountability to be among its core values. Yet the company did little in those areas, especially on transparency. Users' circles were devolving into echo chambers of hyper-partisanship and intolerance. In a 2017 letter, CEO Mark Zuckerberg acknowledged the need to build social infrastructure that facilitated better interaction, but he didn't change the existential vision.

Instead, in 2021 Facebook rebranded itself as Meta. The rationale was likely partly to distance the organization from its troubled past. The move also promised to solve the company's reliance on other platforms by building proprietary technology and applications for the metaverse. A few months before the announcement, Zuckerberg attributed the drop in the company's value to Apple's iOS privacy protection features, which reduced the value of advertising on Meta's platforms.

Aside from expanding into virtual reality, what is Meta's existential vision? Without a clear idea, the organization once again runs the risk of losing its way. It can't focus on enduring priorities over lucrative yet fleeting opportunities. We've seen flashy graphics but have heard little about the company's core values or existential vision. What kind of interaction does Meta intend to foster on its platform? We're still in the early days of this new frontier of digital interaction, but if the new organization lacks an existential vision, it will likely suffer from the same commercial distractions that have plagued its predecessor.

Closing Thoughts

Existentialism provides the fundamental motivation necessary for organizations to achieve the incredible. Each company comes to its vision differently, yet these share certain characteristics.

Existential visions must be big: Their scope must match the level of motivation they inspire. Tesla, Microsoft, Amazon, and Apple all seek to redefine how we go about our lives. Existential goals, and even existential visions, might require reinvention over time. Haier's example demonstrates how organizations need to adapt to shifting circumstances. Finally, people in the organization must align their own existential commitments to their organization's. That's how they'll feel a stake in the transformation process.

Existentialism is the vital engine of truly perpetually innovative organizations—both the source and the means of transformation.

CHAPTER THREE

Customer Obsession

The advantage of being customer focused is that customers are always dissatisfied. They always want more, and so they pull you along. Whereas if you're competitor obsessed, if you're a leader, you can look around and you see everybody running behind you, maybe you slow down a little.

—JEFF BEZOS[38]

Existential purpose together with customer obsession go hand in hand in helping to motivate and direct people toward perpetual innovation. The previous chapter described how Haier, the Chinese appliance giant, decentralized into hundreds of microenterprises in order to serve customers distinct products in distinct markets. That's a sign of the company's attention to customers, but actually that understates their attitude toward customers—it's more about obsession.

I mean *obsession* in a technical sense, not the way advertisers talk about being obsessed with customers. It means being truly willing to listen to them, to attune yourself to their challenges and accommodate them while still staying in business with a reasonable profit. It starts with emotion but leads to concrete changes in how the company operates. Haier and some other companies go beyond what might seem like a normal amount of attention and become obsessed, regardless of whether it's rational for the business.

At Haier, new products or updates can't proceed with a full budget until vetted and deemed desirable by users. When Haier developed the Air Cube, which combined air purification and humidification, the company solicited comments from eight hundred thousand online users even before creating a prototype.[39] Once it had a prototype, it actually posted it on a crowdfunding site through which 7,500 customers purchased a preproduction model. Haier then incorporated the feedback from these 7,500 customers before launching the mass model from which the microenterprises developed their versions.

Each of these painstaking stages enabled the company to "take the temperature" of the market and adjust design and production accordingly. And because the microenterprises are small and focused on specific markets, they can carry out these adjustments quickly and reliably.

Likewise, the company operates on a "zero-distance" principle: Any Haier customer should be able to reach a Haier employee whenever they wish to do so.[40] Employees aim to become not salespeople but trusted advisors and designers. Nor is this an added burden: Haier believes that zero-distance benefits both parties: the customers have their ideas heard, and employees have the privilege of listening.

That close connection with customers is a big part of how Haier avoids the chaos of largely autonomous microenterprises. Shared services platforms also help. Haier has reduced its HR department from 860 employees to only 11, and most microenterprises have no need for anyone dedicated to the function.

The obsession with customers shows up in the company's "Rendanheyi" philosophy. *Ren* means "people" or "person" and refers to employees, *Dan* means "orders" and refers to the needs or demands of users, and *Heyi* means "integration." Thus the company aims to connect employees with customers culturally as well as structurally. An R&D person elsewhere might focus on the lab work, but at Haier, even the labs must be responsible for the final sale—or lack of sales—of products they develop.[41]

That obsession pays off with steady feedback from markets. The company receives millions of user responses per product post, enabling further alignment around what people want.[42] That responsiveness only strengthens customers' ties to the brand—while arousing engagement from employees who can picture buyers better than their counterparts elsewhere.

The Ever-Present External Tug

It's good to have an existential purpose. But it's ultimately an internal motivation that can falter after a while, especially when the business model proves itself. To sustain a company's discipline—to avoid the complacency and internal politicking that come from success, you need an external tug as well. And the best source of that tug is your customers. As Bezos points out, they'll never be satisfied. You can leave your rivals in the dust and still lose sales at the cash register. People will still pester you for lower prices, higher quality, added features, and maybe all of these at once.

To compete in this type of environment, you have to be obsessed with satisfying your customer. Let's clarify what customer obsession means. It goes beyond the usual awareness of customers that almost every company needs in order to stay in business. It's a kind of emotional commitment, beyond rationality, tied to the existential purpose. It makes the company accommodate, listen to, and attune itself to customers' challenges, no matter how frustrating or contradictory. It forces the company to make some questionable choices in the short term that pay off over time, not just in customer satisfaction, but also in employee engagement and overall quality. Customer-obsessed companies also tend to be the first to realize when and how markets are shifting.

This obsession, however, doesn't mean simply surveying to find out what people want and giving it to them. Customers can't simply be data points; they must come alive to developers. That happens in one of two ways.

The first is *cocreation*. To cocreate with customers means to obtain their input at every stage of production. This is how Haier works, and it includes soliciting future product ideas via social media, carrying out beta testing, and maintaining online forums for customers to report issues. Companies act based on what customers say they want, making customers the experts.

Yet *empathetic imagination* is more suitable when a potential product is connected with a novel technology, a new way of thinking, or even a new way of life. As Henry Ford (allegedly) said, "If I had asked my customers what they wanted, they would have said a faster horse." In such situations, companies should not focus on finding out what customers think *right now.* Instead they should ask, "What would a product that could improve the *future* lives of customers look like?"

The focus on the future might come into conflict with short-term profitability. If a technology is new, it will take time for customers to *experience* how it improves their lives. The first wave of adopters needs time to use it, rave about the technology, and get others to try it.

Pioneering with empathetic imagination is therefore certainly riskier, but as Ford showed, with a greater potential payoff. To drive that first wave, would-be pioneers must have the courage to develop a high-quality product. They may seem less connected to customers than cocreators, but they're just obsessed with them in a different way.

Cocreation at Zara: The Customer As the Expert

Amancio Ortega is the founder of Inditex, as well as its powerhouse Zara division that has pioneered fast fashion. Ortega has a simple view of Zara's purpose: to produce "along the lines of what's happening; if the market wants this, let's do it."[43] Ortega didn't believe he knew fashion better than his customers, but he did think that his background in textile production enabled him to build a better contract manufacturing system than other fashion companies. From day one, he let customers take the initiative on designs, while Zara focused on production and distribution. Zara wants to be *the* store where customers have all of their fashion needs met.

This bottom-up model of product development requires genuine attention to and appreciation of everyday customers. It is not about celebrity designers in Paris or New York. As Ortega puts it, "I don't have to see the catwalks: I see the street." In one story, he says, "I was in a car stopped at a light, and a scooter pulled up alongside me ridden by a young man wearing a denim jacket covered in badges. I liked it; I could see that this was new, genuine, trendy. I called my design chief from the car and told him what I was looking at. In two weeks, the jackets were in shops and selling like hotcakes."

That responsiveness requires not only integrating stores with designers, but also a supply chain with space for constant customer input. He says, "We can completely undo any production line if it isn't selling; we can dye the collections with new colors, and we can create styles in just a few days."

Zara's genius is thus in how quickly and systematically it discerns what customers want, translates it into new products, and distributes them globally. Customers don't have to visit every clothing store in their city to find the trendiest items. They often have a notion of a specific item, such as a scarf, and are willing to pay for it immediately if it is of reasonable quality at an affordable price. They want to have all their needs met quickly and conveniently, and they'll pay extra, with greater loyalty, to a company that reliably makes that happen.

The company rarely surveys its customers; instead it relies on data and feedback from stores. When a style sells out, the store tells headquarters to manufacture more of it; styles that sell poorly go on sale. Zara minimizes its risks by keeping the volume of new styles small, hence the need for the advanced information system, connecting store associates with designers at headquarters, as well designers with contract factories. Vertical integration, through information networks, is key to agile cocreation. That's how Zara makes its obsession with customers into a concrete and repeatable business.

Empathetic Imagination at Apple: Anticipating Desire

Cocreation can work well, as Zara and Haier have shown. But it depends on customers already knowing what they want. Steve Jobs had a radically different approach, but Apple feels just as much of a tug as Zara. That's because the company comes up with ideas for products by *empathizing with* the user. As Jobs put it, "People don't know what they want until you show it to them.

That's why I never rely on market research. Our task is to read things that are not yet on the page." He was still obsessed with customers, but his ultimate motivation was to create a product that customers would *come to love.*

The previous chapter described how Jobs and his Apple colleagues focused on the quality and elegance of products rather than early sales. That didn't change even as the company grew into the giant it is today. He acknowledged, "We have a lot of customers, and we have a lot of research into our installed base. We also watch industry trends pretty carefully. But in the end, for something this complicated, it's really hard to design products by focus groups."

Jobs and his cofounders weren't looking simply to make products that would sell; they wanted products that would change their customers' lives. When he returned to Apple, he worked with creative director Jony Ive to combine technological power with simplicity and accessibility. Their innovation was worlds removed from what the typical customer could understand, but their obsession with customers ensured a final product that delighted users. Instead of building what customers seemed to want now, Apple built the most powerful consumer machines possible and then worked from the customer's perspective to ask:

1. How can this help my life?
2. What would I want to do with this?
3. Does this machine give me power that I can easily learn how to use?

They weren't looking for technology for its own sake. Ken Segall, the longtime marketing director, pointed out, "It's important to look through the eyes of others. As a customer, see how you feel about the entire customer experience, from advertising to purchase to learning and using the product or service. Ask yourself one critical question: Is the experience so good that you'd actually tell friends, family, or colleagues about it? If not, why? For example, if the buying process seems confusing, it might be that we're offering too many choices, which can actually backfire, freezing customers into inaction."[44]

The Best Test: Actual Use

Microsoft occupies a middle ground: It emphasizes cocreation, but with a twist tied to its reliance on advanced technology. It's not enough to sell a product once; if customers aren't actually using it, then the company is falling short and will eventually see declining sales. Customer obsession doesn't stop with the sale—all the more important as software companies shift from product purchases to subscriptions.

Brad Anderson, corporate vice president for Enterprise Client and Mobility, explains its focus on usability: "We all know of organizations and companies whose revenue looks healthy, but they're losing customers. If customers really love what you're building, they're using it." Accordingly, under CEO Satya Nadella, the company relies on dashboards that emphasize usage. "What's the growth in the last seven days? What's the growth of the last month? What are people using? What are they not using? It's all grounded one hundred percent in the customer."[45]

Unlike Apple's limited offerings, Microsoft's large suite of products forces the company's R&D to rely on user data, not just internal ideas. But in order to guide innovation, the data captures not what the customers want but what they actually use. That means also watching what they are *not* using. If your products are such high quality, why do your customers clock so little screen time on them? Product development spurred from user data must aim at needs that aren't being met.

Obsessing About the Entire Experience

We can learn from both Apple and Microsoft to step away from conventional market research. If you commit to creating something innovative and powerful for customers, with advanced technology, into a product that's easy to buy and use—customers will thank you for providing what they didn't know they needed.

Tesla operates in a similar fashion, closer to Apple's empathetic imagination. Largely avoiding market research, it develops a high-quality, advanced product and then makes it easy to purchase and to use. The selling point of

Tesla could be its wide range of technological innovations, "a sophisticated computer on wheels."[46] But when the car hits the showroom, it's all about what the product can do *for* the customer. In Tesla showrooms, customers, not technology, have power.

At their core, Tesla and Apple build complex and powerful machines. In their stores, they mask their products with a cloak of simplicity and ease. Tesla doesn't care if customers understand the incredible feat that is a line of fully electric vehicles; what matters is whether customers leave the store having ordered a car that, aside from charging, operates better than cars they owned in the past. This flavor of customer obsession hinges on helping customers obtain innovative products that they never knew could exist and that work in their lives.

Innovation from customer obsession is not limited to the product line; progress can happen in customer service itself. Thus Apple devotes a great deal of time and attention to its in-store and online customer service experience. But maintaining simplicity requires balance. Apple trains store employees to walk through five steps, captured in the acronym APPLE, when they approach a customer:[47]

Approach customers with a personalized, warm welcome.

Probe politely to understand the customer's needs.

Present a solution for the customer to take home today.

Listen for and resolve issues or concerns.

End with a fond farewell and an invitation to return.

The middle step is the key to service on products that, by nature, can be confusing. Employees are trained to present solutions, not to solve problems. Most of them can't fix phones that won't connect or computer screens that glitch. They are trained to hear about the problem, take your item to the back, ship it to a service center, and give you a replacement while you wait. Apple wants every person who enters the store to leave happy with an Apple product in tow, and that certainly includes existing customers, whose loyalty is touted as the best in the world.

The Apple Store itself was a daring move, launched despite the failure of stores by Gateway and other personal computer companies. The Genius Bar and the general openness of the store were both innovative at the time.

Companies obsessed with their customers end up discerning unmet needs and shifts in the market—so they can adjust their offerings before a crisis occurs. Customers can feel that obsession, and they, in turn, will become obsessed with the brand. Apple, Tesla, and other customer-obsessed perpetual innovators work for this loyalty every day by ensuring that their customers feel supported to purchase whichever groundbreaking product they did not even know they needed.

Amazon's Blend of In-House Innovation with Cocreation

Most customer-obsessed companies that aren't committed to high-technology products will refrain from risky empathetic imagination. They'll prefer cocreation. But there's still enormous potential value from a strong dose of empathetic imagination even there. The best example is Amazon, whose customer obsession has been a pillar of its business since its founding. What's most admirable is how it has maintained this obsession while growing into one of the biggest companies ever. It offers both a reliable retail machinery and several breakthrough products and services.

As described in the previous chapter, Amazon aimed to meet a common need: using the internet to get people what they want faster than anyone else. In a 1998 letter to shareholders, Jeff Bezos said simply, "We intend to build the world's most customer-centric company."[48] Bezos, and now his successor, Andy Jassy, have worked to maintain that dedication even as the company has become an enormous organization. The company's start-up mindset (see chapter 5) helps to create urgency, but the foundation is the focus on customers.

Cocreation. That happens by focusing on selection, convenience, and low prices, with close attention to what works and what doesn't. The internet enables rapid results on a variety of experiments, so the company readily innovates in areas where customers ask for more or better. As Bezos pointed out, "To be innovative, you have to experiment. If you want more invention, you have to do more experiments."

The company focuses not on sales or profit, but on helping the customers buy. Bezos again, back in 1997: "We don't make money when we sell things," but "when we help customers make purchase decisions." For example, Bezos denied an investor's request to remove negative reviews on the website, since he saw giving customers complete reviews of items as improving the buying experience.[49]

Empathetic innovation. Yet the company also dares to innovate in fundamental ways—because it knows that customers are never satisfied. There's a danger in incremental improvements because it's easy to slack off, to drop the exhausting discipline.

Let's say that after transforming your current business, you are doing everything right. You identified a consumer need, perhaps only a niche, but you figured out how to meet it better, faster, or cheaper than anyone else. You implemented a streamlined customer feedback system, but you rarely use it, because you identify most pain points before the customer feels a pinch. Your customers love you, your employees believe in the mission, and your competitors are so far behind you that you've forgotten their names. You think to yourself, "Can it get any better than this?" And you'd better say yes.

First of all, few companies actually achieve all of the above. A more realistic example would put you near where Amazon was circa 2005. Also 2007, 2017, and maybe right now. In 2005, Amazon was seemingly doing fine, growing steadily. Amazon Web Services was two years old, and the company had officially entered China through the acquisition of Joyo, which actually ended up not doing well.[50] The company took on fresh new capital, and people were excited about further acquisitions, expansions, and other types of non-customer-oriented business improvements. But Bezos went right back to customers by introducing Prime, which gave subscribing customers free shipping on most products as well as free or discounted access to digital media.

Announced during an earnings call, it served to remind shareholders and employees alike that the company's mission had not changed, that "our consumer franchise is our most valuable asset, and we will nourish it with innovation and hard work."[51] Customers had not asked specifically for something like Prime, but Bezos and his colleagues used their empathetic imagination to develop it and make the numbers work.

Nourishment via innovation is often where highly successful companies turn after completing their initial mission. They can always improve their current dominant product, but there's an emotional payoff in coming out with something new, as well as the reminder to stay disciplined. Bezos said, "We must be committed to constant improvement, experimentation, and innovation at every initiation. We love to be pioneers, it's the DNA of the company, and it's a good thing, too, because we'll need that pioneering spirit to succeed."[52]

The joy of a customer-obsessed company is in creating positive feedback loops and preventing a fall into complacency. Successful companies are always susceptible to the latter; if competitors aren't at the back of your heels, be assured that your customers are assuming that position.

Amazon's obsession has played out time and time again. Fundamental to its process of innovation is to work backward from the intended customer experience. Rather than get caught up on engineering or sales achievements, people have to focus on what customers get out of any investment. The goal is to imagine a product or service, combining empathy and customer data, and then innovate to overcome the barriers to that offering. Nothing stands in the way. When AWS saw its customers' needs changing, it went to the effort of designing custom chips for its servers—no longer relying on what chipmakers were offering. The company had no interest in competing on chip design; it just saw a way to deliver a better customer experience without a higher cost.[53]

In 2007, the company released the Kindle, an electronic reading device starting at $399, followed a year later by acquiring Audible, an audiobook platform quickly integrated with Kindle. Then in 2017, Amazon acquired Whole Foods, with 471 stores and intensely loyal customers.[54] All of these moves offered benefits to *existing* Amazon customers. Kindle and Audible combined for exclusive features and rates for Prime. With Whole Foods, the company didn't just rearrange the stores, add a few signs, and wait to reap the profits. It capitalized on its advanced technology base. It implemented Prime services that enabled customers to shop for groceries for delivery. It seems every innovation Amazon makes circles back, directly or indirectly, to improving the offerings to its customers.

That relentless innovation, despite the company's already great success, stems not from a rational decision, but from the obsession with customers that Bezos infused throughout the company, old, new, and recently acquired. Contrast Amazon with Blockbuster. As will be described in chapter 5, the latter largely stopped innovating after meeting a specific customer need, perfecting the delivery, and acquiring a seemingly loyal fanbase.

It had no scandal, legal trouble, or any other typical cause of its train wreck of an ending. It provided customers with exactly what they wanted: a convenient place to browse, rent, and return movies. While the technology world was blooming, and the definition of convenience was reaching new heights, Blockbuster fell into complacency with incremental improvements. Without a passion for customers, it couldn't get motivated to do the hard work of perpetual innovation. What little innovation it tried involved me-too extensions such as theme parks.

Amazon not only preaches customer obsession, but it empowers employees with tools to serve customers directly. People have easy access to the data and software to build new customer experiences. The AWS investment pays off here, as cloud-based servers lower the cost of innovation.

Companies obsessed with their customers provide something they truly believe customers deserve; something that at first is a product or service, but quickly becomes a staple, a necessity, and terrifyingly enough, a *basic* in their lives. And when have the basics ever been enough for anyone? Your customers need more, and customer-obsessed companies will feel compelled to deliver more. The minute you refuse to fight to get your customers more, you've lost. Your product has become an expectation, and you can only satisfy or disappoint your customers, never impress them. The apathy becomes mutual.

Bezos states it again: "One advantage—perhaps a subtle one—of a customer-driven focus is that it aids a certain type of proactivity. When we're at our best, we don't wait for external pressures. We are *internally* driven to improve our services, adding benefits and features, before we have to. We lower prices and increase value for customers before we have to. We invent before we have to."

Obsession Throughout an Organization

It might seem easy for executives to become obsessed with customers. But how can they spread this obsession throughout the organization? For the offerings to be truly oriented to customers, all employees, knowingly or otherwise, must be on board.

Haier, for example, benefits from its extreme decentralization. Employees have a great deal of autonomy combined with access to customers. Serving customers well is the main point of the microenterprise, so Haier essentially creates a structural imperative to serve its target customers.

For its many distribution employees, Amazon relies on software that forces them to work according to customer-oriented values. Each warehouse has data so specific that each floor, each section, and each employee can have their ideal day's workload drilled down into a rate of units successfully processed (picked or packed) per unit of time, down to intervals of fifteen minutes.[55] Their actual performance, in comparison to the desired rate, becomes the main driver of promotions, probations, and firings. Whether or not an employee actually cares about customers, the job requires him or her to act in the customer's interest.

The internal enforcement of customer obsession may seem harsh, but it improves on frustrated managers running in circles, screeching in miscellaneous expressions of contrived encouragement and anxious contempt. The more a company can draw on its existential purpose, the softer this enforcement becomes. In Apple's retail division, employees work what many would consider a stressful, underpaid, and likely dead-end job.[56] But thanks to the company's training programs, customers see little evidence of this reality. Hiring for a service mentality certainly plays a part, but most of the enthusiasm and care that employees demonstrate comes from the training. The company convinces most employees that their job is not to sell technology, but to dutifully play their part in "enriching people's lives."[57]

The training takes weeks, and sometimes months, before people hit the floor. Much of this training is practical and technical, but a surprisingly large portion is spent telling hires that "they are doing something far grander than just selling or fixing products." With echoes of ordaining a priest or missionary, new hires start in a special ceremony. Existing employees applaud them for what they will soon be equipped to do. The clapping lasts for minutes and ends with gratitude in advance for the lives that the new hires will enrich. Apple pays store employees at best an average wage, yet retention is high because of this belief in serving customers.

In both hard and soft ways, companies can promote this obsession in their organizations. Any company that makes a quality product should be able to convince employees that the product will substantially benefit their customers' lives. In situations where, perhaps due to scale or just a distance from the product, some employees feel disconnected from markets, companies can package customer obsession and ideal employee practices into a single, measurable performance goal.

Silent Customer Service

Beyond employee attitudes, customer-obsessed companies fret about satisfying consumers. They invest in infrastructure to achieve high levels of customer satisfaction, not just through the usual call centers, but also by looking for potential pain points. Customers love knowing that their complaints are being listened to, but nothing can top the experience of having no complaints at all. Mistakes happen everywhere, yet obsessed companies work to prevent those problems from damaging the customer experience.

Amazon makes sure that customers don't suffer from company errors—and then works to keep those errors from recurring. When an order is delayed, the company will, where possible, upgrade it to expedited shipping. That's expensive, but it satisfies customers, who often never notice the delay. Then the company uses its extensive internal database to identify the specific fulfillment center, floor, function, and manager likely responsible for the delay. Investigators identify the root cause of the issue, and the organization adjusts shipment times, logistics, and management teams as needed. To the customer whose near delay caused these sequences of events, the entire procedure goes unnoticed, without inconvenience.[58]

Only an obsessed company would invest in the technical infrastructure and liberality to generate this behind-the-scenes customer service. Amazon does have a conventional customer service department, but it uses the infrastructure combined with its ongoing dedication to predict and fix most incoming complaints. To make the point, Bezos devoted pages of the 2012 shareholder letter describing instances where the company's customer service predicted or fixed customer complaints—part of justifying Amazon's ongoing investment in customer-oriented infrastructure. All of this is "motivated by customer focus rather than by reaction to competition."

These investments go beyond specific offerings, such as expansions of the Kindle Owners' Lending Library and Prime Instant Video. Obsessed companies want to make up for problems that you barely notice, on principle, with moves such as proactive refunds.

Suppose you paid $2.99 for a movie on Amazon Prime Video. You experienced some roughness from greater buffering than normal, but still you enjoyed watching the film, gave it a good rating, and moved on with your life. Out of the blue you get an email: "We noticed that you experienced poor video playback while watching the following rental on Amazon Video: _____. We're sorry for the inconvenience and have issued you a refund for the following amount: $2.99. We hope to see you again soon."

Something similar happens for business customers. As described in earlier chapters, Amazon pioneered cloud-based servers with AWS. The move was enormously successful and profitable. But instead of resting on its laurels, the company also set up AWS Trusted Advisor. This is a software service that continuously monitors how customers are using the suite of services. It makes automated recommendations to improve performance or security, or to save money.[59]

Tesla demonstrates a similar level of dedication to improving customer experience without waiting for complaints. While not as seamless as Amazon, the company uses its software updates and other automated efforts to address predictable pain points before customers actually experience them.

It also sometimes intentionally waits to enter a market even if it has demonstrated strong customer demand. As one former employee put it, "You only get one chance to enter a market."[60] A common problem is that the new market lacks electric chargers. Rather than risk a subpar customer experience, Tesla will often ensure its charging team installs sufficient chargers before beginning deliveries in the area, even if that means a delay.

Like Bezos and Jobs, Musk and his Tesla colleagues stay true to their customer obsession. They'll risk losing short-term sales in order to preserve the brand's commitment to customers. The experience of the car itself remains unchanged, and they expect the vehicles to be worth the extended wait.

Data Is Gold

Emotional commitment is the foundation of customer obsession. Among other benefits, it motivates leaders to improve their intuition on customers. Yet they also rely heavily on data, especially in cocreation at scale. These companies see data as a tool, not an end in itself.

Small companies typically can collect data on customers without large, intentional operations. Their leaders can interact with customers one on one with real conversations. As companies grow, leaders struggle to keep up those interactions, and no one individual can tabulate the opinions and behaviors of their many customers. Hence the need for data with analytics on present and potential customers.

Amazon—the giant of this space—is obsessive about collecting data, drawing from a diverse array and taking the data seriously. Besides validating experiments, data ensures accountability. As a former warehouse manager noted, there "is too much data to hide from."[61] The company's management trainers emphasize the need to confront and make use even of disappointing data—and to accept some failure. Andy Jassy, Bezos's successor as CEO, says, "If you invent a lot, you will fail more often than you wish. Nobody likes this part, but it comes with the territory." Adam Selipsky, who took over AWS after Jassy, encourages employees to focus more on an idea's potential to solve customer problems than on its likelihood of succeeding.[62]

Data is essential to the para-social relationship with customers, vital for adequately meeting their needs, making them want to buy from the company, and responding to shifting needs before competitors fill the gap. That's what happens with Zara's 350 designers. Every morning they dive through sales data from stores across the world to determine what items are selling and to tailor their designs accordingly. They also receive qualitative feedback from empowered sales employees, such as "customers don't like the zipper" or "she wishes it were longer." They might still get inspiration from catwalks and other fashion shows, but customer data drives their designs.

When Zara creates a new item, contract manufacturers in Europe and North Africa release only small batches, and these amount to quick, brief pilots in nearby stores. Sales data on these batches determine whether to order large quantities and distribute them according to anticipated demand for the items.

Zara sets itself apart by investing in analytics to recognize the different customers that shop at each store, differentiated on a neighborhood rather than regional level. The company has found that neighborhoods across the world are more likely to share similarities in their specific markets than stores in the same city. Shoppers at the Fifth Avenue, Manhattan, location share more similarities with the customers at their Ginza, Tokyo, location than they do with those in nearby SoHo. The latter, in turn, share similarities with the Shibuya customer base in Tokyo.[63]

Customer obsession plays out in many ways, but its foundation is a deep-seated commitment to the well-being of users. Whether in cocreation or empathetic imagination, it gives organizations a tangible goal and a vital discipline that discourages complacency.

This commitment is truly an obsession, because individual investments are hard to justify by ROI or other rational metrics. Yet these moves add up to a culture that creates engagement where the most rational, by-the-numbers company would leave employees cold. In order to sustain agile innovation, companies need the continuing enthusiasm that comes most readily from customer obsession.

CHAPTER FOUR

Pygmalion

As your lover describes you, so you are.
—JEANETTE WINTERSON

Steve Jobs was a thoroughly unlikeable guy. Obnoxious and moody, he was known for firing people publicly and for parking in spaces for the disabled. Colleagues made a point of going the long way out of buildings to avoid passing by his office and getting an earful. People were terrified of him. Yet he somehow won over enough of them to create a culture of innovative design, one that put Apple on its way to becoming the most valuable company around.

A clue to his success comes in his focus on recruiting, where his commitment to results shined. One day Apple's then-chief talent officer, Daniel Walker, was trying to convince Patty Shu to join his team as the primary recruiter. Shu, then a top merchandiser at Williams-Sonoma, was skeptical. But on the way out she bumped into Jobs.

Shu introduced herself and explained she was considering joining to lead hiring for the company, and Jobs looked at her and said, "That's a big job . . . are you going to do it?"

Shu confessed, "I don't know. Probably not." But she then took the opportunity to ask Jobs a question: "What do you want out of Dan's team? What do you want him to do?"

Jobs answered, "God forbid that I would ever have more amazing talent than I knew what to do with. That would be heaven for me."

His intense, focused response, full of conviction, won over both of them. Not only did Shu join Apple, but from that day forward, Walker said he made hiring a lot of "amazing talent" his mission. Recruiting got harder, but Jobs's focus on delivering great products created a culture that outweighed his personal difficulties and inspired colleagues to do great work. He had a kind of Pygmalion effect across the sprawling company, winning over people who might never meet Jobs himself.

The Problem of Scale

The previous two chapters praised companies for existential commitments and obsession with customers. But those qualities are hard to promote through direct personal interactions. As companies grow to thousands of employees, how can they create cultures that drive agility and innovation?

The solution comes from an ancient source, the epic poem *Metamorphoses*, written in 8 CE by the Roman poet Ovid. The massive account tells the history of the world from the creation of the universe to the death of Julius Caesar. Narrated through Ovid's mythico-historical framework, it focuses on how people create and maintain change.

Nestled among tales of heroic achievements is the simple story of Pygmalion, a male sculptor in Cyprus who had contempt for the women around him. In his frustration, he shaped his ideal woman out of ivory. After generously pouring his heart and soul into the sculpture, he named it Galatea and showered it with fine jewelry and clothing. He had fallen in love with it.

At a festival in honor of Aphrodite, the goddess of love, Pygmalion offered sacrifices and wished for a bride that would be "the living likeness of my ivory girl." On returning home, he kissed his statue. The lips were warm, and he discovered that Aphrodite had granted his wish—the statue had become a real woman. Pygmalion married Galatea, had a daughter, and lived the rest of his life with the woman of his dreams.

The key to the story is that Pygmalion imbued the best characteristics he could imagine into Galatea. His deep-seated commitment and attention to detail enabled him to create something beyond what should have been humanly possible.

Steve Jobs, Jeff Bezos, and Elon Musk did the modern equivalent in their companies. Rather than create ideal colleagues, they used their zeal to inculcate specific traits and concerns in employees far beyond their own immediate teams. Their influence ran deep into the organization.

In doing so they solved the problem of scale. Their existential commitment and start-up mindset might convert a few dozen managers and other colleagues to the start-up mindset, but they couldn't reach a large organization. Instead they needed to personally promote a strong company culture. With perpetual innovation, it's essential to have a strong, performance-oriented company culture to follow.

It's no surprise that a CEO's efforts matter. Researchers in California analyzed anonymous employee survey data from Fortune 1000 companies and tied these to financial outcomes. They found that CEO personality types had a statistically significant effect on corporate profitability.[64]

Throughout this book, I mention ideas, values, and mindsets that successful company founders embody. The CEOs who manage to achieve a Pygmalion effect throughout their organization not only live out these values in their management and day-to-day responsibilities, but they instill these values and mindsets, among others of their choosing, into the fabric of their company as a whole through their company culture.

Curating an organizational culture becomes more difficult as a company grows. Founders and CEOs can easily mold those around them, especially those who they interact with personally, but it's nearly impossible to mold an entire organization. That's what makes modern-day Pygmalions so special: they influence the mentality of their entire company. Their influence trickles. By weaving specific attributes into a company's DNA, corporate Pygmalions sculpt the employees that they *don't* interact with.

This deep-seated commitment is essential. To achieve the Pygmalion effect throughout their organizations, leaders must not only live out these values in their management, but also instill them into the fabric of their company. That's especially difficult as a company grows. For modern Pygmalions, their influence trickles throughout. By chiseling specific attributes into a company's DNA, they sculpt employees they never see.

Recruiting High-Potential Talent

Many successful entrepreneurs emphasize the need for talented colleagues, but Jobs and other Pygmalions took this concern to the next level. He said recruiting was his most important job. He knew that a company was only as strong as the sum of its parts; his charisma alone would not create a scalable and successful business without a strong team. Likewise Jeff Bezos wrote that "setting the bar high in our approach to hiring has been, and will continue to be, the single most important element of Amazon.com's success."[65]

Elon Musk, who was running SpaceX along with Tesla (and meanwhile developing a solar energy start-up), nevertheless was obsessed with hiring. As late as 2015, when Tesla had twelve thousand employees, he had to personally approve every hire. That meant every single person. Recruiter Marissa Peretz said her team had to provide written bios on everyone hired for a new two-thousand-person factory, from the janitors and cafeteria workers to the assemblers.[66]

Most interesting is the case of Advanced Micro Devices, which was on the brink of bankruptcy in 2014. The board elevated Lisa Su to CEO, and she knew from the start she had to rebuild the company's talent.

A Stanford PhD in electrical engineering who had innovated in semiconductor design, she had real credibility in attracting tech talent. Early on, she spent a portion of her time poaching high-potential people by selling the AMD experience as an opportunity to "learn a ton and make a big impact." As she recounted later, "What you can do as a single smart person is great, but what you can do when you bring ten smart people together, or a hundred, aligned on a vision, is incredible."

She sought those who "want to take a risk, do something very special in the industry, and fight the battle with fewer resources and more freedom." The pitches paid off. AMD's stock price increased thirty times over, and the company recently surpassed longtime industry leader Intel in the high-performance computing market.[67]

Tying "Fit" to a Distinct Company Culture

Musk wasn't concerned just about individuals—he wanted to set expectations for everyone who came on board. In 2010, when the still-small company desperately needed more engineering, design, and software talent, Musk raised the game. He lured over Arnnon Geshuri, then Google's HR director, and told him to hire only champions in their field who fit well with the Tesla culture.

On paper that might not seem much different from how other companies hire. But at most firms, *cultural fit* usually ends up meaning *personal fit*—and a manager's snap judgments about who they'd rather hang out with. Wanting to socialize with a prospective coworker isn't inherently problematic for a company's success, but it can be when it's the deciding factor between talented candidates.[68]

Musk, by contrast, wanted people who would thrive under the intense pressure he was putting on his people. A senior executive who reported to Elon Musk until recently, said it was almost as if the company wore its culture on its sleeve: "Because of the ambition and the goals, people work in a high-performance environment . . . There's this culture and expectation that yes these goals are impossible, but the world needs us to achieve them."

Starting from high expectations, Musk defined a good cultural fit: someone who not only withstands tremendous pressure to create solutions that no one had ever invented, but also someone unwilling to take no for an answer. The Tesla executive pointed out that people absorbed those expectations through a trial by fire: "If you say 'that's not possible,' that's not a productive enough answer for the conversation. Musk learned over time that he can get rid of that person and find someone who can offer a productive no."

Geshuri and others involved in hiring could therefore clearly define "fit," however difficult to find. For them, stamina and willingness to struggle mattered just as much as raw ability, and it inspired people throughout the organization to embrace Musk's single-minded focus on engineering excellence.

In 2014, Musk said, "What I'm really looking for is evidence of exceptional ability. Did the person face really difficult problems and overcome them? You want to make sure if there was some significant accomplishment, were they really responsible or was someone else more responsible? Usually, someone who really had to struggle with a problem, they really understand it and they don't forget."

Especially since many talented candidates apply to Tesla to help ensure a transition to electric cars, the company can find it difficult to differentiate between them. The difference between good and great candidates can be hard to see, but Musk provides clear criteria around overcoming difficult problems. By establishing a specific vision for what his employees should look like, and establishing that his vision is not an aspiration statement but a requirement, he sets his hiring team to identify the optimal candidates.[69]

Over time, culture takes over and leaders need to do less to reinforce it. Musk is famously demanding, but other agile innovators have a similarly distinct culture that drives recruiting. Under cofounders Reed Hastings and Marc Randolph, Netflix made a point of encouraging independent decision-making by employees. People share information openly, broadly, and deliberately; they're extraordinarily candid with each other; and they avoid rules. The company is also quick to fire people who can't or don't want to do the same. That strong sense of identity eventually gets around. As at Tesla, people who chose to work at Netflix knew what they were getting into, and usually wanted that kind of environment—a process of self-selection that only bolsters the Pygmalion effect.[70]

Indeed, a strong sense of identity as a company helps not only with deciding among recruits, but also with reinforcing the Pygmalion effect.

When your company culture is publicly stated and widely known, as at Tesla and Netflix, talented people who *are* a good fit want to come work for you.

Learning from Experts, Not Managers

A strong sense of identity is essential to the modern Pygmalion effect, but it requires hiring people for their expertise and drive, not their skills. Managers tend to assume people can apply their skills from one company to another, when the cultures might be entirely different.

At Apple, Jobs wanted to create visionary and revolutionary products. Doing that, however, required constant learning. To encourage learning, he needed managers who subordinates would respect. That meant hiring experts, not professional managers.

Jobs learned this the hard way. In 1983, he wooed John Sculley for months from his position as the number two executive at Pepsi, famously asking him, "Do you want to sell sugared water for the rest of your life? Or do you want to come with me to change the world?"

Jobs thought Sculley's marketing talents would catapult Apple into personal computer dominance. But a few years into Sculley's tenure as president, he convinced the board to replace Jobs with him as CEO. Jobs told the BBC, "What can I say? I hired the wrong guy and he destroyed everything I'd spent ten years working for."

Too many companies make the mistake of hiring or promoting people who have good organizational skills but little expertise in their area of focus. As Jobs conceded, "We went through that stage in Apple where we thought: 'Oh, we're gonna be a big company, let's hire professional management,' . . . It didn't work at all. . . . They knew how to manage, but they didn't know how to do anything."

In his return to Apple, as he moved the company back to its original identity, Jobs fostered a culture where experts led experts. He wanted to create an environment conducive to learning, which couldn't happen with management by professionals: "If you're a great person, why do you want to work for somebody you can't learn anything from?"[71]

As Joel Podolny and Morten Hansen pointed out:[72]

Apple is not a company where general managers oversee managers; rather, experts lead experts. The assumption is that it's easier to train an expert to manage well than to train a manager to be an expert . . . Hardware experts manage hardware, software experts software, and so on. Deviations from this principle are rare, and it cascades down all levels of the organization through areas of ever-increasing specialization. Apple's leaders believe that world-class talent wants to work for and with other world-class talent in a specialty. It's like joining a sports team where you get to learn from and play with the best.

Jobs said the best managers were experts who never wanted to manage, but decided they had to because only they had the expertise needed to create remarkable innovations. That expertise would induce subordinates to respect, listen to, and learn from them. So managers had to be respected experts. By relying on experts instead of professional managers, Apple ingrained learning into the culture of the company. And learning is essential to perpetual innovation.

Some people saw Jobs as a control freak because he would pay close attention to the design and usability features of Apple's products. But he respected people's expertise too much to tell them what to do. Instead, he invested in getting to know colleagues and getting them to understand his point of view.

Ron Johnson, who created the enormously successful Apple retail stores under Jobs in the early 2000s, found Jobs's approach distinctive:[73]

Jobs wore his opinions on his sleeves, and you knew where he stood every day. When I started working at Apple, he called every night for a year at 8 pm. He said, "Ron I want you to get to know me so well that you'll know how I think." I think the most misunderstood thing about Jobs is that he was the best delegator I've ever met. He was so clear on what he believed in, he had such clarity of purpose, that you could actually operate with a lot of freedom.

While hiring for a specific role or function, it's easy to pick someone with previous experience in that kind of job. But many people who fit this description fail to create an environment where employees want to learn and grow from one another. Steve Jobs knew that if he wanted to create a culture of innovation, he had to create a culture where employees wanted to learn from each other and wanted to listen to what their higher-ups had to say.

During his lifetime, Jobs created visionary and revolutionary products unlike almost any other. To develop new products and bring them to market, Jobs knew that the skill set required to do the impossible was fluid and required constant learning. And creating a company culture where experts led experts helped support, train, and retain remarkable talent.

Crafting a Sense of Belonging

Even when companies hire people who fit into the culture, they still need this diverse, often strong-willed talent to collaborate with each other. That means crafting a sense of belonging.

AMD excels at achieving both diversity and collaboration. It ranks among the most diverse and welcoming companies globally, especially for women and LGBTQ+ people, not just to source more talent but because it believes that diversity, equity, and inclusion are the path to bringing out the best in its employees and fostering a creative workforce. The company has made an effort to increase women engineers and engineers from underrepresented groups.

Metrics and milestones to increase this hiring are part of the company's overall strategy, along with a goal that 70 percent of employees participate in employee resource groups or other inclusion initiatives by 2025. The company has also fostered relationships with historically Black colleges and Hispanic-serving institutions.

Those employee resource groups cater to all kinds of demographics and offer mentors to new employees. Internal surveys suggest that the vast majority of employees are proud to work for AMD. The surveys address employees' performance in engagements (their commitment to AMD, their team, and their job), manager quality (management's ability to engage hearts and minds with day-to-day interactions and decisions), and the Belonging & Inclusion Index (a work environment in which all individuals are treated fairly, have equal access to opportunities and resources, and can contribute fully to their success). As benchmarks, the company uses data from other companies, as well as their own data from past years.[74]

Other companies have found strength in creating a company culture where people feel they belong. Bumble CEO and founder, Whitney Wolfe Herd, labels old concepts about how the office should operate as benefitting the structure of a predominantly male workforce with only one parent working.

Unlike most male-dominated technology companies, Bumble's staff is 85 percent female. Work hours are flexible, and parents can bring children to the office as needed. Employees get reimbursed for wellness services such as gym memberships, therapy sessions, meditation memberships, and even acupuncture visits. Those benefits have encouraged and inspired talented women to join.[75]

Establishing a workplace where everyone thrives enables your company to make the most out of the talent it recruits. Top talent wants to come, and then it wants to stay. Whether by encouraging more women in the organization, or partnering with historically Black colleges and universities, diversity and inclusion are an indispensable part of any business.

When people feel part of a supportive community at work, they are more engaged with their jobs and more productive. Conversely, a lack of community is a leading factor in job burnout. But talented, high-performing innovators aren't easy to get along with. (Jobs was only an extreme version of this problem.) They are strong-willed, ambitious, aggressive, smart, and opinionated, always looking to rise to the next level. Together they cause tremendous tension that can spark further creativity. The danger is that internal goals and personal conflicts will overwhelm attempts at agile innovation.

The challenge is to bring a team of competing individuals into a community and align them to one goal. Thus the crucial follow-up for efforts at inclusion: develop strong mechanisms for decision-making and resolving conflicts. Here it helps to turn managers into coaches, adjudicating disputes rather than laying down the law and creating the perception of favorites. As Bill Campbell emphasized, from his career of mentoring Jeff Bezos, Eric Schmidt, and other tech leaders, a manager's job is to break ties and make people better.[76]

Earning Your Place

Hiring is only half the battle. Beyond the rigorous hiring practices, Pygmalion companies reinforce their culture with aggressive performance requirements. Joining the company is just the beginning of earning your place on the team.

Tesla is serious about expecting high performance, if not the impossible. In 2017 the company made national news when it bulk fired hundreds of employees. Instead of blaming economic trends, business conditions, or overstuffed payrolls, Tesla made it clear that workers were dismissed for subpar performance, not laid off. Musk wanted to send a message to his employees: Either thrive or be fired. The company did say most of those dismissed were working in administrative or sales jobs.[77]

At Amazon, employees must likewise meet high expectations in order to stay. At fulfillment centers, workers packing and sorting packages for delivery are continuously tracked and monitored. Managers expect them to reach ever more ambitious goals. If not, they are at risk of losing their jobs.

Cyrus Afkhami, a former manager at an American fulfillment center, described an aggressive work culture: "If you fall short, you get three warnings, and if you don't improve by the third warning, you get fired." The company gave employees countless opportunities to succeed. "Every week, human resources or my boss's boss would meet with people to ensure that they are performing up to par, particularly employees in the bottom 10 percent." A company culture where employees are constantly put to the test brings out the best in some employees—but it can be brutal. With the help of HR, managers coach employees quite a bit to improve performance and suggest ways to proceed and hear their feedback; they also do a lot of training.

Continual improvement is common under Pygmalion leaders. Lisa Su at AMD set the 5 percent rule, which asks employees to become 5 percent better each quarter. She wants progress to be both attainable and impactful. Employees need not do the impossible, but they must still earn their place at her company. Having a future at AMD requires results—to be measured only by perpetual progress and personal improvement.

At Netflix, employees earn their place with the Keeper Test, an indirect way of indicating low value to the organization. Managers ask themselves: If someone from their team was leaving for a similar position at a rival company, how much would they or other company members fight to keep them here? A low score doesn't mean immediate dismissal, said Jessica Neal, the company's former chief of talent, but it does mean managers need to intervene. "Even if the answer is that you wouldn't fight to keep them, you wouldn't terminate them—maybe they're not in the right role or you haven't given them feedback, and that situation is manageable and can be turned around."

This pressure forces people to internalize the company culture. At Amazon, employees must continually improve; at Tesla, they must regularly innovate. They wear their company culture on their sleeve, and that creates enormous pressure on everyone else to follow along, even if they aren't in immediate danger of dismissal.

Trusting Your Employees

One way to increase influence, paradoxically, is to give employees autonomy. Free to follow their instincts, they end up embracing the overall organization and its culture far more than if they worked under specific directives.

Chapter 2 described how Haier Group decentralized into microenterprises in 2012 to better serve its diverse markets. But that move was only the culmination of the company's long-standing push for employee autonomy. Up to that point, Haier had already maintained a relatively flat organizational structure with few middle managers. The microenterprises went further as self-managed teams that perform many different roles. Each functions as an independent unit, responsible for its own profit and loss, providing each division with autonomy to make business decisions and meet customers' needs.

The company manages the microenterprises largely through internal targets; it's up to each unit to meet goals and compete in internal as well as external markets. Rather than prescribe action plans, Haier inspires innovation by providing the average employee with freedom and support to put their skills to the test. Units that fall short are subject to takeover or dissolution. As observers have pointed out, "Haier doesn't offer employees jobs—it offers them a platform to become entrepreneurs."[78]

Haier trusts its employees, and they, in turn, have maximized their creativity and promoted long-term innovation. After 2012, Haier's stock price more than tripled as it became the world's largest home appliance company.

Steve Jobs put it best: "The greatest people are self-managing. Once they know what is to be done, they'll figure out what to do and they don't need to be managed at all. What they need is a common vision . . . That's leadership." Pygmalion CEOs are leaders who inspire rather than manage their employees, giving them room to grow.

Even without a decentralized structure, Pygmalion influence depends on trust, including trusting your employees to stay. Netflix even encourages employees to apply for jobs elsewhere so they know their market rate and remain happy in their current position. That means Netflix pays top dollar for high performers. If you no longer want to work there, the company doesn't want to hold you hostage. Those who do leave are likely to be the very ones not under Pygmalion influence. Indeed, the company offers generous severance rather than holding on to workers.[79]

Trust is likely to become an even greater differentiator in the near future. Concerned about productivity, especially with remote work, most companies have introduced monitoring software for their desk-bound employees. In the past, companies could say they trusted their employees while still having managers check up on them. When a company requires electronic monitoring, it's impossible to maintain that facade of trust. We'll see a major divide between firms that believe in self-managing, and therefore attract ambitious, talented, confident workers who embrace a specific purpose or vision, and firms that hire people looking for a paycheck while they put their passion elsewhere.[80]

Mentoring

Pygmalion companies are known for high expectations and trust, but they help people reach difficult goals by providing resources, mentorship, and other support. Most companies offer some kind of training and development—they spent $87 billion in 2020, or $1,200 annually per employee. But Pygmalion firms go beyond one-off events or classes to develop a new skill set. Their ongoing programs focus on a specific mentality, set of values, or attitudes that empower them to achieve.

Beyond these general programs, Pygmalion companies take mentoring seriously. Two-thirds of Fortune 500 companies have formal mentorship programs, where typically executives are "voluntold" to develop junior talent in a hierarchical fashion. That's a recipe for tepid influence, not a Pygmalion effect. Relationships are not meaningful unless simultaneously pursued by both parties.[81]

Pygmalion mentoring focuses on the mentality, attitude, and outlook that leads employees to greatness. Companies want mentorship to be difficult but highly rewarding for both participants, and they put in the time and effort to strengthen such relationships. The goal is for the mentoring to cascade throughout the organization, not just through mentoring but general influence on how managers act and talk about the company. That's how you get a scaled-up Pygmalion effect.

While not a conventional mentoring assignment, Steve Jobs's relationship with his then-chief operating officer, Tim Cook, set the tone at Apple. After his cancer diagnosis in 2003, Jobs began spending years cultivating his staff and grooming Cook to take over. With Jobs's passing eight years later, Cook celebrated his legacy of challenging people and enabling them to "see the potential," not only of the world, but also of themselves. Cook had already worked at IBM for twelve years and then briefly at Compaq. But he imbibed the culture that Jobs had striven to create, especially the relentless pursuit of excellence, which he saw as unique. When Cook took over, Apple was worth under $400 billion. It is worth more than five times that today.[82]

At Amazon, Bezos picked one "tech advisor" each year to shadow him and his work. The closeness enabled him to groom future leaders with a mindset for leading high-value projects. That's what happened to Greg Hart, who led the team that launched Alexa into millions of homes.

Beyond one-on-one interactions, leaders can influence the wider organization simply by walking around. Merely rubbing shoulders with a CEO is a meaningful experience for many employees, and when conducted in a way that demonstrates values, it reinforces the company culture.

The CEO of Zara, Amancio Ortega, is known for eating in the main cafeteria and strolling through corridors to lend a hand whenever help might be needed. He breaks down the company's hierarchy so that being in the same room as the CEO is no longer a pipe dream. Those strolls are opportunities for his employees to see him, learn from him, and grow. At most companies, employees may admire their CEO but rarely see him or her. Not at Zara, where Ortega's frequent appearances lessen the sting of hierarchy.

Many talent development programs are onetime occurrences with little lasting impact on employees. At Pygmalion firms, people are continually molded by colleagues in a culture that stresses personal development.

Giving Employees a Voice

Mentoring is hard to scale even if embraced by middle management. Another Pygmalion technique is to invite employees to contribute their own stories of purpose. Those employees may not internalize the existential commitment of the founder and senior leaders, but they can still be influenced by their organization's central purpose. By offering stories in their own words, they mold themselves into what organizations need, with an emotional connection.

KPMG, one of the Big Four global accounting firms, was looking to build engagement among its twenty-seven thousand partners and employees worldwide. The leaders had developed "Inspire Confidence, Empower Change" as the purpose statement, with the tagline, "At KPMG, we shape history!" Then they created the 10,000 Stories Challenge, asking everyone to develop posters highlighting projects of historical or social significance in response to the question, "What do you do at KPMG?"

In a startling display of people's pent-up appetite to express the meaning of their work, they contributed forty-two thousand stories over four months, far exceeding the goal. These ranged from "We Champion Democracy" (certifying election results in South Africa) and "I Combat Terrorism" (combatting money laundering) to "I Help Farms Grow" (helping lenders justify loans to family farms).

A year after the initiative, the firm jumped seventeen spots in Fortune's 100 Best Companies to Work For, leading its rival accountancies for the first time. While engagement rose overall in the firm, internal surveys found the biggest jumps in groups whose managers spoke at length about purpose, while groups whose leaders barely mentioned the initiative saw little gain. The program itself wasn't enough; it needed managers to reinforce the message to achieve the full Pygmalion effect.[83]

Performance Reviews

These are commonplace at big companies, and in theory enable managers to give detailed acknowledgment and constructive criticism. But in reality they do more harm than good because employees focus on impressing their manager rather than performance per se. Microsoft made this problem worse with a stack ranking system, where managers graded people on a bell curve, each grade going to a fixed number of employees.

As one employee remembered, "If you were on a team of ten people, you walked in the first day knowing that, no matter how good everyone was, two people were going to get a great review, seven were going to get mediocre reviews, and one was going to get a terrible review . . . It leads to employees focusing on competing with each other rather than competing with other companies." Another described sabotage, either open and direct, or subtly withholding just enough information to keep colleagues from getting ahead in the rankings. Without trust, managers could not influence anyone.[84]

Until the company finally dropped the practice in 2012, surveys regularly told leaders that employees simply did not want to work together. Performance reviews and stack ranking undermined the company's efforts to build a community around shared values. The new performance management process emphasized teamwork and employee growth, and collaboration—not to mention satisfaction and productivity—increased soon after.

Pygmalion companies favor direct feedback over occasional reviews. Tesla has kept an annual performance review, but employees say it is simply routine because managers communicate feedback continually throughout the year. As one former Tesla employee pointed out, managers focus on the moment: "If people kick ass, tell them right away. And tell them in front of people. If you have to set aside time to do this, it's wrong . . . You want a culture of excellence that's constantly providing feedback so people feel they are growing all of the time."

Employees across organizations have this same qualm with performance reviews. In a Gallup survey, only 14 percent of employees strongly agreed that their reviews inspired them to improve. If managers aren't providing regular feedback, then the feedback comes too little too late; ergo, "by the time the employee is hearing praise or correction, the issues are history—they have either been resolved or are in the distant past." But nearly half of employees said they receive feedback from managers at most a few times a year, even as other surveys suggest that workers who receive weekly rather than annual feedback find that feedback more meaningful and motivating for outstanding work and to make them more engaged overall at work.[85]

While it seems intuitive to provide immediate feedback to employees, few companies actually do so. Managers prefer the control and deliberation that annual (or quarterly) reviews give them—at the cost of discouraging immediate reactions. After Apple abolished its annual performance review, then-chief talent officer Daniel Walker called those reviews the "stupidest thing American companies do." He found them a tremendous waste of time, as there are more effective ways of relaying feedback to employees.

Likewise, Netflix dropped formal reviews in favor of informal conversations year-round—even as employment exceeded ten thousand. Many HR experts can't believe that a company the size of Netflix doesn't hold annual reviews. But former chief talent officer Patty McCord, in a 2014 article, pointed out, "If you talk simply and honestly about performance on a regular basis, you can get good results—probably better ones than a company that grades everyone on a five-point scale."

Jessica Neal, Netflix's chief talent officer 2017–21, conceded that this frequent feedback can be "cold and mechanical." While many people might cringe and be frightened by Netflix's policy, she said others find it exciting. "They know that they're going to work hard and do great work. No one wants to be bogged down by people who won't do the same."

That's in stark contrast to ExxonMobil, which has clung to a variety of twentieth-century norms, including annual performance reviews and internal ranking. As *Businessweek* described, "Those interviewed described an organization trapped in amber, whose insular and fear-based culture—once a beacon of corporate America—has become a drag on innovation, risk-taking, and career satisfaction." The reporters point to the company's slowness in investing in breakthrough technology, such as shale oil drilling, and the departures of employees "fed up with not innovating." The company also discourages collaboration and psychological safety while paying above-average compensation in order to convince talented people to stay.[86]

Annual performance reviews can still further the Pygmalion effect, but only if closely tied to company culture. Amazon regularly checks in with employees regarding their performance, but mainly to promote the company's values. The process begins with the employee discussing three such values of Amazon that he or she achieved that year, and three others to work on the following year. The manager then provides feedback bringing together the values and the performance. The process leads people to internalize the company's values and align their goals with those values.

What matters is not the exact system of performance reviews, but managers' willingness to give frequent, ideally immediate feedback to employees. Feedback that comes out only a few times a year or that pits employees against each other will weaken, not extend, leaders' influence.

Once their company reaches a certain size, too many employees take the business for granted and focus on maximizing their own personal payoff, often through a congenial workplace. The result is mediocrity, however pleasant, as people refrain from the tough, confrontational work of perpetual innovation. Leaders devoted to adding value, however, keep working hard even with success, and they influence the rest of the organization far beyond their immediate lieutenants. With recruiting, performance management, and a variety of cultural moves, they create a Pygmalion effect that keeps the entire organization nimble and creative.

PART TWO

Ferocious

CHAPTER FIVE

The Start-Up Mindset

*We can have the scope and capabilities of a large company and
the spirit and heart of a small one. But we have to choose it.*
—JEFF BEZOS'S 2016 LETTER TO SHAREHOLDERS[87]

In 1994, IBM was easy to mock. Big Blue had missed both the PC revolution, giving enormous profits to Intel and Microsoft, and the IT transformation, yielding dominance to EDS and Andersen Consulting. While CEO Lou Gerstner deserves some of the credit for its eventual and successful shift toward services, the true leaders were people in the middle—people like David Grossman, a staffer ensconced in the company's offices in a building at Cornell University.

Thanks to his access to a supercomputer, Grossman was one of the first people in the world to use the rudimentary Mosaic browser for the graphical world of the web. Soon afterward, the 1994 Winter Olympics began in Norway, and IBM was the chief technology sponsor. On the web, Grossman found that Sun Microsystems had set up a rogue Olympics site that presented IBM's data feed under its own banner. He wasn't surprised—most of his IBM colleagues were still using mainframe terminals, not Unix workstations. But this was just humiliating, and it propelled him into a start-up mindset.

His initial efforts weren't promising. He reached out to corporate marketing and got a response only a few days later—from someone seemingly unaware of the web. He persisted and convinced marketing to have legal send a cease-and-desist letter to Sun that shut down the rogue site.

He could have stopped there, but now he was on a mission. He drove the three-plus hours to headquarters and walked in toting a Unix machine. He soon took over a large closet in order to demonstrate early websites to anyone interested. The overall response was tepid, but he won an ally from the strategy department, John Patrick. The duo enlisted other IBMers excited about the emerging web and decided to infiltrate the company rather than manage a splendidly isolated team. A sympathetic Gerstner gave them air cover but left the assault to them.

With their competitive fires stoked, Patrick and Grossman moved quickly to outpace rival Digital Equipment. That included spending. "It was money I didn't have," Patrick recalled, "but I knew I could find it somehow. If you don't occasionally exceed your formal authority, you are not pushing the envelope." They showed early websites at gatherings of managers, including one by Grossman's six-year-old son.

They won over essential talent by making deals with managers: "If you let me use your best programmer for a month, we'll build an internet product that will showcase your department's achievement."

Still, they continued to meet skepticism. Patrick faced old-timers who discouraged new thinking. "A lot of people were saying, 'How do you make money on this?' I said, 'I have no idea. All I know is that this is the most powerful form of communication both inside and outside the company that has ever existed.'"

Patrick and Grossman also emphasized that the internet was a company-wide opportunity, not something for a specific silo. At the June 1995 Internet World conference, Patrick told his colleagues that, for the next three days, they were the IBM Internet team—not representatives of parochial divisions. Microsoft was still dismissing the web as an insecure medium for e-commerce, but IBM was now investing heavily. By 1996, the Summer Olympics had an official website, and IBM had built it. A year later, investors realized the company was finally leading from the front—and the stock price shot up.

Like start-up companies, Grossman and Patrick acted in very noncorporate ways. They started simple and aimed to grow quickly. They kept an open mind, not pinning themselves down with any one way of thinking. They took risks, made mistakes, and quickly fixed them. "Just enough" was good enough.[88]

The Hero's Journey

They're ordinary people living ordinary lives, but then they encounter something calling them to a higher purpose. Each responds to the call and meets a mentor who shepherds them along what becomes a quest outside of ordinary life. On the journey, they face challenges, make allies, and eventually reach a crisis point where each must self-reflect and find the strength within, in their commitment to the purpose, in order to succeed. After that success, they return to ordinary life. But that ordinary life is now much improved, and other people see them—deeply changed—as saviors.

That's the essence of the hero's journey, an archetypal story that Joseph Campbell distilled from cultures around the world. In *The Hero with a Thousand Faces* (1949), he emphasized the inherent unpredictability of the journey, along with its applicability to everyone's life. "If you can see your path laid out in front of you step by step, you know it's not your path," he pointed out. "Your own path you make with every step you take."

Chapter 2 described the existential commitment necessary for companies to thrive in our current era of rapid technological advance and uncertainty. This chapter lays out the practical consequences of that commitment, and how it can energize not just a few leaders, but many people in the organization. The challenge is to turn that commitment into the kind of mindset that helps start-ups succeed despite immense obstacles.

That start-up mindset is similar to what happens in the hero's journey, and it's essential for large organizations now. Companies need a critical mass of people who embrace the commitment and dare to overcome corporate strictures in order to meet a great challenge. These are heroes who work tirelessly to accomplish what they've been called to do. They bring resilience in the face of challenges and an intense day-to-day focus on what they are accomplishing. They don't just show up to work every day—they're on an epic adventure, fighting battles and creatively overcoming obstacles to fearlessly fulfill their life's purpose. And they enable their companies to do what isn't possible in the usual corporate life.

The Problem of Day 2

As I emphasized in chapter 1, established companies are not built for epic anything. They're all about predictability, churning out high-quality, affordable products and services at scale. They don't want heroes—they want ordinary life. Unless they're about to go bankrupt, their culture favors people who are obedient and focused, who reliably follow what they and their colleagues have done in the past. Innovation is fine as long as it's incremental, small improvements, nothing that would destabilize the system and create inefficiencies.

Most established companies embrace what Jeff Bezos calls Day 2—when a company has successfully demonstrated its business model and can now focus on carrying out that model at scale. Unfortunately, Day 2 leads to several behaviors that make the company vulnerable in today's era of disruption.[89] The company does the following:

- Becomes focused on internal challenges
- Makes bureaucratic, consensus-based decisions
- Invests in entrenched capabilities
- Fears failure and reduces its ambitions
- Creates layered organizational structures or silos
- Prefers large teams with many dependencies
- Prioritizes immediate, short-term value

Bezos warned companies against the united consequences of proxies, which are metrics or processes that in themselves have no value but indicate progress in adding real value. He pointed out, "As companies get larger and more complex, there's a tendency to manage to proxies. This comes in many shapes and sizes, and it's dangerous, subtle, and very Day 2. A common example is process as proxy."

Processes are just a means to an end, often used to make management scalable. But as companies become large and managers become remote from serving customers, processes become an end to themselves, often so complicated that most people don't know how to navigate beyond them. They compromise on customer service in order to meet the requirements of the process. They focus on inputs, not outputs, and lose sight of the connection.[90]

The flame that got the company off the ground eventually flickers out. People treat the company as a given and start looking out for their own interests. They do what they must to stay on the job, as dutiful employees. Many resort to "quiet quitting," putting their energy and creativity elsewhere. Risk-averse leaders believe the company is large enough that they need not be proactive to prevent its failure. In this paradoxical state, they passively rely on their dispersed "owners," or investors, as well as the vagaries of the marketplace. They don't apply their full critical thinking to looming challenges, nor do they implement solutions quickly. They've lost the energy that propelled the early company to success.

Blockbuster, described in chapter 3, is a prime example. It began as a groundbreaking start-up, revolutionizing barcode systems to enable video stores to track ten thousand VHS cassettes rather than the standard one hundred. Its leaders dared to build a massive distribution center that enabled rapid expansion with tailored selections to local demographics. That's how it became a multibillion-dollar company, the largest video-rental chain with four hundred stores.[91]

But then the company went into Day 2. It competed mainly by acquiring rivals and experimenting with copycat ideas such as a theme park. When nascent rival Netflix approached with an offer to sell out for a mere $50 million, Blockbuster's leaders laughed it off. Their company was so big and powerful that it could simply build its own DVD-by-mail approach. In fact it did build up Blockbuster Online, but it couldn't help tying it to the brick-and-mortar stores, which doomed the experiment.

Blockbuster reached its peak in 2004 with nine thousand stores, but six years later it fell into bankruptcy. Its leaders blamed everyone but themselves. CFO Tom Casey pointed to the Great Recession, which hit just as the company was digesting high levels of debt taken on to finance acquisitions.

"Blockbuster had inherited over a billion dollars of debt, and with the debt markets as they were in 2008–2009, we did not have the wherewithal to invest in subscriber growth as Netflix did," Casey said. "If you stack up the two companies side-by-side at that period of time, Blockbuster had over 7,500 stores around the world, had a disk-by-mail business, had a growing digital business. Netflix had a business by mail and a small digital business which didn't really offer very much. So just in terms of the business metrics and business composition, they were both very comparable, both trying to grow subscribers—one company with the capital to grow and the other without."[92]

Netflix had a lot more than low debt. It had the start-up mindset, continually experimenting and innovating. What was happening at Blockbuster? Nothing. Blockbuster operated on the same business model for all twenty-five years of its existence. It excelled at giving customers what they initially wanted: an easy place to browse, rent, and return movies. It assembled a daunting amount of resources over those years, but when the internet arrived and the expectations of convenience changed, Blockbuster was stuck in ordinary life.

By contrast, consider DBS, originally the Development Bank of Singapore and then privatized. One of the largest banks in the city-state, it could have continued to prosper as a giant. But in 2009 it embarked on a digital transformation—with a difference. It aspired not just to add digital capabilities, but to go on offense. Bidyut Dumra, now head of innovation at the bank, put it this way:[93]

If we wanted to be digital to the core and act like a tech company, we needed to learn from the best. These were Google, Apple, Netflix, Amazon, LinkedIn, and Facebook. Our mission was to become the *D* in GANDALF. This has been an amazing rallying call to our employees. It started to make people realize what was possible and made us think about how we could step up to transform into a technology company. To reimagine banking, we re-wired the organization to have a start-up culture and mindset. We established experiential learning platforms, introduced new ways of working, re-designed office spaces, and fostered ecosystem partnerships to encourage our people to embrace a spirit of experimentation and innovation. We created an environment that embraces experimentation. For this, investment in our people is imperative and re-training is key.

But most companies are like Blockbuster in Day 2. Their leaders have lost the energy that propelled them to unexpected heights. They're now momentarily suspended before they fall—and their employees even more so. Gallup polling data suggests shockingly low engagement: A mere 36 percent of surveyed American employees reported being engaged at work, and that's actually better than the 20 percent level at companies in the rest of the world. The survey gauged engagement by employees reporting clarity of expectations, opportunities for development, and opinions counting at work.[94]

The survey results suggest that many employees lack a clear mission to set expectations and goals, as well as paths for career development. They might have opinions on improvement, but they see the company as uninterested.

They sense when their company is merely asking them to maintain the current operation—just more ordinary life.

This lack of engagement is going to be devastating for big companies as the millennial generation comes to dominate workforces by 2030. That group puts a priority on meaningful work that aligns with their beliefs. The subsequent generation, Gen Z, seems to be similarly oriented. They desire a career that challenges and empowers them, which companies stuck in Day 2 can't provide.[95]

Talented employees will therefore gravitate to organizations with a start-up mindset, a trend likely accelerated with the COVID-19 pandemic prompting everyone to rethink their careers. What a terrible waste of the vast resources afforded to large, established companies! We'll see more examples of onetime cultural touchstones such as Xerox and Nokia, which could have become transformative forces in the markets they had already done the hard work of developing—but didn't.

Pan Am was another such company stuck in Day 2, disrupted long before the internet emerged. An aviation pioneer, it was the largest international airline by the 1950s. It was the first American airline to fly jet aircraft, making long nonstop flights possible and bringing air travel to the masses.[96] But those same long flights meant Pan Am suffered especially hard from rising oil prices in the 1970s, and then again with airline deregulation. To recover, Pan Am uncreatively expanded domestically by acquiring other airlines, but to no avail. It gradually sold off assets and eventually declared bankruptcy in 1991.

After many years of making a profit, executives at Pan Am and elsewhere became complacent and content with convenience. They didn't do the hard work of rethinking systems that had worked well for years but now were out of step with the changing world. Leadership was spread thin, isolated from each other and from reality. They couldn't match the creative thinking of rivals challenging their position in the market, so they missed opportunities to pivot and survive. And they didn't engage their employees, including potential David Grossmans, to do the same.

Humble Origins

How can companies shake up organizations settled comfortably into Day 2? It starts with reminding people of not just their purpose (chapter 2), but also the tentativeness of their current standing. No one needs to tell the members of a start-up that their firm is on shaky ground, but people in established companies don't know, and especially don't feel, that tentativeness. In these cases, you start with stories.

One way is through a history of their company, which likely began as a start-up. Even better is a personal background. Amancio Ortega, the founder of Zara, shares a specific story from his childhood in Northern Spain that drove him to a start-up mindset. One afternoon after school, he accompanied his mother to their usual grocery store. Still not tall enough to see over the counter, he heard a man tell his mother, "Josefa, I'm very sorry, but I can't let you have any more credit."

Being turned away from buying food, such a basic need, shook him to his core. He remembers that afternoon, prompting decisions he made throughout his career, pushing him to stop his schooling early and work as a sales assistant in a shirtmaker's studio. Ortega was driven by an origin story that kept his energy going. Rather than approach life as a sequence of days with various events, Ortega threw himself into the "university of life." As Zara grew, he says, he never forgot that event. Just as the hero has humble origins that ground him in his quest, people with a start-up mindset need a personal reason for persevering.[97]

Jeff Bezos likewise came from humble origins and had to forge his own way. He was born to a teen mother still in high school. In Albuquerque in 1964, being a pregnant teenager was extremely difficult—the high school even tried to expel her—and it required grit. Four years later she married Bezos's adoptive father, who was similarly unfaltering, having immigrated from Fidel Castro's Cuba wearing a coat of household rags sewn by his mother. Both put a priority on work and rising ahead. Jeff Bezos remembers family trips canceled at the last minute because the factory called his father in. Reflecting on his childhood, he credits watching his parents overcome obstacles.

They gave Bezos the determination to do big things, while his maternal grandfather taught him to explore the world and pave his own way. The latter had a ranch in Texas where he and young Jeff spent their days maintaining the property and taking care of the cattle. Bezos recalls his grandfather even using homemade needles on the cows to perform his own veterinary work. Those origins instilled a strong sense of responsibility for taking initiative, doing hard work, and remaining curious.[98]

Missionary Purpose

That grit, along with a deep purpose, enables people to keep driving for ambitious goals. After all, most start-ups aren't really trying just to earn more than the cost of capital. They have a big agenda. To spread that feeling beyond founders or leaders, large companies need people not just committed to an existential purpose, but who feel a sense of ownership for the company's trajectory. These people believe that if they don't perform, then the company can't achieve its noble purpose. They're missionaries, not mercenaries. Bezos explained the difference:[99]

> The mercenaries are trying to flip their stock. The missionaries love their product or service, love their customers, and are trying to build something great. The great paradox here is that it's usually the missionaries who make more money.

Ortega likewise says that making money is insufficient motivation for him. Something deeper drives him, the key to his being able to "carry on tirelessly."[100]

Steve Jobs, who grew up with working-class parents, had a powerful drive to make computing technology accessible to ordinary people. It helped bring about the revolutionary Apple II personal computer, and it drove Next, his venture after he left Apple. In an early speech to Next employees, he said:

> More important than building a product, we are in the process of architecting a company that will hopefully be much more incredible—the total will be much more than the sum of its parts, and the cumulative effort of approximately twenty thousand decisions that we're all gonna make over the next two years are gonna define what our company is. One of the things that made Apple great was that, in the early days, it was built from the heart, not by somebody who came in and said I know how to build a company; here's what you do, da, da, da. One of my largest wishes is that we build Next from the heart and that people . . . feel that. We're doing this because we have a passion about it, we're doing this because we really care about the higher educational process. Not because we want to make a quick buck, not because we just want to do it.

Jobs stressed the larger goal, saying there "needs to be someone who is the keeper and reiterator of the vision because there's a ton of work to do . . . and it helps if there's someone there saying 'well we're one step closer.'" He saw that a mission or deeper purpose would keep the company from poor decisions, so he needed at least a small group of people with a sense of ownership to keep that purpose alive.[101]

Pivoting to Avoid Day 2

Most people in organizations have stories of overcoming challenges earlier in their lives. Those experiences epitomize what Jeff Bezos called Day 1, a sense of urgency even as the company grows large. If people feel the organization settling into Day 2, complacent growth, they can pivot back to Day 1 with challenging initiatives geared to the first principles of their existential vision.

Here it helps to follow the lean start-up loop of build, measure, and learn. Companies can design, launch, assess, and iterate on new and old goods thanks to this never-ending cycle. Each stage in the loop involves developing a minimum viable product and testing hypotheses against market reactions, then embodying new hypotheses in an adjusted version.

People can follow the loop as masters of their destiny, free to pursue what needs to be done, even if it's quite different from what's been done before. The lean start-up approach has the advantage of working under tight budgets, which makes it easier for leaders to give product teams the autonomy they need. Those teams can now go boldly, as befits their hero's journey, and ask for forgiveness rather than permission.

To promote this agility, the start-up mindset depends on simplicity. A pared-down organization running at minimum levels of complexity is much easier to understand than a company filled with branches, committees, and overlapping managers. Steve Jobs said, "Sometimes you need to subtract," but it takes courage to keep a large, successful company simple when intuition is telling you to scale your hierarchy to handle your rising impact. Simplicity forces people to be perpetually innovative, rather than throw money and structure at challenges.

Zara strongly favors simplicity. Ortega prefers to clarify problems and to decide directly and quickly. He is not given to lengthy technical expositions—"What are they good for?" He prefers the pragmatic approach, which gets people focused on problems. His ability to simplify complex ideas is an extraordinary quality, and it is something he has done all his life.[102]

Decentralized Decisions

*Use heart and intuition as well as empirical data in making
a big decision. There has to be risk-taking; you have to have
instinct. All good decisions have to be made that way.*

—JEFF BEZOS[103]

While pursuing simplicity, the start-up mindset also treats decision-making as a vital skill for every employee. Large companies make hundreds of decisions daily, but each one can either accelerate or decelerate a company's growth. Under the start-up mindset, every employee can make important decisions. That's how Zara works, and it helps to keep the organization responsive and responsible. In other apparel retailers, the buyers have all the power, but Zara gives salespeople most of that authority. They don't have to deal with orders such as, "You have to buy fifty thousand meters of denim," when this season's fashion isn't jeans. There's no financial team giving orders to a commercial team; the people making decisions are the ones in contact with customers.[104]

Before the era of Zara and fast fashion, clothes and clothing trends were meant to last long term. New styles came up only every once in a while, and most people bought clothes rarely. The dominant brands of the day were luxury and praised for their longevity. Production didn't occur often or fast. Zara's compression strategies transformed the fashion industry.

Because start-ups are already precarious, they seek the full truth from customers, even if it is information that leads to difficult paths. They have no safety net, and they're flexible enough that the truth can help them grow. Their innate curiosity enables them to fully listen to customers.

As Amazon was looking to expand, Bezos reached out to existing customers to find out what they wanted to see, rather than simply choosing what he believed would sell. Given how personal the business was to him, it would have been convenient for him to sell a product he was passionate about. But Bezos's passion was actually in making full use of the internet to change people's lives. It was from this data that he built his vision for what the company would become: a place where people could buy the things they needed but were niche enough that they didn't command shelf space. Especially in Amazon's early days, he kept his eye on the long game and gave up profits for growth, despite much ridicule. And he had an ambitious strategy to boost customer convenience at a low price: "We do not charge more because we can't figure out how to make it cost less. We invent to make it cost less."[105]

Throughout Amazon's development, Bezos modeled the mentality of choosing truth over corporate practicality. He pushed past the conventional thinking on growing a business, continually expanding selection in order to attract customers. He kept saying that when you focus on the business inputs, then the outputs, such as revenue and income, will take care of themselves.[106]

That same commitment to truth helps keep companies with the start-up mindset from sliding into Day 2. Amazon suffered heavy criticism when it started running ads on its website to regain profitability. The company risked navigating customers off the Amazon page, but the move fit with Bezos's ethos of giving customers many options. Then when ads turned out to be a weakness by concealing stagnating sales revenue, Bezos had the courage to backtrack and remove that safety blanket, and encourage leaders to seek other opportunities.[107]

Structural changes can help promote a start-up mindset in large organizations, especially by focusing decisions and accountability in small teams rather than large divisions. The latter often fail to take initiative because of their complexity, so the start-up mindset fades, and self-preservation takes over. Restructuring to remove complexity while still promoting some coordination with other teams is the solution. But carrying out such a transformational restructuring depends on the leaders holding a deep-seated commitment—an existential sense of what we as an organization must do in order to succeed. Haier's microenterprise approach, described in the previous chapter, is one such approach.

Decentralized decisions require a readiness to act to follow up on those decisions, since you can't delegate. And once you see the problem and the solution, you'll want to execute swiftly. Start-ups do this as a matter of course, but big companies can do this, too, if they don't settle firmly into their operations. That readiness to act also builds resilience because the organization can move quickly rather than postpone the inevitable.

Reverting to the Beginner's Mind

Another key aspect of the start-up mindset is the ability to look at market challenges and opportunities with fresh eyes, free of past commitments and biases. Most corporate leaders rise to their position after years or decades of following one or two specific strategies aggressively. They take a point of view and pursue it relentlessly, and their disciplined pursuit wins them promotion.

The problem is that the world is now so unstable that companies need to be open to new ways of approaching markets. They need leaders with a "beginner's mind," who see the world without the categories and solutions developed over years in one specific industry.

The best beginner's minds are in children. They haven't learned what can't be done, so their imagination runs wild. Some children manage to sustain crazy ideas into adulthood but have the intelligence and discipline to pull them off, such as Elon Musk. Other adults can sustain some of the beginner's mind if they pursue nontraditional corporate careers, perhaps working outside of industry for many years before joining a hierarchy.

It may be too much to ask most corporate leaders to unlearn what they've built up over their seemingly successful careers. But companies can force a kind of beginner's mind with processes that challenge conventional mindsets. Toyota, for example, has the five-why technique to get to the root cause of a problem rather than rely on familiar causes. As will be explained in subsequent chapters, several companies make a point of pushing back against "unproductive noes"—lazy reasons why something hard can't be done. The goal is not to humiliate people, but to shake leaders and others out of ideas that limit what the company can do to respond to possibilities.

Spreading the Mentality to All Employees

While structural and process-based changes can help, charisma matters too. The start-up mentality of founders such as Jeff Bezos and Amancio Ortega often becomes contagious. These founders are consumed by their work, and their behaviors are easily noticeable and quickly copied by those around them. Others adapt because the founder is magnetic. These leaders inspire confidence, as employees see that the leader believes in them and the company. To help it grow, the founder is giving everything he or she can, and employees want to do the same.[108]

Some people fall behind, unable to keep up. But the intensity of the start-up mindset usually attracts more than it repels peoples' best work. It pushes employees in the company to meet the pace set by leadership.

In more established companies, the mindset doesn't have to come from the C-suite. IBM was a hide-bound, calcified company in the early 1990s, but thanks to two mid-level employees, it embraced the internet faster than either Apple or Microsoft.

Entrepreneurship has now captured the cultural imagination, but most people aren't willing to live off adrenaline and hope, waiting for an offering to gain traction. Big companies can meet people halfway with intrapreneurship, where employees work within the security of a big company while still building something exciting. As at IBM, people can shape the future in a meaningful way, as long as they embrace the start-up mindset—and leaders encourage them.

After all, companies don't need charismatic founders to sustain a start-up mindset. As Chris Zook and James Allen of Bain have argued, the mindset is about "the attitudes and behaviors shared by the most persistently successful organizations with the most devoted and energized workers."[109]

Encouragement is essential, regardless of an employee's background. Minnesota Mining and Manufacturing, better known as 3M, began in 1902 making sandpaper. But William McKnight, who rose through sales and became the company's general manager in 1914, wanted to diversify the company. He took notice of Richard Drew, a twenty-three-year-old who had dropped out of engineering school and was helping in the sandpaper lab. Drew had noticed painters' frustration with masking tape that left residues or ruined the underlying work. With McKnight's support, Drew worked for two years on finding an appropriate adhesive.

The process was so long and taxing that McKnight even sent Drew a memo saying, "I think it would be better if you returned to your job of helping Mr. Okie with his waterproof sandpaper." But Drew persisted and eventually created 3M's first breakthrough product, Scotch Masking Tape.[110]

Google is famous for promoting intrapreneurship with its 20 percent time rule: Engineers can devote an average of eight hours of their work-week to personal projects that will benefit the company. While less effective over time, the rule did lead to some early successes, such as AdSense. And intrapreneurs such as Salar Kamangar were essential in meeting the company's pivotal challenge: monetizing its industry-leading search function with AdWords.

Even more impressive is Whirlpool, a century-old corporation of seventy thousand employees that has retained a pioneering spirit of innovation. By 1999, CEO David Whitwam and others were intently working to get the company out of Day 2. That meant investing in new offerings that attracted customers, even if these were costly. More important, they set up "structured ideation sessions" to open up creation and development to any employee who has the drive and desire to contribute.[111] The company also devised software for any employee to submit ideas for relevant people to see and then facilitate work on those possibilities.

From the idea stage, Whirlpool has a formalized process so employees feel empowered to work on the idea and take it further, showing a clear advantage to developing a product within a large established company versus on your own with no supervision or assistance. The process the company follows begins at idea development, proceeds to testing and experimentation, and flows into large-scale commercialization.

Presenters at the idea sessions offer "discoveries" of new consumer insights, competitive information, or technology developments. They keep the company apprised of what the world requires in terms of products, a valuable reality check in an established organization even when discoveries don't lead directly to new offerings.

Better yet, the company is realistic about the outcomes of innovation, just how a start-up is aware it may fail. The company expects a "survival rate" of only 10 percent of ideas reaching large-scale commercialization. Whirlpool keeps meticulous records of the ideas that fail, understanding they may be of use later and can inform future projects. That's the kind of mass experimentation and record-keeping of progress that is not feasible with a start-up.

The company's emphasis on innovation, despite the high cost of employee energy, time, and money, reflects its understanding that profitable growth is essential for a company of its size and age—and that it depends on empowering employees. How to balance corporate support and free-ranging innovation is a challenge, not so different from what start-ups face in seeking capital. Whirlpool has a 70/30 split, where innovators must follow 70 percent of the usual R&D process with standard performance metrics and executive review. The remaining 30 percent of the process resembles a start-up environment, where teams are free to explore ideas, structures, and techniques according to what best fits the goal. While funding is abundant, teams must openly compete for it.[112]

Tesla's Mindset

Tesla, the electric car company, has never slid into Day 2, even two decades after its founding and a gargantuan market capitalization. It's an exceptional but still illustrative case.

The start-up mindset began with its existential purpose, to hasten the world's conversion to clean energy. With rising worries about climate change, that purpose gave urgency to what was already the enormous challenge of breaking into the automobile industry. Cofounder and CEO Elon Musk kept telling employees, "Electric vehicles are the key to mitigating the worst effects of climate change on mankind." In doing so, he put himself on the hero's journey, while encouraging others to internalize his drive.

With this focus on the existential purpose, Tesla has resisted the urge to build complexity despite outsize success. It added only the battery and solar divisions, which fit neatly into the purpose. It still lacks much of the bureaucracy of organizations much smaller, such as public relations.

For some employees, Musk's words were enough. But what about everyone else—especially as the car seems far ahead of its electric vehicle rivals? How have he and other leaders promoted this mindset to the rapidly growing workforce? They did so by asking colleagues to do the impossible—yet in a way that made them feel empowered, not helpless. They were working at "110 percent effort," which made others fear falling behind that pace. People felt accountable to the high standards rather than overwhelmed.

Most Tesla employees don't work alongside Musk, but the company has norms that promote innovation without a full mindset shift of potentially thousands of people. Using the cultural dynamics described in the previous chapter, Tesla has spread the start-up mindset throughout the organization.

One is that people should attack problems from first principles, not from conventional wisdom or best practices. That's the only way to solve the tough problems the company is famous for. Another is that an employee should go straight to the source of needed information, no matter how low-ranking the employee and how high up the source. Inversely, Musk is known for going straight to an employee with needed information rather than through his or her supervisor. When he receives reports from teams, he engages them in their process, challenging them and working out solutions as though he is a member.

Through these norms, Musk exemplifies ownership over the work, mental agility in seeking the truth, and a dedication to swift execution. Managers and employees mimic this behavior, creating a powerful culture that prevents Day 2.

Another striking norm is the refusal to accept limitations. Musk has been known to fire employees if they give an "unproductive no" to a proposed solution. Tesla's journey has involved achieving what was previously considered impossible, and pushing the edge is part of the company's strategy. Musk's crazy demands force people to pivot away from systems of thinking that make the task impossible and to have the resilience to keep trying beyond initial difficulties.[113]

That's the heart of the start-up mindset. It takes people on a hero's journey of overcoming daunting challenges by calling up energies they didn't realize they had. It's not for everyone, but many talented people find it exhilarating. And together they can shake a mature company out of its settled ways.

CHAPTER SIX

Managing the
Tempo of Change

*Music is rhythm, and all theater is rhythm. It's
about tempo and change and pulse, whether you're
doing a verse play by Shakespeare or a musical.*
—DIANE PAULUS, AMERICAN DIRECTOR

The 2018 NCAA basketball tournament was about to start, and Virginia coach Tony Bennett was feeling good about his team. In what was supposed to be a rebuilding year, the initially unranked Cavaliers had coasted to a conference title and ended up the top-seeded team in the tournament.

Led by future NBA players Kyle Guy, De'Andre Hunter, and Ty Jerome, the Cavaliers had an unprecedented regular season. Scott Gleeson, a reporter at *USA Today,* praised the team for its "tempo-controlling offense and nation-leading defense."

Yet the team stumbled in its first game in the tournament against the unheralded Retrievers of the University of Maryland at Baltimore County. After a back-and-forth first half, UMBC trounced Virginia in the second half. Gleeson analyzed why: "Virginia got beat in transition, which rarely happens. The Cavaliers let the opponent drive the lane and get to the basket at a higher rate than any game this season. Everything, including their hedging on ball screens, was slow . . . The Retrievers dictated tempo from the start."

Virginia had been one of the most efficient teams all season, but they had become complacent and didn't do the extra work to control the tempo. A less-talented newcomer came to play harder, and Virginia couldn't keep up. It wasn't about speed alone. The biggest upset in college basketball history was all about tempo.[114]

Why Tempo Matters

The world of business is about more than just speed. It's also about tempo—controlling the pace of activity, speeding up or slowing down as needed. Moving fast all the time isn't sustainable, but too many companies settle for a fairly fixed, somewhat relaxed speed. Perpetual innovative companies have a high-tempo culture. They follow simple rules to quickly step up the pace when opportunity strikes, and even when they slow down, they maintain a deliberate and alert disposition.[115] As Bob Sutton points out, when companies keep moving fast, "people get confused, upset, and things will go wrong all over the place." The key is to pause or slow down at times, especially when there's complexity or high risk.[116]

Let's move from college basketball to the animal world. On the list of beloved beasts, lions have to be in the top ten. They always seem to be the good guys: Think *The Wizard of Oz, Chronicles of Narnia, Lion King,* and heartwarming videos of kids "roaring like a lion." The association between lions and strength runs deep, and for good reason: Lions are one of the fiercest animals out there. The lion is such a strong force, but why?

Lions are masters of tempo. For the majority of their lives, they're calm. Anyone who spots lions likely sees them relaxing, yet they are physically powerful enough to command respect. The juxtaposition between the lion's strength and serenity is how any person would want to be, powerful but calm.

A group of lions living and hunting together is called a pride. It's a fitting term: Lions are strong and inspiring, with strengths to be proud of. Directing the pride are lionesses: They lead the hunts and raise the children in the matriarchal society that is lion life. (Male lions focus on protecting the pride's territory from rival lions.) Cubs look up to the lionesses, as they are led by example.[117]

Tempo Like a Lion

We can learn a lot from lions, especially about tempo. When a pride goes on the hunt, the lionesses know to vary the tempo. They start off patiently, often stalking their prey for long periods. In the same way, agile, innovative companies don't rush out products. They take the time to discover what customers might want, and possibilities for capitalizing on it—then they pounce.

The tempo changes abruptly. When the lionesses come out of hiding to chase the prey, they have no time to waste. They speed toward the target, working together to give the prey no chance of escape. If the lionesses falter in their pursuit, the hunt will fail; if the leaders lose the tempo, the organization falters. Tempo in an organization must start from the top and spread from there.

A hunt therefore involves two distinct segments and two speeds. The stalk is the longest: The lions stealthily follow the prey, often a large group of animals, deciding how to position themselves and which animals to target. They plan, plot, and make strategic decisions. Then comes the action. The lions sprint after the prey relentlessly, at a blazing speed, up to fifty miles per hour! They make lightning-fast decisions, not stopping for breath until they've chased down their prey.

Tempo is thus about decisions as well as movement. That's the first simple rule. Jeff Bezos outlined something similar in business when he distinguished between type-one and type-two decisions.

Type one corresponds to the stalk, what Bezos called "one-way doors." These are high-magnitude decisions with low reversibility. They involve a lot of data and deliberation, as the stakes are high. You're still on offense, but you move deliberately.

Type-two decisions, on the other hand, are highly reversible and less important, individually. These can be made by a skilled person quickly, with limited data. Any of the lionesses in the pride can reach the prey first, but it takes the leaders to decide which prey to stalk in the first place.

Settling on the target is a big commitment—if the prey is too fast, too large, or in a tough position, the pride doesn't get another chance. The prey escapes, and the lions go hungry. When it's time to pounce, the analysis has already been done, and speedy decisions are key. Lions rely on instinct and reflexes to chase down their prey.

Differentiating between these types of decisions can be the difference between a slow-moving organization and a quick one. Getting a type-two decision wrong can be a bump in the road, while extended thinking on it is disastrous. The reverse is true for type-one decisions, where deliberation is appropriate—though even these decisions can't be put off for long; at some point the organization has to move. Bottling up skilled workers, in an organization too scared to push the limits, is the recipe for stagnation.

As Kathy Eisenhardt found in the fast-moving computer industry, companies need to move reasonably quickly even for strategic decisions. They still deliberate extensively, with a great deal of information, but with disciplined heuristics that prevent them from lingering over decisions.[118]

Imagine you are leading a new racing team. Type-one decisions are which kind of race to enter, what car to buy, and who the core of the team are: the driver, the head mechanic, and so on. These decisions shape the team's future and require careful consideration.

Should the team spend five hours deciding on the color of its logo? No, that's a five-minute decision for one or two people, type two. In order to get the fastest car, the team has to move at the proper tempo. A few extra hours spent working on the engine could be the difference in a photo finish, and the same holds for a new product on the market.

Consciously Choosing Sprints

The second rule is about staying ready to sprint. Frequent sprints are an essential part of agile product development. The goal here is to push ahead quickly in creating a minimum viable product or some other result that can yield vital information on what customers want. Extreme time pressures force teams to overcome the usual cautiousness and inability to choose among plausible features that delay most projects. A sprint clears the air—teams have no time to get bogged down, and they know whatever they generate will be rough. Sprints force product developers to move quickly to get the all-important market information.

But sprints also make sense throughout agile, innovative organizations when threats or opportunities arise. Teams must quickly develop and implement a new idea or strategy, without getting stuck in type-one deliberation. Before that point, teams (or leaders) have been carefully watching and planning their attack (or defense). Then suddenly it's time to move quickly.[119]

To work, teams in sprints need extra freedom from day-to-day responsibilities. They must focus on challenges in a fairly narrow task, with quick decisions. Leaders need to support the teams so people can focus on the immediate issues.

Here the inspiration is the world-renowned soccer player Lionel Messi, an Argentinian currently playing for a French team. When analysts assessed his movements in a typical game, they found he walked far more than other players, and he rarely ran at all in the first few minutes of a game. He was not only conserving energy, but also assessing the field and the other team and formulating strategies for attack. He was moving slowly so he could move fast at the right time—and score more goals and assists than any other player of his time. He was a master of sprinting when appropriate.[120]

Like Messi, companies can't sprint all the time. When teams consciously slow down, while staying committed to an urgent goal, they can go deeper and ultimately faster into their objectives. Their operational speed might slow down (how fast they move), but their strategic speed will pick up (how fast they deliver value). They're working on those type-one decisions before exploding into a type-two sprint.[121]

Tempo Is More than Speed

We can learn more from lions than just going fast or slow. Here are a few more simple rules:

Stay alert. The advantages of tempo depend on being alert for opportunities—and avoiding complacency. Lions need to rest and recover after a hunt to recharge so they can give it their all on the next hunt. But the lionesses must always be looking out for opportunities. In the same way, individual people need rest and recovery to avoid burnout so they can give their all to the next pursuit at work. Yet while they get to rest, organizations as a whole can never sleep. Hence Amazon's Day 1 mentality, described in the previous chapter on the start-up mindset.

This was why the Virginia basketball team fell short in 2018. They had adjusted tempo brilliantly in the regular season, saving their energy for when it mattered. They defied expectations and achieved great success. But then they became complacent and stopped reacting quickly, right when they needed it the most. They lost to a team weaker than several they had beaten that year, and their season ended. They had a Day 2 mindset in that game, and it cost them.

That alertness goes beyond addressing an immediate threat or opportunity. In 2014, Amazon was revamping its delivery system, building sorting centers to improve the efficiency of their holiday delivery. Key to the process was a steady flow of packages every day. But the company's main shippers, UPS and FedEx, refused to deliver on Sundays.[122]

Amazon executive Dave Clark found a clever solution: a landmark deal with the United States Postal Service (USPS) to deliver on Sundays, working around the conflict with UPS and FedEx. Keeping deliveries steady over the weekend lowered costs significantly. Yet Amazon wasn't satisfied.

The ordeal led the company to remodel its entire delivery system by developing relationships with independent contractors. Not only would most deliveries cost less, but the company would depend less on the big delivery partners. The USPS breakthrough was a big improvement over the current system, but management didn't sit back and congratulate themselves. They saw an opportunity for more, and they pounced.

If lions stopped hunting for long, they would simply starve. Even if the last hunt was the most delicious prey ever, they wouldn't stop hunting. Other animals would get their prey, and they wouldn't survive. A business needs the same mentality, or it will die from complacency. A company with great tempo that doesn't become complacent will achieve amazing success. Just look at Amazon now.

Leaders must balance opportunity with long-term stamina, so they need to be alert to the organization as well. A healthy workforce is much more productive than a burned-out one, and companies must watch energy levels in order to get the most out of employees. Bumble, the "feminist dating app," was having a busy year in 2021 with a stock market debut and massive growth in its user numbers. So founder and CEO Whitney Wolfe Herd told the seven hundred employees worldwide to take a paid week off in June and go fully offline. She knew that in order to stay hungry as an organization, the people couldn't be tired. Organizations keep moving, but people need rest.

Stay paranoid. When lions are on the hunt, they worry that the prey will escape. They don't get cocky or assume they've won before the hunt is over. Lions relentlessly chase their prey until they've achieved their goal. If people moved with the same sense of healthy paranoia, they would stay locked in. That paranoia motivates them to stay alert. The companies that lose paranoia get complacent, and the same happens with people. Paranoia is key to tempo. It ensures that you keep your rhythm.

Look at Intel's success as the internet emerged. CEO Andrew Grove wouldn't let the company become confident of its market position in personal computing. He believed that fear, even a touch of paranoia—a suspicion that the world is changing against you—was a healthy antidote to the complacency that success often breeds.[123]

Grove regularly questioned himself and tried new approaches to problems. Type-two decisions still need to be made instinctively, but a constant paranoia that you aren't using the optimal methods is healthy in keeping up with the times. The biggest collapses occur when a business refuses to acknowledge its ways are outdated.

That paranoia kept the company ready to adapt to the quickly evolving market, and it survived while many of the first giants of the internet did not. A prominent failure from complacency, as described in the chapter on the start-up mindset, is Blockbuster. As one observer noted, "They were too busy making money in their video stores to imagine a time when people would no longer want or need them."[124]

Imagine you're the driver of the race team described above. If you run a practice lap on an empty track, you might drive pretty well. Then imagine driving a second lap, where if you don't drive fast enough, you won't qualify for the championship race. You'd probably drive much faster, since a poor performance might end your season.

This is not to say that the threat of negative repercussions is the right way to motivate people to move faster. The threat of punishment often actually does worse than positive incentives to speed up work, and I actually recommend neither. Much better is a general, purposeful paranoia that everyone embraces.

Think back to the Virginia basketball team. A purposefully paranoid team would have come out against their low-seeded opponent with full alertness, and would have won, probably pretty easily. Virginia lost the paranoia that inspired them to excel all season, so they lost control of the tempo.

Look broadly. One reason we call lions "kings" of the jungle is their wide, unbounded vision. They're scanning the environment, looking for threats and opportunities, while other animals focus on their immediate surroundings.

In 2017, Amazon had become the top-selling speaker company in the world, powered by the domestic success of its Alexa software and Echo product line. In typical Amazon fashion, the project had developed at breakneck speed, with teams all over the country focused on Alexa. The company even offered every new hire the opportunity to work their intended job or switch over to a position in the Alexa division.[125]

But that wasn't enough. Google had just released its own smart speaker, and Amazon's leaders wanted more success. They kept an unbounded vision. After receiving a late-night email asking why the speakers weren't being sold in other countries, Bezos had teams working to sell Alexa overseas the next morning. He never let Amazon stop climbing.

Combining that ambition and paranoia, you get a refusal to accept the usual time estimates. When people expect to finish a project in five weeks, ask why they can't do it in one. Companies with the best tempo always move faster than others think possible, partly because they save their energy for when it matters. Said one car industry veteran who joined Musk's automotive powerhouse: "What took a single meeting and five days at Tesla would have required a six-month process at Renault or Audi."[126]

Lions don't stop until they dominate their territory. You don't want your business to be somewhere in the middle of the food chain, or trapped by someone else's decisions like a housecat. You want your business to be at the top of its sector. Don't limit yourself.

Control the Tempo to Keep Agile

How can a struggling organization gain or regain control over the tempo? Let's see how Virginia's basketball team responded to that shocking early loss in the 2018 tournament. Not only did it have a strong regular season, but this time it went all the way through the NCAA tournament and became the national champion in 2019. (For the record, I'm not a fan of the team; they just make an interesting example.)

After the 2018 tournament, Coach Bennett knew that something had to change. The team's tempo was solid—the defense excelled, and the offense already operated like a lion, moving slowly and pouncing whenever scoring opportunities opened up. But he instituted regular playmaking to discourage complacency. He added flexibility to the game plan to free up his players to get better opportunities on offense.[127]

Scott Gleeson reported that "the Cavaliers still played slower than any team in college basketball, but mixing in continuous ball-screen offense with the blocker-mover system allowed them to pair an elite offense with their already great defense. Bennett isn't going to compromise his defense and is more than okay playing methodically on offense, but he isn't afraid to make tweaks." With those adjustments, the team regained control over the tempo and went undefeated in the 2019 tournament.

Flexibility is the key for many companies in controlling the tempo and sustaining agility in responding to ever-shifting markets. Zara, the global clothing retailer introduced in chapter 3 on customer obsession, does this well. Its stores change more than a third of their stock every week, and they replenish their stock every three days. While other stores set their collections only once for an entire season, Zara frequently changes its products to suit what people ask for.[128]

By operating on low-profit margins for each item of clothing, Zara gains a large market share that generates profit on volume. Rapid replenishment enables stores to ditch underperforming or outdated products with little cost, enabling them to adapt and improve faster than their competitors. Doing so is essential in the clothing industry, where trends change continually, but the concept applies to any industry. The model assumes that half or more of the offerings will succeed, so a company isn't overwhelmed; it has enough rest so it can handle replacements for those offerings that disappoint.

Tesla is another firm that excels at adapting to new trends or demands in the market. Its culture of responsiveness with low bureaucracy (see chapter 5) enables it to adapt to customers quicker than its rivals. Workers often get emails from CEO Musk, even in the middle of the night, updating them with new developments or concerns and demanding action. With its fast response, the company capitalizes on change and gets a massive competitive advantage.[129]

One company that lacked flexibility and tempo, and therefore failed spectacularly, was BlackBerry. In the early 2000s, BlackBerry came out with the first smartphone and was a major force in the market. It dominated the new industry—but then it relaxed and neglected to continue innovation. When Apple and other competitors adopted touchscreens and new camera technology, BlackBerry couldn't change its tempo and speed up to adapt, so it lost its enormous first-mover advantage.[130]

Play the Stars

Many organizations, once they have a set of popular products or services, are inclined to support all of them close to equally. But tempo-driven organizations, like the Virginia team, know better. They give the stars disproportionate playing time.

In 2019, all three of the Cavaliers' star players returned, and each averaged about thirty-three minutes, or 83 percent of a forty-minute game. Only two other players averaged over twenty minutes, and the rest of the roster averaged under ten minutes. This emphasis on playing the stars is common among college and professional teams but underappreciated in business.[131]

To maximize returns on capital and remain relevant in the marketplace, companies shouldn't fear diverting resources from underperforming products. Any new offering needs an initial commitment with time for experimentation and learning through failure, but after a while, effective organizations need to give up on subpar projects and focus resources elsewhere. That goes not just for offerings with disappointing revenue, but also those that fail to keep up with nonmarket requirements. Hanging on to the past slows down your ability to keep up with the present.

Not surprisingly, Zara does this well. Inditex, Zara's parent, shut down a tenth of its stores because they couldn't keep up with the company's internal standards. That's key to keeping up the tempo, because the pieces of the organization must fit together.[132]

This logic applies to employees as well. At Netflix, as described in chapter 4 on the Pygmalion effect, only people who perform at a high level can continue with the organization; everyone else is encouraged or forced to leave. It's better for people to leave than for the company to expend more resources on those who are unlikely to fit in. As one employee said, "Being on a dream team is not right for everyone, and that is OK."[133]

Tesla likewise readily prunes its people. And that's in addition to the close attention paid to hiring, as described in chapter 5. People who can't keep up are usually forced out, less by HR and more by the company culture. The tempo is such that no one wants to let anyone else down. People either keep up with the pace or move on.

Amazon, a far larger organization with many semiskilled employees, works to prune people while providing more support. Fulfillment centers have advanced tracking metrics to see who lags behind and who performs well. Supervisors and HR readily reach out to the bottom 10 percent to help improve efficiency. Most of those 10 percent do eventually improve.[134]

Build from the Inside

Controlling tempo is hard. It requires rapid adjustment in real time, which in turn depends on substantial trust among the key participants. That's best done by building talent internally. All three of Virginia's stars during their national championship run had arrived on campus as freshmen, not transfers, and had already had at least one season together.

Companies can foster that same trust through vertical integration, so suppliers and distributors are colleagues rather than contractors. The more of the process you control, the faster you can adjust speed and chase opportunities. Outsourcing can lower prices and boost efficiency through specialization, and every company must embrace it to succeed nowadays. But organizations should limit outsourcing for activities that could be crucial for future success. Or if the economics of outsourcing are compelling, you can do the extra work to integrate with suppliers and build trust.

Thus Apple made a momentous decision in the 2010s to work with a contract manufacturer to develop its own line of computer chips. CEO Tim Cook said the company had a "long-term strategy of owning and controlling the primary technologies behind the products we make." Amazon has also developed its own chips rather than buying from established suppliers such as Intel.[135]

Establish a Cadence

Continual speedups and slowdowns can wreak havoc on people's plans, not to mention their nerves. Most agile, innovative companies have policies to promote at least a somewhat orderly tempo.

One common policy is "heartbeats, not handcuffs." The goal is to keep pace with external developments, matching that "heartbeat," so developers don't fall so far behind as to require "handcuffs" to avoid missing an opportunity. Another is to match likely internal dynamics, and a third is to institute quick but regular check-ins. The goal is to establish a semi-predictable structure while allowing sudden changes as needed.[136]

Another approach is to double down on flexibility by keeping structures loose. Amazon, for example, has a constantly shifting senior leadership team. Other companies tend to have a fairly fixed C-suite, with six to eight executives heading up the major units and functions of the company. That stability makes for easier office politics, but it creates fiefdoms that prevent the coordination and rapid adjustment necessary for reaching possibilities—and proves highly disruptive when crises do occur.

Amazon's "S-team" has about twenty executives, with membership frequently changing according to the needs and opportunities of the moment. The team sets strategy, shapes culture, and responds to crises. So it has a great deal of power but without the positional authority of fixed placement on the team. With frequent changes, it might be hard to keep the team aligned, but the company insists on forcing each issue into a six-page narrative. An S-team member works long hours to distill an issue into a memo that everyone can quickly read, digest, and discuss. The clarity and alignment ensure that when the company does change its tempo, it does so with full and strong commitment.[137]

Flexibility makes it easier for companies to set a cadence that matches their capabilities in the moment—but doesn't trap them when circumstances change. To prevent people from resorting to tired, slow explanations, Apple empowers employees to keep asking questions to get to "deep knowledge," to what's really going on. Anyone can escalate a problem if he or she isn't satisfied with the answers being given.

Organizational Structure and Processes

Here are some structural ways to enable companies to control tempo. After all, an organization's structure and processes have a lot to do with determining how quickly it can adjust speed. There's no perfect layout, since different models work better in different industries, cultures, and settings. But some imperatives apply regardless of your specific form.

Eliminate barriers. All organizations develop bureaucracies as they grow beyond the point where everyone knows everyone else. But perpetually innovative companies reduce the frictions that slow down the all-important adjustments. These frictions include not just silos, but also demeaning, overtaxing, or contentious tasks that add little value.

This was especially true for Microsoft. Before Satya Nadella became CEO in 2014 (see chapter 2), engineers thought that their ideas weren't translating into success. As Nadella recalled, "They came to Microsoft with big dreams, but it felt like all they really did was deal with upper management, execute taxing processes, and bicker in meetings."

Nadella reduced hierarchies and freed engineers from most of the institutional controls so they could carry out their dreams. As he pointed out, "They became Microsoft's mainstream, rather than fighting daily battles as renegades." And with them on board, the company could enlist them to address sudden opportunities and threats, often with the help of their ideas.

Likewise at Netflix, according to Jessica Neal, its former chief of talent: "I haven't seen many organizations figure out how to allow talented people to come into the organization, and feel truly empowered and valued, like they're the owners. I think most companies as they grow get scared of the chaos, so they start to implement processes, policies, and rules that end up slowing everybody down. But then what happens is that high performers get really frustrated, because they just want to run with their ideas, so they go somewhere else. Netflix hired the best people, empowered them to do great work, and didn't make it hard for them to get stuff done."[138]

In particular, the company trusts employees to sign contracts and charge expenses at levels most firms wouldn't accept, so people don't get bogged down in the weeds and can focus on speeding up or slowing down as needed. This freedom has continued even as subscriber growth slowed in 2022, forcing Netflix to cut costs in other ways.[139]

Purge inefficiencies. Besides outright restrictions are a variety of practices that impede efficient work. Large teams, for example, are often hard to coordinate and can lead to overdeliberation and slow decisions. Hence Amazon's two-pizza rule: Most projects can involve no more than ten people—a group that can reasonably be fed by two pizzas. That limit gives teams enough people for creative friction, but not so many for the noncreative frictions of dealing with many voices. That means teams can focus on customers, decide quickly, and channel their energy productively.

Often the same person will lead multiple teams, which helps with complex projects such as Alexa, to minimize overlap and conflict while coordinating on the overall objective. The teams still operate largely independently, but some targeted guidance from leaders and higher-ups maximizes the teams' collaboration. After all, when teams have fewer restrictions over pursuing their ideas, they'll commit more energy to those ideas—including applying them to current challenges.

Agility is the hallmark of Amazon culture. Its leaders noticed that the two-pizza team concept wasn't working beyond product development, because the team leaders were working part-time on several projects—they weren't responsible from end to end of a project. So they replaced the two-pizza teams with the single-threaded leader. Amazon found out that the keys to success and agility in teams were not the size of the team but rather the quality and the span of control of its leader. They made each team leader focus on doing whatever it took to successfully deliver the project. As SVP of devices, Dave Limp, pointed out, "The best way to fail at inventing something is by making it somebody's part-time job."

These single-threaded-leader (STL) teams had leaders who could work on only one project at a time. But an STL can lead the development of projects that are quite large, not just small teams. He or she has the freedom and autonomy to assess the novel product problems that need to be solved and decide what and how many teams they need, how the responsibilities should be divided up among the teams, and how big each team should be.[140] The result is faster innovation due to faster decision-making, greater creativity, and higher accountability.

What's more, Amazon shortens training periods and expects people to learn mainly through experience. One former manager at a fulfillment center pointed out that he was supervising a few dozen people within two months of accepting the job, even though he had no management experience. Thanks to a supportive HR department, he learned as he went and quickly developed skills and responsibilities. The fulfillment center in turn got a new manager on the job much faster than if he'd had conventional training. The company trusted people to rise to the occasion.

Clear goals. Organizations that control tempo need an endpoint to work toward. How they get there will depend on shifting trends in markets and the competition, but clear goals anchor the organization and facilitate collaboration. That's how Alibaba works on the frontier of digital technology and commerce. It relies increasingly on artificial intelligence, guided by the leadership. That clarity gives the firm a competitive edge at a time of fast-moving technology. As one employee explained:

> Digital evangelists must understand what the future will look like and how their industries will evolve in response to societal, economic, and technological changes. They cannot describe concrete steps to realize their companies' goals because the environment is too fluid and the capabilities they will require are unknowable. Instead, they must define what the firm seeks to achieve and create an environment in which

workers can quickly string together experimental products and services, test the market, and scale the ideas that elicit a positive response. Digital leaders no longer manage; rather, they enable workers to innovate and facilitate the core feedback loop of user responses to firm decisions and execution.

It's easiest for existential leaders to provide clear goals, and in doing so, they cultivate a culture of creativity and innovation through their clarity. To quote a sports mantra, "Clear eyes, full heart, can't lose."

Thus a former Tesla executive pointed out that CEO Musk has a hyper-focus on clarity. He distills the outward vision down to specific priorities, which is what attracts talent. But he insists that if you're doing your job and hiring smart people, you need to be clear about the rules of the road. He defines the goalpost, and from there, people have to figure out their own tasks.

Frequent check-ins. Large or numerous meetings reduce productivity. But regular, quick gatherings and updates do work to keep the organization's many activities on track, at the proper speed. How frequent the check-in will depend on the urgency or complexity of the project and the desired cadence.

Periodic meetings also help to establish a rhythm and stay on pace. These can feed into deadlines that prod teams to work faster than they would have otherwise. Some projects might have only one final deliverable, but regular updates keep leadership and other teams informed while ensuring a steady pace. While teams need a great deal of freedom, everyone should be kept in the loop and encouraged to move forward.

Controlling the Chaos

That's the dilemma of twenty-first-century business: giving teams autonomy but coordinating them to accomplish some activities quickly and others at a sustainable pace. Every company, like Virginia's basketball team at the 2018 NCAA tournament, is tempted to relax and lose control of its tempo. That opens the door to an inferior rival who can win out by speeding up to grab opportunities. When Virginia regained its tempo the following year, it couldn't be stopped.

The COVID-19 pandemic gave the world an unprecedented opportunity to see which companies couldn't adjust their tempo and which ones could. Start with Peloton, which sells exercise bikes and treadmills to consumers. As gyms closed, the company saw a rapid increase in demand. This tragic event could have been a massive opportunity, but the company didn't rise to the occasion. We can point to three deficiencies:

Failed recognition. Peloton didn't see how the pandemic would shake global markets and reshape daily life. It wasn't looking broadly at its environment.

Slow reaction. When the company finally realized that the world had changed, it still moved slowly to change operations. The reasons aren't clear, but numerous meetings, structural barriers, unclear goals—all of these might have played a role. The company wasn't sufficiently alert or paranoid to move quickly, so it couldn't keep up with the increase in demand.

Slow execution. Partly because it moved slowly, when it finally did increase orders and production capacity, its supply chains were bottlenecked. It also underestimated the health risks to employees, who couldn't be rushed as the company wanted. The pacing was all wrong.

While Peloton has avoided bankruptcy, it missed out on a significant opportunity. It overcompensated in 2021 to make up for delays in 2020, leaving it with a huge surplus of products as in-person gyms reopened.

For contrast, look at Etsy, an e-commerce platform that connects artisans to consumers. It had a similar experience when demand for masks, then a minor product, spiked at the start of the pandemic. Its leaders reacted quickly in mobilizing Etsy's artisans to switch, and the company's revenues took off. Etsy succeeded because it shifted gears and ramped up production in certain areas to capture a sudden opportunity—thanks to its broad awareness and digitally enabled agility.[141]

Like the Cavaliers in 2018, big companies have a lot of advantages, but they'll get passed if they lose control over the tempo. Don't let up.

CHAPTER SEVEN

Bimodal

CIOs can't transform their old IT organization into a digital
start-up, but they can turn it into a bimodal IT organization.
—PETER SONDERGAARD, FORMER EVP, GARTNER

It was 2008, and SpaceX was on its last legs. The company had a daring strategy to develop reusable rockets, and its first three launches of the *Falcon* rocket had failed. But the fourth attempt, on September 28, finally worked. Soon the company was landing and reusing rocket tanks on a regular basis.

Those innovations got most of the buzz, along with the company's plans for Starship and other innovative products. The company's founder and CEO, Elon Musk, was famous for bold predictions that never came out on time—but still eventually happened. As COO Gwynne Shotwell points out, "We aim high. We have always achieved what we wanted to, never in the timeline. We fail on timeline, but that feels like the right fail to make as opposed to not achieving what you are trying to achieve technically."[142]

But meanwhile much of the company was working on incremental gains. The company's mission was to make space travel affordable so humanity could become a multiplanet species. Breakthroughs such as reusable rockets were essential, but so were small improvements that progressively lowered the cost of lift-offs without compromising reliability. SpaceX's growing engineering corps had groups working on those problems just as it had groups on the breakthroughs. Its greatest achievement was not the breakthroughs alone, but running an operation that combined the breakthroughs with the incremental advances.

The Bimodal Advantage

The last two chapters of this book, on the start-up mindset and controlling tempo, described how certain companies work ferociously to raise their game. They attack problems with the fervor of missionaries, not mercenaries, and vary their pace in order to reserve the energy to grab opportunities with speed. Perpetually innovative organizations typically pursue a two-speed tempo: a steady, sustainable pace most of the time, moving deliberately with big decisions, and an intense, high-speed pursuit in response to opportunities or threats. Most companies typically proceed at a static tempo, generally the same speed regardless of the situation. Here we're looking at another divergence in company operations: bimodal versus unimodal.

Perpetual innovators tend to operate in two modes: compression for predictable or commodity activities, and experiential development for new or differentiated areas. Other companies typically settle into a single mode, usually a lighter version of compression, so they fall short both in cutting costs and in creating new kinds of value.

At least since the 1990s, companies have been shedding noncore assets and activities. Why manage the cafeteria at headquarters, or the janitorial service, when specialized firms will do it better and cheaper? Many have gone further, contracting for marketing, manufacturing, distribution, or even product development, when these are not intrinsic to the strategy. This outsourcing led to a wave of downsizing as companies focused on their core competencies.

Yet a great many activities have remained that companies cannot fully outsource, usually because these are too complex or integrated into the main operations. The solution for ambitious companies is compression, or accelerating the overall ongoing push for efficiency. Every company tries to add efficiency to its activities as it learns and scales up, but compression adds pressure and discipline to the process. Often that work is essential for corporate success. Predictable operations, where the organization has little left to learn and where differentiation has minimal payoff, can account for much of a company's costs. Compression adds discipline and urgency to this process, especially for complicated operations that haven't already been routinized. The goal here is to standardize, automate, and push hard to remove costs.

Compression also works for projects with incremental improvements and minimal market or technical uncertainty. Leaders can ask those teams for detailed end-to-end schedules.

This chapter, more than most, draws on my own research over the years, especially in the global computer industry. In the 1990s I worked with colleagues on multiple studies that focused on bimodal development. My subsequent consulting and research have confirmed the findings we published back then.

The following chart neatly lays out the differences in the two modes. Note that unpredictability, not complexity, per se, determines how much to rely on experiential development. Agile innovators relegate complex but predictable projects to compression.

	Predictable	Unpredictable
Simple	✓	Experiential-focus
Complex	Compression	Compression/ Experiential-focus

They go in the opposite direction for most of their core strategic operations. Here they downplay efficiency altogether and encourage managers to pursue multiple options and hypotheses. Their experiential approach emphasizes learning and discovery, though still with a focus and milestones to ensure discipline and accountability.

Breakthrough projects won't have detailed timelines. Instead, overseers will look for interactive schedules with milestones for discussing findings and new paths. Smart leaders need to distinguish these projects sharply from those that benefit from compression so the same team doesn't work in both modes.

Many companies have moved toward a superficial bimodal approach by cutting costs in operations while boosting budgets for innovation. But bimodal isn't about a neat division between continuing operations and product development. Some seemingly ordinary operations might be highly strategic or differentiating, and benefit from an experiential approach. As for product development, much of it is actually highly derivative or incremental, and can benefit from compression. And budgeting is only one part of project management. Most companies take the easier approach of running all their projects the same way, pushing for efficiency while blandly encouraging innovation if it appears promising.

And that's how bimodal differs from the dual-tempo approach described earlier. Shifts in speed can affect an entire organization, depending on the threat or opportunity. The bimodal approach divides the organization into activities to be compressed and activities to be developed experientially. That division continues over time, separate from short-term changes in speed.

Here's how to apply each mode. For compression: Set a clear plan for the activity, delegate it to accountable managers, lower the costs over time according to a learning curve, and consolidate related activities over time. These steps are all about taking a process a company already knows well and doing it even better.

For an experiential activity: Develop multiple options, test each, and set frequent milestones under a leader's guidance to ensure learning and progress. The emphasis here is on discovery, so openness and curiosity are essential, not hard discipline.

Accordingly, compression works well for developing derivative products, while experiential is better for developing new products or platforms. The chart below brings together these points.[143]

	Compression	Experiential-focus
Key Learning	Complexity	Uncertainty
Image of Product Development	Complex series of steps	Foggy path through shifting markets
Strategy for Product	Rationalize plan (yet deliberate action)	Improvise
Strategy for Speed	Rationalize (plan) Delegate (suppliers) Compress (CAD) Compress (overlap) Cross-functional Reward	Search on more fronts (iterations) Uncover errors (test) Focus (milestone) Big picture (leader)

Compression

Compression comes from civil engineering and uses such familiar techniques as the critical path method, PERT, reengineering, and concurrent engineering. Carmakers rely on it for large assembly products, but it's also popular in the mainframe segment of the computer industry. That's a mature niche where customers, competition, and technology are fairly stable and technology improves slowly. For all we talk about disruption, plenty of corporate activities still operate in relatively stable environments. (see figure: A Bimodal Approach to New Product Development).

The process works for any predictable operation, however complicated. To accelerate the efficiencies, companies must manage aggressively, identifying opportunities for improvement and pursuing these with discipline. Over time they can simplify the steps, which often enables them to delegate more to suppliers, but serves mainly to shorten the time it takes to complete each step. Simplifying also encourages overlapping development. Overall, this strategy involves rationalizing or reengineering the process to streamline it, then squeezing it together to reduce cost, time, or both.

A Bimodal Approach to New Product Development		
	Experiential	Compression
Uncertainty	High	Low
Definition of specifications	Specifications evolve over time before final definition	Specifications are completed within a few days
Initial staffing of team	Staffed with only key employees	Fully staffed with all employees involved in product development
Milestones	Early: Long intervals between milestones Later: Short intervals	Short intervals between well-defined milestones

It's similar to the "hurry-up offense" in American football. After enough practice, teams can eliminate huddles, accelerate snap counts, and run rapidly developing plays. Companies reduce time or cost by streamlining the process, eliminating delays, and squeezing together design steps. Let's delve into the four key steps:

Planning and monitoring. Above all, this involves close attention to what's actually needed for the operation. Planners can use their comprehensive view to eliminate a great deal of unnecessary activity while fixing some steps that work poorly in practice. Planning squeezes development time with a blueprint that organizes and coordinates different parts of the project team. Plans have political benefits too: while reducing costs overall, they ease the path to necessary resources, as senior executives are more generous with funding and personnel when plans are thorough.

Amazon excels at compression, especially at its fulfillment centers. These warehouses, which pick, package, and ship products, run with overlapping steps and operate at all times of the day. They rely on assistive technology to reduce wasted time by workers and compound productivity. Software prompts guide workers in picking out products, as they "are not meant to have to think long about what they're retrieving."[144] They just go where the software tells them. The centers as a whole are given critical pull times (CPTs) that mark exactly when certain loads are to be shipped out. Extensive planning and analytics go into calculating these CPTs, so the centers can meet their targets.

Beyond those targets, the company tracks timing metrics for each employee and department every hour. Planners use these metrics to scope out operations in advance while increasing the targets as people move along the learning curve. These times motivate employees to speed up everything overall, and the whole system is a positive feedback loop of compression. Managers also have weekly individual check-in meetings to ensure problems are solved quickly. The system is so intense that "a swing of a second or two in the average time to complete a task can make the difference between getting kudos from a manager or a warning about job performance."

Workers (and union activists) say the incentives prod them to cut times by engaging in dangerous actions. Indeed, the pressures induce everyone to pick up the pace, overcoming the complacency and laxity that often arises from routinized activities. But just as with the introduction of the assembly line at Ford Motor Company in 1913, the intensity stresses many employees who aren't meant for such structured, driven work.

With all this tracking information, each center's human resources staff meets with managers weekly to discuss the bottom 10 percent of employees and how to boost their efficiency. Workers who consistently fall short get a written warning each week; after three such warnings, they are fired. That's a worst-case scenario; more likely, the collaboration with the manager and HR helps workers get to the root of problems and improve substantially. Amazon plans out the process thoroughly to deal with inefficient work as it arises and to minimize time spent on extraneous problem-solving.

That careful attention has also enabled the company to get a head start on automation—supplementing the human pickers with robots. In 2012 it bought Kiva Systems, using its robots to rearrange shelves according to a computer system. The "click-to-ship" cycle was taking over sixty minutes; Kiva robots cut that cycle down to fifteen minutes, and the warehouses could now hold substantially more inventory. Amazon is still a few years away from replacing human pickers outright, but this heightened attention has given the company a remarkable lead in reducing shipping times and costs. With compression based on planning, assistive technology, and analytics, its global advantage in consumer shipping may be hard to overtake.[145]

Delegating to others. Once the planners know the value and compressibility of each task in a process, they can usually outsource some of those tasks, including design. That frees the work teams to focus on tasks involving their competencies. The in-house developers might focus on a brand-specific aspect of the design, essential for integrating the item with the rest of the product line, while leaving the rest of the design to suppliers.

For predictable products such as mainframes and minicomputers, companies benefitted from involving suppliers early and extensively in the development process. The latter often had excellent product ideas and valuable insights regarding downstream manufacturing issues. Well-known standards and interfaces clarified the delegation of design tasks.

Delegation also works internally, as in AMD's $49 billion acquisition of another chipmaker, Xilinx, in 2022. Chapter 4 explained that AMD rose from near bankruptcy with a bold strategy to leapfrog the technology of market leader Intel. The strategy succeeded as AMD released the most advanced chip in the industry, but then the company lacked the resources to pursue a full product line of chips. So it bought rival Xilinx to support a varied offering of chip types.

AMD could have tried to broaden its offerings on its own, but Xilinx speeded up the process because it focused on the compression work to support AMD's experiential successes. The joint expansion, with Xilinx putting out chips blending the two companies' technologies, carried out the strategy better than if AMD had gone it alone. Most delegation happens as outsourcing, but acquisition is another approach.

AMD had already done the fundamental innovation in chip design, but needed to scale up this advance into a broad product line. That work wasn't especially innovative, and Xilinx could handle it quickly and at much less cost than if AMD had tried to expand itself. AMD's leaders just had to oversee the legacy Xilinx teams and managers separately.[146]

Shortening the design stages. Companies can compress with brute force by adding personnel, requiring overtime, and enforcing tight time goals. But it's more sustainable to rely on technology, especially computer-aided design. CAD works particularly well to speed incremental innovation with faster engineering computations, greater reuse of past designs, and easier communication among designers.

Apple excels at shorter design stages. Every fall, the company releases a new model of the iPhone, now at 14 as of 2022. One reviewer highlighted the compression challenge: "The problem with so much great innovation is that upgrades are now so iterative that it has become difficult to know what to write about them each year."[147]

Most customers don't replace an iPhone annually, but enough people do to make it a big event—and that puts pressure on the company to include some innovation in every new model. Yet the changes have to be quick and disciplined to keep to the annual schedule. So Apple has to aggressively shorten the design cycle. Otherwise, with the smartphone market now saturated, the company might fall behind a rival.

With so much experience, and such a hard schedule, Apple has become an expert at compression. Each model begins with extensive planning to maximize efficiency. Design stages take place simultaneously, and engineers likewise work on multiple projects for multiple phone models. When the time comes and a new model must go out, the company releases updates periodically to appease current iPhone owners while still working on new features and technologies for future releases. Meanwhile a separate experiential team explores possibilities for major advances.[148]

When speed is the essence of a competitive advantage, overlapping is essential. Zara emphasizes overlapping production stages because its business model requires a rapid response to fashion trends. At any given moment, a new fashion line is on its way to stores, its factories are generating a newer line, people at headquarters are designing an even newer line, and store employees are reporting on emerging preferences for what will be the newest lines of all. As soon as one piece of clothing is approved and rapidly produced, a new style immediately enters production—and customers will want something new a week after that.

While rivals take months to design and produce a new style, Zara moves in a matter of days. As soon as designs are approved, the company's vertical integration realizes the idea quickly, void of intermediaries that could slow down the release of new clothing through lengthy approvals or simply favoring other customers. The stores drastically reduce wait times for customers, with the process unfolding rapidly through multiple stages at once.

Zara's high-speed process helps compression in multiple ways. It forces Zara to collect data at every step of the way, so it can both discover inefficiencies and predict trends better than rivals. The overall urgency encourages managers to find and address minor hindrances that counterparts at slower companies might ignore.

Compression has worked wonders for Zara, giving it a solid foothold in the fashion industry. One early article raved that Zara has "an amazing capacity to sense fashion trends, take them on board, and turn them into reality at bargain basement prices. And all within twenty days!" While margins on each item are low, the strategy enables the company to sell the stock at full price and at such high volume that it commands a large segment of the market with substantial profits. Through compression, this scale has made it difficult for rivals to overtake it.

While some designs do fail, Zara's can rapidly adapt and minimize losses. After the devastating terrorist attacks on September 11, 2001, Americans' somber mood made them unreceptive to the floral styles that designers and brands had been pushing. While most companies struggled with tepid sales, Zara quickly switched to dark, quiet shades that sold much better—and expanded its market share.[149]

Keep the innovation simple. In order to maintain a steady pace of incremental improvement, companies must resist the temptation of frequent big changes. Nike has mastered this approach with its shortened design stages.

Nike has the largest share of athletic shoes, with a strong following. Sneakerheads, as superfans of shoes are referred to, eagerly await new drops of the next model of the company's centerpiece Air Jordans. Yet most models have little in the way of advances—often just a new colorway or design. How does Nike manage to make so much money off of shoe releases that are hardly better than existing models?

Nike has mastered the art of compression, not just marketing. Yes, Nike pays a large group of celebrities to advertise for them. It also creates some scarcity, producing limited quantities of new releases in order to drive up demand and prices. But it could not have trained sneakerheads to focus on regular releases without a highly disciplined investment in compression.

As ESPN writer Scoop Jackson put it, "The business model set in place by Jordan brand's practice of annually releasing something new, and numbering it into a marketplace that stays connected to a singular item, has always been revolutionary." Without the compression techniques employed by Nike to maintain this level of consistent production and evolution, the Jordan brand wouldn't maintain such high demand.

Central to its success is Nike's extensive use of planning. The company sets the release of new models several months in advance—sneakerheads can go online and find the release dates of new models of Air Jordans periodically to be dropped over the next several months. Each model is usually the "nth" iteration of an original model: Air Jordan 6 Retro Low "CNY," Air Jordan 12 Retro "Playoffs," Air Jordan 4 Women's "Canvas," and so on. Consumers know that each release won't be a significant improvement on the last one, most likely an incremental gain in technology. But the superfans still buy.

As for simultaneous and shortened stages, different teams of designers are constantly working on different new models and colorways of new iterations of a shoe at the same time. Old designs are constantly reused and slightly improved upon to get a head start on production. That way, releases can be staggered with a short wait time in between, so consumers are never waiting long for a new release, which keeps them attached.

At its start, Air Jordans represented a significant leap in shoe technology for athletes. Now that Nike has garnered so much traction, it stands to profit by periodically releasing new models that are only incremental improvements. Through compression, by intensive planning in the design stages,

Nike can drive up demand as much as possible. As a result, the Jordan brand makes a few billion dollars in revenue every year.[150]

Experiential Development

Many business projects, however, lack a predictable path. Innovating beyond incremental improvements is a foggy journey through shifting markets and technology. Here ambitious companies must resort to experiential development, an approach that came from drama and jazz, where improvisation is a finely honed art form. We discovered it in the fast-moving segments of the computer industry, especially laptop and hand-held models.

Because innovation is inherently unpredictable, the key challenge is to build up information and a degree of predictability to propel the work forward at a good clip. So the process starts by creating and testing multiple options, with frequent milestones giving people enough focus, motivation, and discovery to cope with the uncertainty. Where compression resembles a hurry-up offense in American football, the experiential approach corresponds to the fast break in basketball. Players must rely on intuition and teamwork, but still within the context of rules and roles. The experiential strategy involves four steps:

Multiple options. Development teams generate possibilities as parallel alternative designs, sequential iterations of previous designs, or some combination of the two. These can take the form of simple ideas and sketches, virtual computer simulations, or palpable prototypes such as mock-ups and preproduction models. It's similar to a team launching a fast break with multiple players in position to score depending on where the defense commits.

The overall idea is to accelerate product development by creating multiple design options at key decision points. Options provide flexibility to keep the team moving despite setbacks. If the leading option won't work, developers can quickly switch to a known alternative. Emotionally, the multiple choices make developers less vested in a single approach, so they can switch designs as warranted.

Generating multiple options is the opposite of the planning for compression. In the mid-1990s, my team and I studied twenty-eight next-generation product-development projects at fourteen high-tech companies. Most companies failed to complete those projects on schedule. Of the companies we studied, ranging from $500 million to $10 billion in annual sales, only four saw their projects meet expectations for schedule, specification, and market share. The products of five companies appeared successful to outside observers but fell short of internal goals or market-share aspirations. New products from the remaining five failed entirely. We found that in every case of delays and difficulties, these originated in the definition phase of development, before the organization had committed to a specific product design. Multiple options enable teams to proceed without resolving the uncertainty.[151]

Above all, though, the different designs give developers an intuitive feel for how the design parameters play out in the real world. Most people struggle to evaluate a single proposal in uncertain situations, so forcing multiple options increases the team's knowledge of both the options and the situation.

While Apple now seeks compression with most aspects of its phones, it emphasized experiential development in creating the original iPhone—especially the multiple options. A device that revolutionized how our world operates, the iPhone didn't originate out of thin air. The touchscreen, for example, wasn't a common feature at the time, so Apple considered alternative options. Even the grid of apps, taken for granted today, was debated and iterated upon. Teams experimented with different possibilities until they finally found one that stuck.

When the developers committed to specific options, they found the resulting whole incoherent. A designer recalled that "the fragments might have been impressive, but there was no narrative drawing the disparate parts together; it was a jumble of half apps and ideas." That's sometimes how the experiential model works—teams pursuing various ideas, iterations, and nearly finished innovations, with little attention to the finished, profitable product. Steve Jobs gave the overall project team a two-week ultimatum to get together a working prototype. That requirement often pushes some developmental projects to failure, but not the iPhone.

Even after the initial design, Apple had two main options: Make the iPhone a miniature version of a Macintosh desktop computer or transform the iPod technology into a phone. Indeed, the team split into two separate projects, and the competition became intense. People were fired and quit, and the whole situation was almost like a war. Both teams had difficulties. The iPod team struggled to put together a touchscreen way to make calls, at one point even using a radio-like wheel. Meanwhile, the Mac team treated the design almost like a research project, with absurdly long loading times. After iterations and painstaking experimentation, the leaders fashioned a brilliant compromise: The Mac team handled the software, and the iPodders took over hardware. It was the best of both worlds, and the iPhone became a raging success—all thanks to optionality from the very beginning.

Our research found the same benefits of multiple options. Successful companies moved quickly to develop multiple prototypes of the key subsystems of their new product—and then of the entire system. Because they skipped the usual proof-of-concept stage, their prototypes often weren't perfect, requiring software fixes, rewiring, and even minor redesign. But the delays thus incurred were small and cheap relative to the advantages gained. Early multiple prototypes excited and energized the product team in ways that less palpable representations of the new product or its subsystems could not. With prototypes available, team members' discussions were focused and concrete, and decisions were made quickly.[152]

Testing. Closely related to multiple options, frequent testing accelerates development by creating a series of small, quick failures mixed in with success. Continual testing maximizes learning because it captures developers' attention without triggering their defense mechanisms. It surfaces problems early in the development process, when these are easier to correct. It's also astute, as it grounds debates in concrete outcomes, which limits the conflict and politicking based on opinion and hunch, not fact.

While we criticize Facebook elsewhere in the book, it does excel in testing. With billions of users interacting daily, the company has a massive vault of data to learn from. We can debate the ethics of this data usage, but Facebook's testing with this data has undoubtedly led to much of its success financially. Even the notorious experiments on emotion, claimed head of content policy Monika Bickert, helped to generate innovative new features.

The company constantly tweaks its settings and user experience, even without the user knowing, to find solutions. "At any given point in time," said CEO Mark Zuckerberg, "there isn't just one version of Facebook running; there are probably ten thousand. Any engineer can basically decide that they want to test something."

Facebook tests a variety of features, from new reaction buttons to closer integration with other platforms such as Instagram. These tests ensure that engineers can gather real data on how new features work without taking large risks that could affect the entire platform. Any new feature rolled out on a large scale will have been extensively tested, ensuring maximum effectiveness.

With the constant feedback of user data, engineers can thus learn from their mistakes and test out the success of new ideas in real time. With thousands of versions running at once, designers are continually learning and gaining experience; inevitably, a few ideas lead to noticeable gains and make it into the main version of Facebook. With ever-improving user and customer experiences, the company has monetized its massive engagement through targeted advertisements—85 percent of its revenue comes from ads.

With hundreds of millions of regular users, Facebook can test just about every feature of the website, and it emphasizes split testing in advertisements. The company launches multiple versions of ads, testing font choice, text color, target audience—basically anything an advertiser would want to change. Advertisers can even design their own split tests. The company's commitment to experiential development has enabled this painstaking learning, and while Facebook/Meta has struggled in recent years, it remains far ahead of its rivals in user experiences.[153]

Frequent milestones. Even a highly experiential development process can cause designers to lose focus and veer off track, dazzled by the possibilities. Confusion and chaos can reign. Just as in fast-break basketball or improvisational drama and jazz, product developers need an overarching sense of structure.

Ongoing, short milestones impose a structure without time-consuming, bureaucratic reviews. These typically involve weekly or biweekly looks at the current state of the design. They force developers to calibrate the fit of the design to market and technology changes, correcting as needed, while also coping with emotional roadblocks. They promote speed by coordinating the diverse activities of development teams. The milestones create a relentless sense of urgency that combats procrastination while building a confident sense of task accomplishment.

Powerful project leader. While the teams do the main work, strong leaders can gather needed resources and shield developers from bureaucracy. The best ones provide a disciplined vision that focuses the project and keeps the chaos of the experiential strategy under control.

Jeff Bezos was one such leader, even in a failure as notable as the Fire Phone. In 2010 he saw companies staking out claims in the smartphone market, and he decided Amazon could still claim a space as an innovator. He devised the grand idea of the Fire Phone and had visions of technology unlike anything else in the smartphone market—a three-dimensional display, the ability to detect gestures in midair.

In sharp contrast to his focus on customer feedback in other parts of Amazon's business, Bezos doubted that listening to potential users would result in dramatic product inventions. Instead he urged creative "wandering," which he believed was the path to dramatic breakthroughs. He encouraged designers to dream big and aim to revolutionize the smartphone, despite the doubts of his employees.

His powerful leadership wasn't enough: The Fire Phone failed spectacularly in its launch in 2014. The company wrote off $170 million, and production of the phone stopped within a year. But Bezos reassured employees that failures were the price of success. As he prophetically wrote to shareholders in the year before, "Inventing is messy, and over time, it's certain that we'll fail at some big bets too." He didn't punish the executives in charge of the Fire project. He wanted to send a message that taking positive risks would be rewarded.

Indeed, experiential development can lead to long-term gains even if the original project fails. The Fire project taught the company a great deal, such as the intricacies of small-scale hardware design, as well as efficient ways to work with chipset vendors and manufacturers. Amazon didn't use those lessons for a better phone, but it did apply them to products such as the Echo speakers for its popular Alexa offering. One magazine even called the failed Fire Phone "the best thing that happened to Alexa." Without Bezos encouraging and bolstering all of this experiential learning, the company might never have realized those gains.[154]

Most project leaders won't be CEOs; they'll be managers throughout the organization. But they should all be close to the senior team so their project gets patient support regardless of the mode.

Caveats

Experiential development can thus succeed even when it apparently fails, but companies still need substantial discipline to pull it off. Here are some dangers:

Overplanning. While careful planning is critical, technical and market uncertainties are high, and companies can fall into the trap of "planningitis." In that mid-1990s study, we found that most failures of next-generation product development came from the "fuzzy front end," when companies were defining their expectations for the product without hampering their developers' creativity. A common failing was putting many resources into the project but giving little attention to the definition. At one company, an executive complained, "We had too many engineers spinning their wheels while the definition kept changing."[155]

Senior management is often part of the problem. In one company, executives held back project launches until they had a detailed schedule and budget. That practice was appropriate in the more predictable settings where many of these leaders earned their spurs, and it gave them extensive control over the project. But it needlessly delayed serious design efforts for experiential initiatives.

Developers themselves are also susceptible. In one firm attempting to cross over to desktops from workstations, planning was the easy way out. Marketers and engineers debated endlessly over the fine points of features such as keyboard size and trackball design, as well as the likelihood of advances in screen and communication interfaces. Since they could not agree on the shape of the future, planning was a way to avoid conflict. The planning process ended not with logical closure, but only in panicked reaction to a potential competitive product. A better approach would have been to crystallize those disagreements into varied options to be tested.

Overusing CAD. We found that computer-aided design slashed development time in slower-moving categories, but actually slowed development in the faster-moving ones. Why?

The answer is complex. As mentioned above, most CAD systems do several things well. Some simulation systems support "virtual" prototypes for multiple options, while stereolithography and 3D modeling can help create physical prototypes. But CAD isn't flexible enough to help with rapid idea generation and testing, which are essential to experiential development. Relying on CAD can indirectly discourage the open thinking necessary for those projects.

Faulty implementation is another problem. Some CAD systems take a long time to learn to use effectively. People resist learning new systems, so firms end up with incompatible CAD. Some CAD designers become caught up in computer "hacking" and lose focus on their development tasks. Such hacking can crush otherwise useful customizations of CAD packages.

Finally, many companies develop in-house packages and interfaces for their CAD tools that function poorly for new projects. In the wake of one disaster, an engineer lamented, "To foul up takes a human, to really foul up takes a computer." The bottom line is that CAD can aid in experiential development, but only if the package fits the product development strategy and is appropriately implemented.

Reliance on suppliers. Suppliers can be a big help in compressing product innovation, but not in experiential development. In the fastest-moving segments of the computer industry, for example, suppliers helped little, and only the slower product developers relied on them.

When product development is no longer predictable, it's difficult to coordinate work with suppliers. Advancing engineering and shifting interfaces keep complicating the relationship. Committing to a supplier also locks a company into a supplier's technology that may get leapfrogged by rivals. Yet companies are still tempted to rely on suppliers in order to paper over weaknesses in their development organization.

We found in the 1990s that several companies elected to form partnerships with key suppliers to develop new-platform products. In some cases, the codeveloper brought a set of skills and experiences that complemented the strengths of the marketing partner; in others, the partner offered financial resources or useful technology. In several cases, however, major differences in style, priorities, and motivation created costly delays and revisions. Working closely with suppliers brings a high degree of risk.

If a company lacks some vital capabilities, it can still control the process. It should rely on its in-house competences, supplemented by relationships with one, two, or possibly three premier suppliers of cutting-edge knowledge. It can safely use off-the-shelf parts for everything else. That's not ideal, but is more likely to yield a breakthrough product than working closely with a supplier from the beginning.

Neglecting derivative opportunities. When companies do succeed at developing a breakthrough, they often fail to plug the marketplace gaps between current and future offerings with derivative products. Many customers are likely to want something in between the existing and breakthrough offerings. Providing such a product shouldn't be difficult, but companies need the discipline and awareness to pull in a compression team to fill that gap before a competitor does. Here's where bimodal is urgent: the same area needs both the experiential and compression treatments.[156]

Golden Rules

Besides these factors, we found two rules of thumb for experiential development. These dictates applied across a wide range of products.

Seek multifunctional teams. It's tempting to limit product development teams to the R&D group, as these are the people who understand what needs to be done and have the key skills for success. But it's much better to cast a wide net, with people from engineering, manufacturing, marketing, and even purchasing and accounting. Their multiple perspectives reveal more opportunities for overlapping stages, generate more creative ideas, identify design flaws faster, and build more effective prototypes. In contrast, firms that still used "over the wall" or "functional silo" approaches suffered from marketplace misfits and downstream incompatibilities in procurement, manufacturing, and logistics.

As for placing multifunctional teams in "skunkworks," semi-independent units outside the management hierarchy, this is no panacea. Companies were more likely to launch breakthrough products from autonomous multifunctional teams within the hierarchy than with functional teams or multifunctional teams in skunkworks.

Breakthrough teams had the best of both worlds: cross-fertilization of ideas from the diverse team members; integration with the main business to draw on cash, talent, expertise, and customers as needed; and autonomy to keep "business as usual" from overwhelming a team's distinctive processes and culture.

Don't reward teams for meeting a schedule. In the face of uncertainty, companies are tempted to encourage developers by rewarding them simply for meeting scheduled requirements. But developers focused on schedules will end up neglecting outcomes that add value but are hard to predict, such as quality or new features. Not surprisingly, they design for schedule rather than for spec. Schedule-based incentives at one major software firm led developers to cut corners, make inappropriate trade-offs on product quality, and sow the seeds for subsequent delays and other surprises. At a large computer vendor, the result was the sapping of morale among engineers who prided themselves on innovative design. Rewarding for schedule was often how the slowest product developers attempted to speed up, but doing so usually left them further behind.

Our research didn't point to a single best incentive structure. But it's likely wise to reward for a broad range of outcomes, including the product's ultimate market performance and ideally some marker for learning from experimentation.

Some Projects Need Both

Most companies would make substantial progress just by adopting a bimodal approach, where breakthrough projects get the openness of the experiential treatment while others meet the strict discipline of compression. But once a company establishes this approach, it can take up advanced challenges. Sometimes in product development, it isn't clear whether to pursue compression or experiential development. With projects that are both highly complex and unpredictable, a company might want to mix its modes and prod the project team to move in both modes.

In studying the global computer industry, we found the following general points, regardless of the mode chosen:

1. Build multifunctional teams, and reward them for more than just meeting schedules. This advice is essential for experiential development, as just mentioned, but it benefits compression as well as long as the incentives match the directives.

2. Be sure to plan, but set limits on the time. If planning is difficult, that's a clear signal to go with experiential development.

3. Assess the project's type as you learn more. If the development appears predictable, move to compression, and if uncertain or novel, lean toward the experiential. If the project has a high level of complexity, consider dividing the development into compression and experiential segments.

4. Carefully introduce CAD. Understand what CAD does well: support communication, reuse designs, and enable simulation; and

what it can hinder: idea generation and testing. Make sure your CAD systems are compatible. Keep an eye out for designers turned hackers.[157]

Building a bimodal organization may be the most difficult challenge in the book, requiring both attention and flexibility. It takes not only the tactics emphasized here, but also a deep appreciation of both compression and experiential strategies. It requires teams willing to commit to one approach, while teams with another approach might get all the glory.

Leaders must recognize the dangers of compression in limiting developers' attention to new opportunities, while realizing that the experiential strategy will seem too experimental, uncontrolled, and counterintuitive to many managers, marketers, and engineers. Perpetually innovative companies need cultures that promote bimodal development throughout the organization and hierarchy.

The bimodal approach can have a large strategic payoff, but it is not a trivial accomplishment. Managers must overcome cognitive, social, and emotional roadblocks. That's why the bimodal approach comes only after the elements described in the earlier chapters. Only ambitious companies should apply.

PART THREE

Courageous

CHAPTER EIGHT

Go Boldly

Whatever you dream you can do, begin it. Boldness has genius,
power, and magic in it. Begin it now.
—JOHANN WOLFGANG VON GOETHE

By 2000, Amazon was on its way to becoming the "Everything Store." Rapidly expanding its product categories, it was taking on incumbent retailers and brands in much of the economy. It was also moving toward handling most of its inventory through a growing network of warehouses. To handle the burgeoning online marketplace and logistics operation, it relied on the computer servers of a few large suppliers.

Those third-party servers, however, began to slip on speed and reliability. They couldn't scale up at Amazon's rate of growth. Rather than cast around for more or better suppliers, the company stepped back and had a bold thought. If its suppliers' servers struggled to handle growth, then other growing companies must be having those same troubles. Instead of searching for an outside solution, Amazon decided to make its own—even as the prevailing corporate wisdom was to focus on core competencies and outsource everything else.

Benjamin Black led a team that had worked on website engineering, and they now explored this new possibility. The timing was perfect: frustrated with delays in software projects, the company had just done the hard work of requiring standard APIs for new software applications in order to scale up solutions to specific problems.

Black remembered that his team wasn't sure how to build a solution, but they knew that if they got there, they could create a lot of value both for Amazon and for other companies. That realization was enough, as it built on ideas that had already been bubbling at the executive level. CEO Jeff Bezos approved the idea in 2003, and Black's team began to build what became Amazon Web Services (AWS).

"Right off the bat," he said, "we just thought it would be an interesting thing to do. It took a while to get to a point of realizing that this is actually transformative."

For a company specializing in shipping and online sales, the decision to build its own, better servers was ambitious, risky, and potentially a fruitless use of resources. Why should an online retailer be able to build a better server than specialists? But the project ended up recasting Amazon's standing in the world of technology. A decade later, AWS reported $4.6 billion in revenue and accounted for most of the company's profits. It continues to be the world's most popular cloud computing service. Bezos's recent successor, Andy Jassy, came out of AWS and was Black's boss.[158]

Amazon could have just remained in its e-commerce realm and waited for another company to pioneer cloud computing or some other solution. But the company was too restless to wait, and it boldly decided to fix the problem itself. In doing so, it became a leader in an entirely new industry.

Yet throughout this transformation, the company's mainstay e-commerce business never diminished; all sides of the company grew in unison. This multi-industry dominance gave Amazon a sense of security that enabled further bold risks, which followed a similar story of development. In 2007, for example, the company ventured into consumer electronics with the Kindle e-reader. Even failures such as the Fire smartphone helped it achieve later breakthroughs with the software-intensive Alexa/Echo in 2014.[159]

The Strategic Benefits of Boldness

So far in this book we've described how perpetual innovators need to be generous—with an existential commitment to adding value in the world, especially for customers, with a culture to drive a shared commitment. Then we explained that companies have to attack opportunities and threats in a ferocious but measured way, with a start-up mindset, a varying tempo, and a bimodal approach to problem-solving. But all of these virtues aren't enough: Companies still need to act courageously to make sustained change. A tepid, cautious approach to products and services won't work because it won't draw on the emotional energy that comes from boldness.

As Black and Bezos realized, overcoming tough problems can create enormous value. Elon Musk, at Tesla, SpaceX, and other companies, has essentially turned that approach into a strategy. A gifted engineer who inspires other talented people to persist at challenges, he focuses on the daunting problems whose solutions would yield high returns in markets. Boldness is risky, but success is the ultimate differentiator, and it catapults his companies from their competition. After all, if you refrain from boldness, you'll always have to deal with rivals, and you'll never get much respect from investors.

In automobiles, that's what happened with conventional producers. General Motors actually released an electric car back in the 1990s, but mostly for regulatory reasons, not because it believed in the technology. The car failed to take off, the regulations changed, and the company stopped all work in the area. When Tesla had the crazy goal of disrupting the industry with electric vehicles, it had a wide-open market, and now its market value exceeds car companies producing far more units.

Something similar happened at SpaceX, whose reusable rockets were an outlandish idea when Musk founded the company in 2002. SpaceX almost went bankrupt, but it stayed afloat with a successful test launch and kept perfecting the technology to the point where it has outpaced the giant incumbents. And it seems to be happening at Neuralink and the Boring

Company. Musk finds hard problems that he believes are solvable with enough engineering talent and resources, and invests accordingly.[160]

Besides impressing investors, a strategy of boldness has two major benefits. One is that trailblazers can achieve sustainable competitive advantage if they continue to invest in focused innovation. Even now, Tesla cars offer features that the legacy carmakers, from their foundation in combustion engine technology, had failed to match. After ten years, those carmakers have finally started selling electric vehicles, but have yet to master the regular software updates that are a hallmark of Tesla.

The second is that boldness attracts high-level talent. Ambitious people want to work for ambitious companies because they know they'll work on major innovations that could change the world. With high-level talent, bold companies are in a better position to achieve their goals than companies with less-skilled employees. Boldness, when carried out with the other elements discussed in this book, becomes a positive feedback loop.

Creating a Bold Organization

It's easy for a start-up to move boldly, but much harder for a large, established company that has already achieved success. For the latter, why take a chance when the company's already doing fine? Big companies have established structures and routines designed around reliability, not major innovation. Even if the founders are still in charge, they're likely to remember their difficult early times and prefer the current smooth sailing.

As a result, most successful companies lapse into conformity. Sometimes that conformity is obvious, as when the firm copies every move of a successful competitor. Sometimes it's sneaky, where the company digitally replicates a physical product that people already love, without making improvements.

Even when big companies have the ambition to undertake a major innovation, they often proceed cautiously. The head of Meta's virtual reality headset division resigned in 2022 over the company's slowness and especially its inefficiency. The plentiful resources created fiefdoms that kept it from stopping work on weak ideas—wasting billions of dollars and delaying focused commitments.[161]

It takes boldness to actively resist the tendency to stick to the safety of conformity and fiefdoms. That's what happened at Amazon. Founder Jeff Bezos remembered that early on, "It was tempting back then to believe that an online bookstore should have all the features of a physical bookstore." But he was bold enough to demand something else: "Instead of trying to duplicate physical bookstores, we've been inspired by them and worked to find things we could do in the new medium that could never be done in the old one."

Likewise, the Kindle aimed to improve upon the book without trying to copy all of its features. It was admittedly a tall task, but Bezos turned the design team's attention to "the list of useful things that can only be done in the long medium." He fought conformity with provocative questions, and he kept pushing until he got either success or, as with the Fire Phone, a strong marketplace reaction against his bold move.[162]

Organizational Boldness

We tend to think of boldness as something that happens only from individuals. A heroic leader, for example, can move a mass of people in a new direction through force of will or charisma. Musk himself is certainly an extraordinary leader who seems to thrive on tough challenges. Having already assured his place in business history with successes at Tesla and SpaceX, in 2022 he couldn't resist buying Twitter and boldly transforming it into a broader platform.

Yet organizations can become bold at every level. Like the other key traits described in the book, people at all levels have to work at least somewhat independently from the leader.

Start with you. Boldness has to start somewhere, and it has the greatest effect from the top. Know, be, lead: This organizing principle should guide how company leaders go about any sort of institutional change. First, articulate your great dream for the organization. Then know yourself, your strengths, your weaknesses, and your ultimate desires. Know what compromises you can make, and know what you absolutely will not settle for.

Then, actually become this bold person, inwardly and outwardly. Take advantage of your strengths, improve on your weaknesses, and ensure that your inner values are reflected in any changes you make. Finally, lead others to do the same, and trust that they are emboldened by the example you have set. The energy you'll get from pursuing your dream will catalyze energy in others.

When embarking on a bold project, know that every step of that process can be challenging. Even if your main business isn't struggling, it's uncomfortable to shift resources into something new. You'll face financial, psychological, and emotional roadblocks. Going boldly isn't about a single decision, but about continually rejecting conformity and imitation.

That's also what happened with Amazon's Alexa. Its engineers cautiously predicted its main use would be for music, so they thought they had only to create a speaker that wakened people and responded to vocal commands. Bezos pushed; he wanted more, even though the company was still recovering from the disappointing Fire Phone that critics dismissed as overambitious. The Alexa team may have taken the Fire Phone lesson to heart, but Bezos did not. He wanted to try again.

Greg Hart, an executive involved with the project, remembers that "he wouldn't let go of it being a more generalized computer. He told us, 'You are going about this the wrong way. First tell me what would be a magical product, then tell me how to get there.'"

Bezos was so determined that when his in-house team failed to make what he wanted in time, Amazon acquired Evi, a Siri-imitating app that had already achieved the question-and-answer functionality his team was struggling to develop. For $26 million, Bezos reaffirmed his belief in the product and brought his team's focus back to the worthwhile struggle: innovating features that didn't exist.

He also wanted a speaker that would converse, which no product on the market could do. Alexa's engineers noted how "people were uncomfortable with the idea of programming a machine to respond to 'hello.'"

Deep learning was the answer, but acquiring the necessary data would take decades. Bezos came up with a bold shortcut: He partnered with a data-collection firm to rent houses, plant Amazon devices, and send workers in to read from scripts for eight hours a day, letting the Amazon database soak in every word. The multimillion-dollar program was a fraction of the total amount of time and money spent on Alexa's development, and it paid off. Within two years, the company had sold over a million Alexa-powered Echo devices.

What is most notable about these transformative ventures is that they were all entirely voluntary. Amazon was not on the brink of failure or losing customers. With AWS, for example, it was dealing with only minor server issues. Most companies would likely have declined to invest manpower and capital when their main product was still growing rapidly and offering plenty of opportunities. With Alexa, if companies tried to make something at all, they would have aimed simply at offering music, but Bezos pushed hard to go further, despite enormous expense and risk. He was comfortable with taking big risks, and he brought people along to make things happen.

As for Musk's companies, they pursued bold initiatives when they were still small—but they've continued to innovate even after achieving success. Tesla moved into the mass market and trucking, while SpaceX developed a moon lander.

Resist the sunk cost fallacy. Most companies tend to make big moves only when their original, once-successful product is no longer growing enough to sustain the enterprise. Even then, they struggle to overcome their emotional attachments to the original offering. Clinging to their sunk costs, they keep wanting to give that product another chance. So they pour time, effort, and capital into a failing endeavor—delaying their pivot to a better direction. Coupled with risk aversion, the sunk cost fallacy induces even struggling companies to sit still rather than change.

Courageous leaders can resist this bias by sending a strong message: Regardless of past accomplishments, current resources should go to the products and the people that can bring success. Previous chapters described how in 2014, Microsoft dramatically pivoted away from its long-standing strategy under new CEO Satya Nadella. The company's once highly profit-able suite of products was anything but innovative: The Windows operating system struggled against Google's free Chrome, while Office lost ground to numerous less-pricey productivity bundles. Investments in the next gener-ation of products, especially smartphones with the Nokia acquisition, were draining resources needed for areas where Microsoft had a chance to succeed.

Nadella saw right away that the dead weight had to go, so he halted any work on updating Windows. That was Microsoft's supposed crown jewel; first released in 1985, it took up much of the company's engineering efforts to push out annual updates. Despite its past, Nadella saw that the Windows business model was no longer serving the company or the customers well. As such, Nadella decided to shift internal focus away from the product and, shockingly, to give it away for free.

Like Jassy at Amazon, Nadella had risen through the fast-growing cloud computing division, so it was probably easier for him to give an objective assessment of Windows' potential relative to other uses of those resources. Still, it was a courageous move, and one of many that kicked off Microsoft's digital transformation and total reinvention.

Nadella shifted decisively away from smartphones, losing the $7.2 bil-lion paid for Nokia but gaining manpower that could go to better oppor-tunities. He acknowledged giving up on the time and money recently spent on Windows, Nokia, and other declining endeavors, but insisted that catching up with industry leaders was practically impossible. "We were chasing our competitors' tail lights," he told colleagues.

Stagnating with its current hardware and software lineup, and too far behind to build anything innovative there from the ground up, Nadella looked to use Microsoft's capital as a springboard into adding high-demand products and services. Where were these new opportunities, and how could the company get there? Nadella set a new strategy emphasizing video games, social media, cloud development, and artificial intelligence: all fields where Microsoft had some assets but was certainly behind, and had never truly built before. Yet the company saw growth and opportunity. So Nadella launched a series of bold, risky acquisitions. The company bought over a hundred businesses, hardware and software, with most expanding on a preexisting Microsoft service.

The biggest one, which Nadella said would "provide building blocks for the metaverse," brought in video game developer Activision Blizzard for $68.7 billion in 2022. Also important was game developer ZeniMax for $7.5 billion in 2021 and social media platform LinkedIn for $26.2 billion in 2016. Others beefed up cloud services to the point where its Azure service is now the biggest rival to AWS.

Those outlays were possible only because investors saw the company move from its traditional hardware-and-software pursuits to growth areas—and kept rewarding that boldness. As of December 2022, Microsoft's market value was $1.8 trillion, up from $340 million in 2014.

Nadella embodies the idea that boldness requires continuing unrest. Frequent maneuvers in and out of new fields and old products is the only way for such a massive company to sustain its working products while minimizing how much it falls behind. We can expect the company to shift again if the metaverse, say, or AI falls short of expectations.

Simplify the structure. You can't move boldly if your organization has a large body of middle managers who can strangle or dilute any bold move from the top (or bottom). So boldness usually requires a lean organizational layer.

That's how Paul Polman worked when he became CEO of Unilever, whose organizational chart had twelve layers. He simplified and consolidated the chart down to five layers, and then proposed a bold strategy around social purpose and stakeholders. The push worked well for several years. Then after stagnating under successor Alan Jope, the company resumed its push for simplification by selling off major brands in tea and ice cream.[163]

Getting to Bold

What if you'd like to move boldly, but worry that you'll move too fast or too far? You can reduce risk by seeking out information broadly, beyond your usual circles. All the data in the world won't give you certainty; you'll still need to make a subjective judgment. And that takes a level of maturity, risk-taking, and creativity that many leaders lack. As CEO advisor Ram Charan explains, "You need the mental capability and tenacity to knit your inferences into something meaningful, and the imagination to think of new options."[164]

That means confronting the fear of failure that keeps most CEOs up at night. The fear often stems from perfectionism, the irrational sense that what really matters is carrying out initiatives exactly right. Business is notoriously messy—even in high-performing companies, leaders typically spend much of their time fighting fires. So fear of failure is usually about fear of humiliation.

But the only way to fight an emotion is with another emotion. As the writer Arthur Brooks points out, you have to build up your reserves of courage, which he recommends doing by focusing on the present, visualizing a courageous act, and stating your desire to overcome your fears. These steps help you marshal the energy to overcome your fears and still act boldly.[165]

While these are a good start, most bold decisions in business proceed methodically. We don't hear about the many bold decisions that even bold leaders resist, often for good reason. As scholar Kathleen Reardon has argued, courageous business leaders refrain from moves with a very low chance of success and with little to be gained along the way. They also don't squander their political and economic capital on low-priority areas, and they also seek less risky ways to accomplish their goals. Only when they have no alternative do they go for the bold move—and this process gives them the courage to do so.[166]

I'll add only that leaders also gain courage from their existential commitment to the company's purpose. That commitment doesn't take away the risk, but it gives them the emotional energy to override the usual worries in order to achieve the longed-for result. Boldness ultimately has to be partly emotional—especially now, markets are too uncertain and volatile to support simple rationality.

Boldly Pulling Back

Boldness is less about chasing volume or speed and more about quality: Are we effectively building a sustainable business for the company? At times of rapid growth, a company can lose sight of the basics as they struggle to keep up with scale. They might realize that standards are slipping, but actually slowing down and scaling back to firm these up takes real courage. A temporary pullback will upset some customers, but can be crucial to ensuring that the product quality remains high.

When Apple began, cofounders Steve Jobs and Steve Wozniak focused on innovation and quality. Customers were an afterthought. In 1984, when the company released the Macintosh personal computer, sales were so disappointing that it led to Jobs's departure from the company. Yet its quality was so remarkable that it eventually changed the world. As explained in chapter 4, Jobs didn't care about the sales.

What did bother Jobs? Low quality in any of his products, even though he knew that, for most customers, the technology was so advanced that he could cut hundreds of corners and still satisfy them.

When you're a carpenter making a beautiful chest of drawers, you're not going to use a piece of plywood on the back, even though it faces the wall and nobody will ever see it. You'll know it's there, so you're going to use a beautiful piece of wood on the back. For you to sleep well at night, the aesthetic, the quality, has to be carried all the way through.

While Jobs was away from Apple, from 1985 to 1997, the company focused on profit, not quality. Led by marketing expert John Sculley, the company paid less attention to innovation, and it foundered. It was time for renewed boldness. When Jobs returned, he scaled back the offerings that Apple created in his absence. While some of these products were profitable, he wanted to create groundbreaking offerings, which had gained Apple its initial reputation. The results were extraordinary: a series of revolutionary products, from the iPhone and App Store to the iPod, that catapulted Apple into the most valuable company in the world. Profits soared, far exceeding what Sculley had achieved. Jobs shared his philosophy:

> My passion has been to build an enduring company where people were motivated to make great products. Everything else was secondary. Sure, it was great to make a profit, because that was what allowed you to make great products. But the products, not the profits, were the motivation. Sculley flipped these priorities to where the goal was to make money. It's a subtle difference, but it ends up meaning everything—the people you hire, who gets promoted, what you discuss in meetings.

Jobs was likewise bold in developing new sales channels. Apple could have built a conventional retail store and done just fine, but he wanted something centered on how customers actually lived their lives. As Ron Johnson remembered:[167]

> As we were driving to meet my team, in charge of designing the stores, I told Steve I'd been thinking that the store is organized all wrong—we've organized it like a retail store around products but we should organize it around themes like music and movies and things people do, and he looked at me said, "Do you know how big a change that is? I don't have the time to redesign the store. You might be right but I don't want you to say a word about this to

anybody." As soon as we met the team, the first thing Steve said was, "Ron thinks our store is all wrong and he's right, so I'm going to leave now and Ron you work with the team." Later that day Steve called me and said, "You reminded me of something I learned with every movie I did at Pixar. At some point when we're about to release, we realize the script could be better, the ending's not quite right, and this character isn't exactly how should be. And at Pixar, we always had the willingness to not worry about the movie release date, but to get the movie right. You only get one chance to create a movie; you only get one chance to launch a store. So it's not about how fast you do it. It's about doing your absolute best."

Advanced Micro Devices (AMD) similarly pulled back to focus on the basics. A leading semiconductor maker in the 1970s through the '90s, the company neared bankruptcy in 2015 due to debt from failing ventures, a divisive internal culture, and a sharp decline in personal computer sales. It had poured $200 million into manufacturing plants in the early 2000s, yet archrival Intel solidified its lead in conventional computer chips within central processing units.

Some engineers and executives were eager to move on and turn their efforts toward graphics processing units, letting Intel run away without competition. Others, perhaps blinded by the sunk cost fallacy, were adamant that with more iteration, their CPUs could still compete. This dispute, said to have led to "shortcomings in product quality," prompted Lisa Su's becoming CEO.

As described in the chapters on Pygmalion and bimodal, Su had an extensive technical background in semiconductors and decades of experience in the industry. As much as anyone, she understood the seemingly limitless potential of those chips. Yet her first major decision was to *cut*.

Su noted that the flood of expertise into the industry had made it seem oversaturated. When *every* company is technically talented, success comes from carefully allocating resources:

> It's important when you're a technology company to decide what you are really, really good at because you have to be the best, number one or number two . . . It's all about focusing on, "Hey, this is the DNA of the company, let's make it as great as possible in terms of what we can bring to the market."

Su saw the company's greatest strength was in high-performance chips for the fast-growing gaming and data center areas. For the next year, she focused nearly all internal engineering efforts on creating the most advanced chips, largely abandoning the mainstay CPU market to Intel.

The pullback worked. Finding a new groove in the gaming industry, AMD's revenue grew from $6 billion in 2014 to $14 billion in 2021. When companies are struggling to compete, execution can trump creativity. Having the courage to take steps back will eventually enable the organization to move forward.

Boldness does require a keen strategic sense. Bumble, under CEO Whitney Wolfe Herd, gained initial success with a contrarian focus on online dating apps. While rivals focused on user engagement, new features, and subscription plans, Wolfe Herd (introduced in the Pygmalion chapter) designed Bumble around safety. To support this mindset, the app has an AI algorithm that blocks users who are just *predicted* to act inappropriately. As Wolfe Herd put it, "What Bumble is really selling is a sense of control over the mysterious alchemy of human relationships."

That niche strategy not only gained Bumble significant market share in the United States, where it has a far higher percentage of women users than its rivals, but also guided international expansion. In 2018, the company boldly entered India, where sexual violence and inconsistent law enforcement have discouraged many women from online dating lest they be stalked. Wolfe Herd and her team spent months understanding what would help Indian women feel comfortable in online dating. They stripped the app of some features taken for granted in the United States, but that were a distraction in India. Boldness involves the courage to cut as well as add—and it has paid off for Bumble.[168]

Conformity and Risk Aversion

Boldness is all the more remarkable in its absence. When a failing company lacks the ambition to remake its marketplace with bold moves, it can easily blame external factors for its troubles. The collapse of Blockbuster, described in the chapter on the start-up mindset, shows the typical corporate response to failure when leaders prefer complacency over courage. Blockbuster's former CFO, Tom Casey, repeatedly blamed the company's collapse not on its strategic decisions (including declining to acquire Netflix in 2007), but on the difficult timing of a stock market drop when it was still digesting debt from its spinoff from Viacom. His attempt to draw an equivalency between the two companies falls flat when we consider the timeline. In 2010, when Blockbuster filed for bankruptcy, it had been delivering largely the same product for a decade. Netflix, on the other hand, was innovating. Casey's analysis reflects not bad luck, but the fact that Blockbuster's entire business model was a mere side pursuit for Netflix. After its 2004 launch of Blockbuster Online, its by-mail business, the company kept it tethered to the physical stores and made no major improvements. Meanwhile Netflix developed digital by-mail, streaming, and original content in one decade.

Nokia similarly failed to be bold in falling short. As pointed out in the preface, Nokia lacked courageous and innovative products that customers would love. In other words, the world changed, and the company failed to adapt and innovate accordingly. Blockbuster and Nokia, without boldness, hesitated before each step. But their leaders could still find plausible excuses for their failure—business is so complex that you can always find something else to blame. That's the power of complacency: It deadens your perspective and makes you vulnerable to outside forces. Boldness sets you free and energizes you to overcome the obstacles that stop timid organizations.

Freeing Employees to Go Boldly

It isn't enough for leaders to be bold—they must create an organization and culture that encourages audacity. Psychological safety gets a lot of attention, and it's surely important. Research suggests that employees feel most comfortable taking risks where they feel settled and supported. People won't make big moves if they fear reprimands, or worse, if their ideas don't work out.

Engagement, however, is equally important, and often overlooked. Before taking up a difficult task, people do best when their team morale is solid. They need both confidence in themselves and appreciation for their teams.

Unfortunately, rates of employee engagement at work are generally low; most people seem to be checked out. Even when they feel psychologically supported to take risks, they simply may not care enough to want to make the company better.

We can imagine this happening at Blockbuster. When people join a company that has run on the same business model for over a decade, they're unlikely to propose big new ideas. Complacent companies are less likely to seek out and listen to a fresh perspective or encourage the sharing of insights. A new Blockbuster employee might have been bursting with ideas, but he or she would have felt little inducement to champion them.

Engagement depends on giving your employees a consistent outlet for creativity and idea sharing. Contrast the complacent approach with Zara, where employee feedback is part of the business model.

As explained in the chapter on the start-up mindset, Zara differentiates itself by cocreating fast fashion with customers. Since 1975, the company has developed a supply chain with space for continual customer inputs. As technology has developed, the transfer of data from stores to designers has only accelerated. Founder Amancio Ortega didn't believe he knew fashion better than his customers, and never hired designers who did. Instead, he believed he could build a manufacturing system so responsive to customer feedback that it would prevail over companies focused on innovative designs. This risky business model *required* high rates of employee engagement.

As a result, Zara's store employees have the added responsibility of compiling and communicating customer feedback. The company makes this communication technically simple, with store managers responsible for ensuring that employees are actively engaging. The story of the pink scarf shows the model in action.

In 2015, over the course of two days, three women asked about pink scarves in separate stores: Tokyo, San Francisco, and Toronto. None of those women bought anything in the store that day.

Alert, engaged sales associates reported those requests, and within a week, two thousand Zara stores received five hundred thousand pink scarves. In just three days, every store sold out of their scarves. The company combined its famously fast production capabilities with engaged, responsive employees to deliver a customer-driven design within a week. By not just appreciating but *relying* on employee input, Zara made employee engagement a requirement of the job.

Some companies get engagement from the culture of autonomy described in earlier chapters. Netflix essentially requires employees to stay alert and make their own decisions, a risky approach that relies on trust. CEO and cofounder Reed Hastings says this autonomy is essential in creative companies, where the much greater risk is that you won't get the innovation you need.

Netflix expects only two things from workers: to deliver their work and to constantly improve it. There's no dress code or set hours; vacation days are unlimited; and expenses are automatically paid. But no one's job is secure, and Hastings admits that "our culture memo says things like adequate performance gets a generous severance package."

This relaxed yet hypercompetitive environment fits with the company's strategy, which depends on honest, harsh feedback to ensure that shows, products, and employees remain in the company only by continuing to show value. Transparency about this environment ensures that newcomers know what they are getting into, and likely serves to recruit people bored in their current job and seeking a fast-paced, highly engaging challenge.

Both of these companies drive engagement by factoring it into the business model. Zara needs store associates to pass on customer feedback, while Netflix needs creative people to keep its product offerings attractive. As they attract and engage new employees, leaders must build an environment where people feel safe and capable enough to think boldly about their workstreams.

Boldness Brings Clarity

The chapter began with the famous quote about the creative power of boldness. That's inspiring, but what does it really mean? It has to mean more than simply the energy of a determined leader.

In connection with an existential purpose, boldness brings clarity that can overcome the minor frictions and disputes that slow down conventional companies. A former executive at Tesla notes that people have no real job security at the company—as at Netflix, merely adequate performance likely leads to dismissal. As noted already, CEO Elon Musk pays little attention to hierarchies or protocols. When he sees a critical issue or bottleneck, his bold vision empowers him to go straight to the source and engage them aggressively, focused on the specific issue:[169]

> Musk operates on first principles, and the fastest way to get something resolved is to go directly to the manager whose job it is to resolve it, rather than go through a network of middle management where the issue could get held up for various reasons, but also the issue could get clouded and a very clear problem statement might turn into something that is less defined.

Despite this disruptive approach, the work proceeds remarkably smoothly at Tesla. Political disputes are surprisingly rare, while employee engagement is high—thanks to boldness, the same former executive contends:

> A lot of people there believe in the mission. They are empowered to do amazing things because of the ambition of those goals, and they work in a super-high-performance environment. There's this culture and expectation that, yes, these goals are impossible but the world needs us to achieve them. And everyone else here is so freaking good at their job, they're going to do their part and I don't want to let them down.

Something similar seems to have happened in military and political situations. When Russia invaded Ukraine, Western observers expected the latter to fall quickly. After all, Ukraine was badly outmatched militarily and was surrounded on three sides by invaders. Many of its citizens either spoke Russian fluently or sympathized with Russian intervention in order to address the country's widespread corruption. NATO even offered Ukrainian president Volodymyr Zelensky a private plane so he could safely evacuate from the capital.

But Zelensky famously replied, "I don't need a ride, I need ammunition." He rallied his fellow citizens to resist the invasion. While they benefitted from military hardware that NATO donated, as well as Russian mistakes and incompetence, they turned the tide mostly with their own valor and determination. Ukrainians may have had a nuanced national identity before the war, but Zelensky's boldness galvanized everyone to draw on inner reserves that their complacent adversaries couldn't.

Likewise, Mohandas Gandhi boldly sought Indian independence from the British empire. He identified the empire's weakness, but knew it would take extraordinary courage to attack it. So he trained his followers in nonviolent protests that utterly unnerved the imperials, and eventually accomplished his goal. Martin Luther King Jr. learned from Gandhi's success and accomplished something similar in the 1960s civil rights movement in the United States. Their boldness created a moral clarity that unified followers and reduced the frictions and infighting that slow down most organizations.

All change requires courage, but most companies change only to get up to speed with the norm. Actually rejecting conformity is rare, expensive, and risky; it takes courage that most companies lack. That's especially true when a company is thriving, as Amazon was when it developed cloud computing. But even in rough patches, such as Microsoft had in 2014, bold initiatives are hard. The company needed a new CEO to let go of sunk costs and invest in future opportunities. Blockbuster offers the more common example: a company that excelled at its initial offering, but complacently continued to provide that service with little reinvention in sight.

Sometimes boldness requires scaling back. Continuing to make units of a profitable product may look good on paper without being sustainable. A bolder course of action is to reallocate efforts to areas with greater potential. Thus Apple and AMD had to cut before they could grow again.

All the same, bold leaders require bold organizations. And that depends on a culture and a structure that promote employee engagement and initiative—and discourage complacency. Whether passing on information or creating new offerings, people at all ranks need to go boldly, not just meekly follow a leader.

Above all, boldness requires a kind of restlessness—never accepting a successful approach for long. Most leaders lack the extraordinary gifts of a Jeff Bezos or Elon Musk, but they can adopt their techniques around insisting on the mission and daring to add major value.

CHAPTER NINE

Radical Collaboration

*How did we cure polio and smallpox, and send a
man to the moon? How did we decode the human genome in
just thirteen years? Collaboration.*

—MARGARET CUOMO

Back in 1906, the British statistician and polymath Francis Galton attended a county fair where people estimated the weight of an ox. Afterward, Galton borrowed the cards with the guesses and found, to his surprise, that the average of the 787 entries was almost exactly the actual weight of the animal. It was more accurate than the estimates of any of the individual butchers and farmers, who presumably had an eye for such things.

Galton's conclusion became the principle of the "wisdom of crowds," that groups of people can be smarter than even the most expert individuals among them. Researchers in multiple fields have shown that aggregating a variety of judgments can dramatically increase accuracy, as individual errors cancel themselves out. Crowdsourced judgments have improved medical diagnoses, scientific research, and economic forecasts.

A variety of judgments is essential. Like stock market bubbles, crowds of like-minded people can run an organization off a cliff, hence the need for a diversity of perspectives in any collective intelligence. The wisest crowds include individuals who disagree with one another. In practice, that means fostering collaboration widely across an organization.[170]

Why Is Collaboration Hard?

So far we've emphasized the role of talented people energized by a common purpose in agile innovation. But individual talent isn't enough; companies also need people working together to create something bigger than any could achieve on his or her own. It turns out that true collaboration is very difficult—only courageous companies can sustain it for long across the organization.

More often than not, two heads are better than one. At work, at school, and at home, the biggest challenges we face are always easier to overcome as a team than alone. It stands to reason that the larger the organization, the more complex its challenges. So why do some organizations achieve collaboration more than others?

Every company says it values collaboration, but aside from high-performance companies, little real collaboration actually seems to take place beyond formally established teams.[171] To understand why, we have to appreciate the power of silos. When companies are small, everyone knows everyone else, and it's both easy and essential to collaborate across the organization. You're just trying to survive, and everyone is motivated to help. But if the company succeeds, it typically grows and expands its offerings. It now has so many people and so many complicated activities that each function becomes a world in itself, with less to do with the other functions.

In this new state, leaders often take survival for granted and start building mini-fiefdoms under their management. Everyone is looking for security, and a solid organization that they control often appears to be the best way to get there. The most successful companies grow and diversify so much that they must create discrete, stand-alone operations—a multidivisional form. All those silos are good for handling complexity, but at the cost of making it difficult for people to work across functions and divisions. Managers and employees are all motivated to protect their fiefdoms and maximize their resources.

In theory, broad organizational collaboration should still happen at the level of senior executives. But in reality, executives are human like everyone else and tend to care more about protecting their areas than risking what they have with collaboration. What if that collaboration results in a loss of resources or respect from the CEO?

Silos are essential for scaling up complicated processes. You need people specialized in each area who can run those processes reliably and at a low cost. Silos are how we got the abundant, high-quality products and services of the mid-to-late-twentieth century. They gave us modern affluence.

Silos made sense when markets were fairly stable as they were for much of the twentieth century. But they're risky now that most companies are facing upheaval from technological advances. Upheaval doesn't happen in a neat way; it affects activities throughout the organization, and overcoming it requires rapidly collecting information, generating new ideas, and pivoting to exploit them. Hence the need for radical collaboration: an environment where people seek solutions for their organization unhindered by structural or cultural constraints.

In practice, this looks like a senior executive frequently consulting with experts far down the chain of command, or creative engineers working across functions to develop new solutions. It can manifest in many different ways, all of which are useful to ensure organizational agility.

The problem is not the functional or divisional structures themselves, but the attitudes that turn those structures into silos. Perpetual innovators still need to organize their activities, and those structures need not be counterproductive. What matters is the company's readiness to reap the benefits of extensive collaboration regardless of how it is organized. That readiness comes from the following:

1. An openness to new solutions, no matter where they come from or how unprecedented they are

2. A company ethos that encourages collaboration and puts little emphasis on fiefdoms

3. A structure that's porous enough to allow broad collaboration

To get a sense of the difficulty here, realize that if companies actually valued collaboration as much as they say they do, many of them would have to make that a greater value than respect for the hierarchy. A company that actually gives collaboration priority is Tesla, which prizes subject-area expertise over managerial position. When a team at Tesla encounters challenges, it can bypass the chain of command and cross silos. As mentioned in earlier chapters, team leaders are expected to go straight to the person with the knowledge to solve the problem and resolve the issue quickly. CEO Elon Musk shows the way in his actions and words:

> Anyone at Tesla can and should email or talk to anyone else according to what they think is the fastest way to solve a problem for the benefit of the whole company. Moreover, you should consider yourself obligated to do so until the right thing happens.

With radical cooperation an everyday reality at Tesla, people have extra motivation to develop mastery over their areas—they can't rely on the security of their silos to protect them from challenges. They need to be comfortable working with others across functions, people who may respect them only for their expertise. The company values results and is willing to disrespect silos and hierarchies in order to achieve them.

That's the essence of radical collaboration. It goes beyond the ordinary collaboration that encourages people to get help for complex problems. Perpetual innovators believe that only by collaborating aggressively can they keep up with fast-changing markets. The key to their radical collaboration is as much structural as cultural.

Collaboration across Different Structures

A collaborative organization can take many forms. Some perpetual innovators are extremely decentralized. As explained in chapter 2 on existential purpose, Haier evolved to focus on delivering quality appliances to a great many distinct markets around the world. In order to generate a diverse array of new products at volume, it decentralized its operations into many miniature firms within an internal entrepreneurial ecosystem. At the other extreme is a company like Apple, highly centralized and organized functionally, in order to generate revolutionary, user-friendly innovation. Both achieve impressive levels of collaboration across their structures for innovation appropriate to their business models.

Most people at Haier work in thousands of separate microenterprises focused on a specific product and market. Each microenterprise is responsible for creating a solid business with its own profit and loss. Those that fail are broken up and the resources and responsibilities absorbed by other units. To succeed, most of these units must gain expertise in relevant technologies and production, and that requires collaborating with colleagues elsewhere. The company thus creates a discipline for broad collaboration to create products that users in each locality need.

That collaboration has only increased with the rising technical complexity of Haier's products, especially as it introduces the Internet of Things into appliances. Supporting each "ecosystem of micro-communities"—either a product or geographical agglomeration—are two coordinating structures: an Experience EMC to help the units stay attuned to evolving user needs and a Solution EMC to help create products and services that address user pain points.

That's the flip side of radical collaboration: The company can give units autonomy over their own businesses because it knows the units will seek help across units as needed. For example, a unit responsible for producing refrigerators in a market realized that "smart" refrigerators created opportunities for helping consumers purchase, prepare, and store food. The unit collaborated with experts in other units to pinpoint those opportunities and construct the offerings—and if the initiative is profitable, the unit expects colleagues elsewhere to seek its help. Everyone is motivated to help because they know the only path to success is sharing knowledge and resources.

Apple, on the other hand, is a very different type of organization, focused on breakthroughs in consumer electronics. The company has transformed multiple aspects of how we all interact with technology, all in service of the company's existential commitment to create innovative products for people's daily lives. Apple not only invents new products, but also works to continually improve on its present offerings.

When Steve Jobs returned to Apple in 1997, the company looked very different from how it does today. His successors had divided the company into separate business units, each managed by a cohort of general managers—often with MBAs—focused on their own profitability. This conventional approach to organizational structure created insulated silos, each of which had little incentive to work with the others.

Jobs took drastic measures to fix this problem. He fired nearly all of the company's general managers, dissolved the business units, and replaced them with functional hierarchies that converged only at the executive level. Apple now works with divisions such as design, marketing, and engineering, rather than an iPad, iPhone, Mac, and other product groups.

The functional structure enables the company to concentrate subject matter expertise in specific areas at scale, leading to greater insights than if each product group had its own designers or engineers. Haier, which doesn't operate on the cutting edge of technology, has no need to concentrate expertise.

Indeed, rather than have individual business units for each product that may compete and cannibalize each other, Apple puts its best minds in a subject area in one place and encourages them to collaborate with colleagues elsewhere. In this manner, the company has repeatedly delivered astounding yet practical innovations.

Jobs restored some middle management, but not in the usual sense. At Apple, managers do not oversee experts—all that does is develop individuals who are good at managing. Instead, experts lead experts. Hardware experts manage hardware teams, software experts software, and so on. The company needs the most talented people to join the enterprise, and those people won't put up with anyone without their expertise telling them what to do. By concentrating these individuals within the organization, individuals of great capability are able to work together and learn from each other to surmount the next big innovation challenge.

That specialization in turn requires extensive collaboration to actually generate products. The functional structure creates hundreds of horizontal dependencies. A VP in charge of camera engineering must work closely with designers working on products that include cameras. This pressure leads the company to promote people who combine technical expertise with the ability to collaborate. The functional structure thus makes radical collaboration a vital skill—and a driver of agile innovation.

When Apple wanted to introduce the portrait mode on cameras across all devices, the camera engineers (software and hardware) didn't work alone. Unintended consequences and unforeseen challenges in the course of development led to long discussions with the user experience, firmware, algorithms, and other functions. Working together, the teams identified and addressed a great many issues. When it finally released the new mode, the company had achieved a feature for mobile cameras previously thought impossible.

Jobs had replaced one kind of silo, product divisions, with another, functional divisions—only the latter had no choice but to collaborate to add value to the company's offerings. Haier's microenterprises are more self-sufficient, but they are under intense pressure to succeed economically and must still collaborate widely to get the capabilities they need. The lesson here is that most large companies are siloed in some form or another. What matters is how much those structures require collaboration and induce the silos to be porous.

Relying on Collaborative Teams

Another approach is to employ a conventional organizational structure but lay over it collaborative work teams that do the main work of innovation. That's what Amazon does. Despite dominating online commerce, Amazon has avoided complacency and silos and is known to move quickly in organizing new business lines and adjusting high-level strategy. By relying on cross-functional teams for innovation, it makes this internal collaboration necessary for success.

As explained in chapter 6 on tempo, Amazon initially organized most of its development work in "two-pizza teams": No team should be bigger than what two pizzas can feed. By staying small, only six to eight people, teams could move quickly as needed. The teams were large enough to include both engineers and nonengineers, often from different departments, who were to collaborate in order to bring their complementary skill sets to bear on potential solutions.

By working across silos, the teams focused not on organizational turf but on customers. And because each team had autonomy in working out its specific module, it worked informally and was empowered to make decisions about their tasks much quicker than a middle manager could. The success of each team depended on the success of others in its solution space, so it was in everyone's interest to solve problems quickly. If one team fell behind schedule, all the related teams ended up late.

Because the teams had to learn to work well together from the outset, they had greater motivation and better coordination within the team. The small size made people more likely to take ownership of the problem they were solving. Small teams could also pivot quickly on receiving new information.

But collaboration by itself isn't enough—teams still need strong leaders to facilitate. The two-pizza teams worked well only for product development, where small size and autonomy were essential for avoiding the tangled dependencies that often stymied innovation. For other projects, especially ambitious initiatives that affected much of the company, the company found that the team leader's full-time focus was essential. Many of the team leaders worked on multiple projects, diluting the responsibility. As noted in chapter 6, substantial innovation requires a full-time commitment.

For example, the company wanted to offer logistical services to merchants (Fulfillment by Amazon). Everyone thought it was a good idea, but the idea went nowhere until the company told a vice president to drop all other responsibilities and focus on making it happen. He had full authority to hire and staff a team with the autonomy to develop the service—without the need to coordinate with other teams.[172]

This phenomenon plays out in organizations besides Amazon. A McKinsey study (see chapter 6 on tempo) suggests that such agile team structures are more likely than conventional (usually department-based) teams to solve problems, because these teams quickly test new ideas and gather data. These diverse, multi-perspective teams can therefore rapidly iterate through product updates and improvements because they have a broader understanding of what the company and the customer need. Most importantly, the teams reported a better ability to double down on areas of strength and potential opportunities due to their collaborative nature. Decision-making bottlenecks and redundant dependencies become apparent when teams are constantly coordinating and communicating with each other.

Amazon evaluated its own approach to team structure by using organizational network analysis. Its self-assessment found that not only do its teams collaborate to solve their own problems, but also they function as bridges across disparate parts of the organization. The smaller team structure also reduced the number of meetings and bureaucratic approvals, along with the misalignment of priorities. With these insights in hand, the company doubled down on the two-pizza structure and added weekly business review meetings between team leaders to further align team priorities—before ultimately switching to the single-threaded-leader approach.

The fruits of radical collaboration often lie in unexpected places. When people are disposed toward comfortable channels—established partnerships and specific working groups within an organization—they tend to overlook other sources for the next idea. Sometimes those sources are beyond the organization itself, in small, agile firms with strengths that are inaccessible to larger organizations, or even direct rivals with complementary attributes unlockable through partnership.

Batteries Included

Structure isn't enough to ensure collaboration, nor are performance measures that can be gamed. Companies also need talented people who, as at Apple, are inclined to collaborate. A critical mass of collaborators can even influence the mindset and culture to make collaboration normal, even expected.

Every organization has people naturally inclined to work, but most companies rely on only a small group to do much of the collaboration. One study suggested that a third of the added value from collaboration came from only 5 percent of the employees.[173] How can companies hire or promote so they have more people inclined to collaborate?

An insight here comes from Jack Altman, the founder and CEO of Lattice, a workplace management platform. Altman divides employees into two groups: those who bring positive energy to the colleagues around them and those who require energy from others in order to stay positive. Others divide people "with batteries included," who create energy for those around them, from people "with batteries not included," who rely on others to create that energy for them.[174]

That's a key distinction, because in most organizations, collaboration takes enormous energy and positive thinking as well as courage. Employees have their set tasks and challenges, and collaboration is an option that they can decline. Only people who are confident, ambitious, and, yes, energetic will make an effort to collaborate with someone outside their group or division. They need to be internally motivated, disciplined, consistent, and accountable in order to get colleagues on the outside to trust and work with them.

Every company, of course, wants to hire people "with batteries included." But that's especially important for those looking to up their collaboration, which should be many if not most companies.

Collaborating Beyond the Organization

Structure isn't enough, nor is energy: Radical collaboration also requires bravery. People have to be willing not only to pursue new ideas, but also to approach colleagues they may not know at all—especially outside the organization altogether.

As companies collaborate, the focus is often inward. People in the same organization undoubtedly work faster and more effectively than people from separate organizations. This strategy also tends to be more profitable because the gains to innovation all stay in-house. That was Microsoft's strategy for many years. When Apple and Samsung saw historic success with their smartphones, Microsoft released the Windows Phone in a vain effort to compete. Likewise, the company delayed issuing versions of its products for Apple's operating system, even as Apple's products became ever more popular. Just as with Windows, Office, and Internet Explorer, they wanted control over products and had succeeded with me-too responses to innovations that strengthened those platforms.

That approach changed in 2015 under new CEO Satya Nadella (see chapter 2). At a major Salesforce event, he took the stage and did the unthinkable—used an iPhone for a product demo. He added that the phone was fully loaded with iOS versions of Microsoft software—from cornerstone products like Word, Excel, and PowerPoint, to recent additions such as OneNote and OneDrive. Soon after, Microsoft's head of Office products joined an Apple event to launch the new iPad Pro.

The dramatic demo emphasized not just the company's existential shift, but also its new priority of collaboration. The company was now going to help customers access its products regardless of platform, so it had to connect with companies it had earlier held at arm's length. Instead of a "confederation of fiefdoms," the company had to focus on doing what mattered for customers—which would often mean going outside people's comfort zone.

Hence the company's new "partner-positive" strategy, which culminated in outbidding Google to acquire the open-source platform GitHub in 2018 and in establishing the Microsoft Partner Network in 2019 (now Microsoft

Cloud Partner Program). Both moves enabled Microsoft and suppliers to share resources, create solutions, and generate business. To encourage participation, the company offers suppliers many of its development programs and business tools. The small firms in turn provide agility and specialized expertise. The network thus enables the software giant to tackle problems that were otherwise too niche for it to address.

ScienceSoft, for example, had technology for faster search functions and better collaboration on documents—but it lacked a strong corporate internet platform to show off its capabilities. After joining the Partner Network, it used Microsoft SharePoint software to demonstrate its offerings in customizable business intranets. That collaboration continued as ScienceSoft helped Microsoft improve its 365 suite of software.

Unlike Haier and Apple, Microsoft did not overhaul its organizational structure to promote collaboration. It relied instead on top-down messaging and dramatic events such as the Salesforce event. But the company's previous all-in-house strategy had demonstrably failed by 2015, and Nadella could rely on an army of talented software engineers eager to maximize their impact. He just needed to give them encouragement and permission. Unlike Apple, Microsoft didn't need to be on the cutting edge, but it did need its software to work flawlessly with its partners, so effective collaboration was essential.

Radical collaboration requires openness to all kinds of opportunities—even those that offer benefits to competitors. Collaborating with rivals like Apple unlocked access to previously untapped customers, and working with small, agile firms like ScienceSoft provided deep subject matter expertise.

Cultivating an Ethos of Collaboration

Encouraging that openness isn't automatic. Employees' default action is to proceed within ordinary parameters, readily working with immediate colleagues but approaching others only hesitantly, and rarely even thinking of going outside the organization.

Some companies let collaboration trickle down from the top, while others expect it to rise up from the organization. There's no single answer for cultivating collaboration, but one easy way to discourage it: internal competition. Pitting employees against each other may seem an effective way to get people motivated to do better. But like monitoring individual productivity, it shatters an employee's trust. Once people see colleagues as competitors, especially outside their silos, true collaboration ends.

Before Satya Nadella became Microsoft's CEO, the company's leaders encouraged middle managers to give a certain proportion of negative performance reviews, regardless of employee performance. The policy understandably discouraged collaboration, as everyone now competed with their teammates. By contrast, Tesla, described above, has perhaps the strongest culture of collaboration, almost a prime directive in order to thrive in the highly competitive world of electric vehicles. People are expected to pay little heed to hierarchy at all—expertise is what matters, not position.

Yet a culture of collaboration doesn't mean deciding by consensus, where everyone has equal authority. Nadella may have quashed mandatory negative performance reviews, but he still saw the need for strong leadership to keep the organization together and moving in a single direction—a necessary foundation for collaboration. As he put it:

One thing I had learned from my dad's experience as a senior Indian government official was that few tasks are more difficult than building a lasting institution. The choice of leading through consensus versus fiat is a false one. Any institution-building comes from having a clear vision and culture that works to motivate progress both top-down and bottom-up.

Instead of an extremely open structure, Microsoft under Nadella emphasized collaboration with what became the world's largest private hackathon.

The event's explicit purpose was to encourage Microsoft employees to work together, across silos and functions, to solve problems through fast-paced collaboration.

The program has been a huge success: After two years, the annual event was drawing eighteen thousand people across four hundred cities and seventy-five countries, working collaboratively on shared ideas. The company has since invited customer teams to the party. The COVID-19 pandemic made the hackathon fully virtual, but it has continued its original mission.

The event gives employees connections across the organization that they would never make in ordinary business and gets them used to working together on unfamiliar challenges. By forcing creative cooperation, it influences the rest of Microsoft's operations, encouraging participants to bring a newfound network and novel ideas back to their everyday functions. The event even resulted in some products, such as Seeing AI, an app that narrates the world around users with visual impairments; Learning Tools for OneNote, an add-on for students with reading challenges such as dyslexia; and EyeGaze, an app for paralyzed users that interfaces with computers through eye movements.[175]

Collaborative Leaders

Nadella relied on much more than top-down messaging to drive collaboration. He also sought a collaborative leadership team. Radical collaboration matters at least as much at the head of an organization as it does in its body organization. Collaboration in the latter means little if the overall direction is fragmented or disjointed. As a result, leadership teams in particular need to embody the spirit of radical collaboration this chapter has been espousing. Organizations need to ensure that their senior leaders are highly motivated to seek solutions, often by selecting the top team with this criterion in mind—batteries included.

Nadella realized early that the senior team he inherited was like a group of individuals working in their own individually successful silos. Meetings were an exercise in poking holes in each other's ideas. Despite the depth of individual talent, a collaborative attitude was missing. Nadella said:

> The poet John Donne wrote, "No man is an island," but he'd feel otherwise had he joined our meetings. Each leader in the group was, in essence, CEO of a self-sustaining business. Each lived and operated in a silo, and most had been doing so for a very long time. My portfolio had no center of gravity.

This center of gravity is crucial to kickstarting collaboration, as teams need some sort of organizing principle to work together around. With this in mind, Nadella assembled a new senior team. He hired a head of business development, tasked with striking deals to acquire and partner with exciting new products and services. He also found a new chief people officer to support the upcoming cultural transformation around external collaboration. Others included a chief strategist, a chief marketer, and a new head for Cloud and Enterprise, Microsoft's fastest-growing business.

While these hires immediately clarified the strategic shift, they also shared a collaborative mindset—which enabled them to use their complementary skills productively and then generate high-quality consensus on major decisions. In order for the company to carry out bold strategic moves, these executives had to be radically open to collaboration—and then drive that collaboration into the organization.

In practice, that means not just debate and disagreement, but also brainstorming to generate ideas—and then reach high-quality agreement. Executives need a collaborative spirit that matches their individual motivation and unifies the company's priorities and its execution. As Nadella says: "When we are an inch apart on strategy at the leadership level, our product teams end up miles apart in execution."

Only if senior leaders are willing to work collaboratively and productively can they lean into each other's problems and help each other address them. They can also serve as the organization's archetype of radical collaboration, with the team using their skill sets to tackle tough problems. The chief financial officer keeps the organization intellectually honest and accountable for its actions, the chief strategy officer remains rigorous about company plans, and the chief people officer represents employees. Similarly, product leaders ensure alignment on specific offerings.

In Nadella's new Microsoft, the company is no longer a "confederation of fiefdoms." Since industry phenomena do not follow organizational boundaries, he encourages colleagues to transcend silos as well. The goal is to do what matters for customers, which often means going outside the comfort zone. Nadella even promotes an open-source mentality:

> One group may create code and intellectual property, but it's open and available for inspection and improvement from other groups inside and outside the company. I tell my colleagues they get to own a customer scenario, not the code. Our code may need to be tailored one way for a small business and another way for a public-sector customer. It's our ability to work together that makes our dreams believable and, ultimately, achievable. We must learn to build on the ideas of others and collaborate across boundaries to bring the best of Microsoft to our customers as one—one Microsoft.

The Limits of Radical Collaboration

Given the benefits of this openness, why have hierarchical structures at all? Several business thinkers have called for extreme versions of collaboration without management at all. Self-managed teams would bubble up on a specific project or initiative and then dissolve after meeting goals. Anyone in the organization could decide on a path as long as he or she made the thought process vulnerable to examination and critique by others.

Frequent internal job fairs would lay out new and potential projects for colleagues to join as they chose. In order to enforce accountability, everyone becomes a virtual company of one, with a transparent balance sheet and profit and loss, with salaries resulting from negotiated commitments made along the value stream and the surpluses that result.[176]

While some companies have made moves in this direction, notably Zappos under Tony Hsieh, none have approached this ideal. It's easy to see why—extreme collaboration depends on people who are so independently minded that they are likely to prefer freelance contracting over working for a large organization in any case. Without structure, it's also hard to coordinate investment in large amounts of capital in a way that would satisfy investors. But we can appreciate the growing interest in these extreme designs as reflecting a discomfort with conventional hierarchy and limited collaboration.

Silos at Myspace

Let's remember that most companies, even highly successful ones, tend to resist deep-seated collaboration—to their long-term detriment. At companies without an urgency for collaboration, even a strong market position isn't enough for sustained success.

Until 2006, the pioneering social media platform Myspace was the internet's biggest website by traffic. It surpassed Google and Yahoo, and benefited from continually marketing to new users. But the warning signs of its decline were already in place. The actual technical functionality of the website paled in comparison to its upcoming rivals such as Facebook. While it had built a community around people and their interests in entertainment and music, it lacked the necessary social features to compete with peers, such as news feeds and status updates.

Those new features failed to emerge because of the company's structure, which was ill-suited for intensive collaboration. The company's functional divisions amounted to silos that separated customer-focused groups from the technical groups that implemented features. Without small teams or other policies to force interaction, the silos had minimal communication or collaboration. So the teams with their finger on the pulse of user experience had little to do with the teams responsible for meeting those user demands—but people didn't worry because they believed they had a competitive advantage of network effects—you had to be on Myspace if you mattered in social media.

The engineering teams ended up pouring time and energy into features that users cared little about, and the online experience, as well as the company, stagnated. The insular organizational hierarchy proved to be the fatal flaw for a company that needed to continually evolve according to user demands. By contrast, Facebook was hungry and driven, with enough cross-functional collaboration to keep adapting and adding new features. Its status as an innovative follower helped its managers resist complacency and in-fighting, while its ambitious yet collaborative founder pushed hard for his vision.

Myspace's success depended on user experience, so its structure should have facilitated collaboration there—and didn't. Evaluating your company strategy and results can quickly reveal whether you have an urgent collaboration problem—and whether your company's silos are slowing it down.

Insular Leadership at WeWork

Companies without collaborative leaders often face major difficulties. WeWork, for instance, was known for its purposeful, single-minded leadership from charismatic founder and CEO Adam Neumann. The company was on track to IPO with a valuation of over $40 billion, and it was attracting enormous publicity for breaking down the silos of personal workspaces in much of corporate America. Neumann evangelized the potential of informal workspaces that promoted collaboration.

Yet Neumann had insulated his senior team from the rest of the company. Collaboration doesn't just solve problems; it also promotes transparency and communication, which helps companies identify problems sooner. When organizations lack collaborative executive teams, they lose this important driver of accountability. They risk having an isolated leadership structure free to act outside of the company's interests.

That's what happened at WeWork, which Neumann led with little oversight. He was free to engage in the self-enriching practices that crashed the company's catastrophic initial public offering—leasing buildings to the company that he personally owned and borrowing money against his personal stake in the company. If he had assembled a senior team of collaborative individuals, they would have been an implicit source of accountability.

A collaborative senior team still leaves room for visionary leadership that goes against the grain, assuming its members share the vision. But the collaborative approach encourages colleagues to dissect and cross-examine strategies, which in turn keeps irresponsible business practices from flourishing. Truly collaborative organizations tend to be transparent in their operations, leaving little room for individuals leading the ship astray.

Promoting Collaboration in Practice

Let's get concrete. While CEOs can promote collaboration through structures, strategic shifts, and senior hires, they can also work directly to help people up and down the organization engage with people beyond their comfort zone. Leaders have found many ways to do this, with AMD CEO Lisa Su (see chapters 4 and 7) among the most prominent.

Su maintains a strong open-door policy, where people at any level of the company can message her with comments and feedback. That's a start, and then she makes an effort to solicit this feedback from employees who might otherwise resist giving comments and ideas to the boss.

Su began doing that in her career at IBM, where she managed a team of ten people. She had been motivated purely by the project at hand, and was surprised when her boss asked whether she had spoken with her team members. She realized speaking with the teams she led was essential to understanding what drove them, which in turn was critical to engaging them in the work.

At AMD, people at lower levels and even entirely outside of the company have provided insights into what works and what doesn't. Su discourages barriers to collaboration based on seniority or rank. She emphasizes feedback on the company's work, so the company takes the radically collaborative approach of making that as easy as possible.

Whitney Wolfe Herd, Bumble's founder and CEO (see chapters 4 and 8), goes further. She established dual leadership, where executives oversee multiple areas, to discourage intraorganizational competition: "Who says only one person can lead a business unit or define what success looks like for a team? We have worked to build partnerships at the top of some of our key functional areas, so you have a creative mind complemented by a strategic one, or an operator sitting next to a visionary—rather than competing with one another to be the only 'VP of XYZ.'"

Companies can't adopt radical collaboration half-heartedly. It's such a difficult practice that an organization must live and breathe it in order to prod people to actually do it. No single strategy will make this happen in every company, but a few principles are worth keeping in mind.

First is the simple openness to all opportunities for collaboration, which can lead to otherwise daring policies like Amazon's "two-pizza" teams. These groups stay small and focused, dealing with individual problems and collaborating to make sure the final product is cohesive. Large teams end up consumed with internal politics, fighting internally for resources, and unable to pivot as they discover opportunities.

Second is to remember the payoff from collaboration with entities outside the organization. Small firms often have deep subject-area knowledge that a large organization cannot replicate but that nicely complements the latter's resources, as Microsoft found with its network of partners.

Third, make sure to adjust your collaboration according to strategic goals. Thus Haier decentralizes according to product markets overseen by entrepreneurial teams, while Apple relies on an expert-driven functional organization. Both force collaboration, but in very different ways, and correspondingly use different structures.

Fourth, encourage not just collaborative structures but also a collaborative ethos, from Tesla's formal policy to Microsoft's worldwide hackathon. Both go far in making people comfortable working outside of the hierarchy in order to solve problems. Remember, most employees would rather keep working with people they know. Collaboration is an unnatural act even for brave people, so it requires cultural and even structural encouragement.

Ultimately, radical collaboration depends on an organizational mindset. Company policy and strategy need to be rooted in this mindset in order to fully achieve perpetual innovation. Every company preaches collaboration, but radical collaboration is a way of life.

Thus there is an important distinction between everyday cooperation and radical collaboration. At the end of the day, embracing collaboration in all its forms, and organizing your company around it, is vital. Companies that collaborate not out of necessity but as a way of life make collaboration truly radical. If they can sustain that embrace, they can achieve impressive results.

CHAPTER TEN

Putting It All Together

As you've read this book, I hope you've seen a connection across the eight main drivers of perpetual innovation. In order to transform your organization for long-term success, you'll likely need all eight drivers to some degree. Above all, you need a deep commitment: transformation is not a one-day event or corporate initiative, but a continual and self-sustaining effort.

A company that has been losing steam can still achieve a significant transformation. But getting there takes the strong direction and concerted effort that only someone in leadership can achieve. It helps if that person is the CEO, but if you are a manager or above, you can still apply the concepts of this book to your team or department.

The main barrier is bureaucracy, even in midsize organizations. Most large-scale transformations fail to boost profitability or growth while wasting billions of dollars in lost time and consulting expenses. Sometimes the best time to reorient the organization is when new leadership comes into office, although it is not necessary.

We've already seen how Apple, Microsoft, Amazon, Tesla, and other companies achieved perpetual innovation through a combination of these drivers. Here is a case study of Starbucks under its founder and longtime leader, Howard Schultz. Starbucks makes a strong example because it offers a service largely through brick-and-mortar retail stores, not the high-digital offerings of many perpetual innovators. It transformed itself twice and is now in the middle of what may be a third turnaround under changing circumstances. Stories of Satya Nadella's and Howard Schultz's transformative efforts are reminders that companies sometimes need different degrees of nudge or transformation when they veer off the track of perpetual innovation.

Starbucks's Existential Purpose

In 1983, Howard Schultz was overseeing operations for Starbucks, then a small chain in Seattle that sold only coffee beans. He went on a trip to Milan, Italy, where he had an epiphany. Inspired by the city's vibrant cafes to create a "third place" between work and home, he left Starbucks and raised enough money to start a single shop to offer the espresso and other specialty coffees of Europe. The idea worked, and he soon bought the Starbucks chain to power his vision of excellent coffee in an engaged meeting place. After transforming Starbucks, he took the idea national and then worldwide.

In later recalling his motivation, he went back much earlier, to 1970, when he was seven years old. He and his family were living in public housing in Brooklyn, and a fluke slip on ice left his father out of work for several months. The family had no health insurance or worker's compensation. Schultz described his father as being "ground down by the world."[177]

That despair inspired the son both to work hard in life to avoid that state and to offer generous benefits to employees—fundamental to the vision from the beginning. It motivated him to dare to change the world for the better with his vision of people coming together over a good beverage experience. Founders inspired by an event early on in life can draw on deep commitment and resist the temptation to fixate on profits; they'd rather make a difference in customers' lives. With that existential commitment, Schultz started off as a missionary more than a mercenary. Pursuing the chain's purpose, even if it hurt the company in the short term, came naturally to him.

The company's first mission statement, in 1990, aimed to "establish Starbucks as the premier purveyor of the finest coffee in the world while maintaining our uncompromising principles as we grow."[178] But Schultz maintained that commitment even after retiring as CEO in 2000 and then returning in 2008. In a 2018 letter to employees on those principles, as he left the company for the third time, Schultz said he sought to balance "profitability and social conscience." Until recently, "social conscience" were words CEOs rarely uttered.

Starbucks took stances on issues that have surely lost them customers, from immigration and same-sex marriage to gun control and racism.[179]

The greatest test came at the peak of the 2008 financial crisis, when Starbucks was facing a rapidly plummeting share price in the midst of a spiraling broader economy. The firm's own rapid expansion had turned out to be its Achilles' heel. The speed with which the organization was building new branches, without a strong conception of what the organization stood for, led to the growth of bureaucracy, not unlike Microsoft's. This bureaucracy, over time, had lost touch with the needs of the customer and neglected the essence of the organization.

For instance, employees from this time period described management blaming dairy prices and logistical factors for the company's slump, causing them to raise prices in the heat of the recession. This orientation to problem-solving had taken the company's focus away from its emphasis on *experience and ethical business.* The company was losing its niche: competing with (and losing to) McDonald's and Dunkin' Donuts, where they once offered entirely different in-store experiences.

The key to regaining competitiveness lies in "preserving [Starbucks's] soul," as Schultz put it. The board brought him back as CEO, and he worked to return the company to his vision. Among his efforts was a three-day conference in New Orleans that gathered ten thousand Starbucks managers. The conference cost $30 million, which the Starbucks board resisted because the company was facing a cash crunch, but Schultz insisted.[180]

Besides attending working sessions, participants helped neighborhoods still recovering from Hurricane Katrina. They partook in exercises that reinforced Starbucks's values and the new company vision: "To inspire and nurture the human spirit, one person, one cup, and one neighborhood at a time."[181] Schultz announced a partnership to direct proceeds from holiday sales to AIDS relief programs in Africa.

The greater attention to ethical sourcing and environmental impact, as well as the introduction of technology partnerships and innovative growth platforms, were major shifts in priority. However, on closer inspection, the transformation agenda still retained certain core Starbucks values at its center: to be a "coffee authority" and the "heart of the neighborhood."

Schultz believed that maintaining the organization's values through a period of upheaval was crucial to his strategy's success. It allowed everyone—from senior leadership to the staff on the ground—to buy into the new vision. It provided staff members a sense of continuity. And it paid off: while many large businesses were still struggling with the aftereffects of the financial crisis, Starbucks boasted year after year of record revenues and profitable growth.[182]

Obsessed with the Customer Experience

For all his concern about coffee quality, Schultz cared most about connecting to what customers need now. In 2009, twenty years after he had relaunched Starbucks as a "third place" based on sophisticated beverages, he had an open mind about what people wanted now. Other big companies might have conducted research to determine how consumers would react to particular store elements—a process that's susceptible to manipulation by executives with a preconceived agenda, but Schultz kept things simple, as he went directly to his customers, with two unbranded coffee shops in the heart of Seattle.

That's not to say that Starbucks ignores conventional customer data. It has a dedicated data science team, led by a senior vice president, to collect and analyze information on the thirty thousand stores and one hundred million weekly transactions. Much of this data comes from the Starbucks mobile app, which tracks browsing as well as purchasing habits. The data helps the company decide on running promotions on any particular item.[183]

Promoting Pygmalion

By the time of the New Orleans conference, Schultz had already replaced many of the company's executives. But he knew he and a few colleagues couldn't transform the company on their own. So he made a point of talking at length to the managers in attendance. People got to hear from him directly, learn from him, and become inspired. He also had them partake in exercises that reinforced the company's values.

With echoes of Pygmalion, he needed to reenergize everyone to the company's values of service to their customers and their communities. Hence the conference's emphasis on the new vision: "To inspire and nurture the human spirit, one person, one cup, and one neighborhood at a time."[184] Schultz's transformation agenda included seven principles:[185]

1. Be the undisputed coffee authority.
2. Engage and inspire partners (staff).
3. Ignite the emotional attachment to customers.
4. Expand globally while making each store the heart of its neighborhood.
5. Be the leader in ethical sourcing and environmental impact.
6. Create innovative growth platforms worthy of Starbucks coffee.
7. Deliver a sustainable economic model.

Many, if not most, of these principles departed from the company's current approach. Yet the agenda retained core Starbucks values.[186]

Regaining a Start-Up Mindset

Schultz didn't found Starbucks, but he transformed it from what it had been. He saw it with a start-up mindset, quite different from the small goals of the actual founders or the calculations of a professionally schooled manager focused on profit and loss. He had no patience for a "small business"; he wanted to become a giant. In his dogged pursuit of purpose, he went through many iterations of offerings, trying slight variations until his team found a mix that attracted customers while still fitting his vision.

Nevertheless, his humble origins kept him focused on the vision, not on his own success. Instead of building an empire at headquarters for himself, he traveled regularly and continued developing the company's culture.

His commitment to building a distinct service came out clearly in 2008, when he returned as CEO. The company had expanded aggressively without a strong sense of purpose. The start-up years were a distant memory.

It was time for a transformation by regaining the old start-up mindset, hence the three-day conference in New Orleans.[187]

Nancy Koehn, a professor at Harvard Business School, explained why he was determined to put on the conference: "Schultz understood that what saves and breaks businesses is much more than cash. In the midst of so much turbulence, it's all too easy to pull levers on the low-hanging fruit of cash and logistics. But you don't save a business and turn it around without speaking to, focusing, and calling on the spirit of your people." He had to reinvigorate what had become a lumbering giant.

Controlling the Tempo

Schultz also knew to control the tempo, when to be patient and when to hustle. In early 2007, when he had only a part-time job as chief strategist at the company, he saw that the company needed rejuvenation. The leadership looked into launching a Starbucks instant coffee, but the research and development leaders estimated it would take at least thirty-two months to develop the perfect recipe.[188]

As he described in his book *Onward*, Schultz was deeply unsatisfied with the estimates of such a long time for R&D. He knew that if it took several years to launch the product, Starbucks might lose a lot of market share. He understood better than anyone that keeping the tempo is key.

In response to the head of R&D Tom Jones, Schultz erupted, "Why must it take so long? If Apple could develop the iPod in less than a year, we can do this!" The infamous "iPod meeting" shook the entire team working on the instant coffee endeavor. In thirty-two months, they not only developed a strong recipe for Starbucks-quality instant coffee, but the company had launched and was selling in stores across the United States.

Like a pack of patient lions on the hunt, the company didn't invest heavily in instant coffee right away. But when the leaders discovered the demand and the possibility of capitalizing on it, they pounced. Tempo in an organization must start from the top and spread from there.

But Schultz could slow things down and disinvest as well. Successful companies need to divert resources away from underperforming products or discontinue them altogether. When Schultz worked to revitalize the store culture, he knew the company couldn't waste time trying to keep struggling stores open. So he closed hundreds of them, most of them in the US.

Meanwhile he invested in the remaining seven thousand stores, including replacing all the espresso machines with the Mastrena, a sophisticated Swiss-made device known for fast and high-quality coffee. Then he ordered all the thousands of US stores to close for three hours on the same day, even though it would cost the company $6 million in lost sales. He thought the organization had fallen off in the quality of espresso, a core part of its brand and mission. During these three hours, baristas watched a video made by Schultz himself demonstrating how to pour the coffee to produce strong, full, but not bitter espresso. Then the stores reopened, and everyone got back to business.

The move became a national spectacle, with Schultz noting how "others covered the closings with an odd sense of wonder, as if it had snowed in summer." It challenged another essential part of the brand, its reliability and convenience. Customers know that they can always go to a nearby store, order their favorite drink, and be back on their way in only a few minutes. The backlash to the three-hour shutdown was far larger than Schultz predicted, but he had no regrets since he regarded quality as being mission critical.

In responding to the media attention, Schultz asked, "How could it be wrong to invest in our people?" He soon won vindication. Espresso sales went up, along with positive stories of customers from baristas. Going slow (temporarily) paid off.

Schultz also moved deliberately in moving into the equivalent of financial services. In 2008, the company introduced a loyalty program that rewarded frequent purchases at the stores and tied it to physical gift cards. Customers could reload the cards, use them for their frequent purchases, and earn free refills and other benefits over time. Usage increased further in 2010 with the Starbucks app for mobile phones, freeing customers from having to present an actual card for purchases. Four years later, the company added mobile ordering and pickup, and soon a quarter of all purchases were done entirely by phone.

The gradual steps ensured that this potentially glitchy offering came out seamlessly and customers were ready for it. By 2021, the company had twenty-five million active rewards members, with $1.6 billion in deposits. While focusing on its "third place" vision, Starbucks had become one of the largest participants in what soon became known as "fintech."[189]

Bimodal in Action

Schultz expected this transformation in store culture to proceed gradually, with a few big events supported by relentless messaging and support from headquarters. While he pushed hard for the instant coffee product, he was open to exploring new ideas in a relaxed time frame. He had patience for other projects with greater uncertainty, so he was comfortable with different parts of the organization moving at different speeds.

After he became company chairman in 2017, his successor Kevin Johnson built on his approach with the Tryer Center, a laboratory for agile innovation. The lab continually tries out new ideas, and many of them end up in real stores. Only when ideas emerge does the staff use rapid prototyping to put projects into action—and then the goal is to roll out each new idea into stores within one hundred days. After six months, the lab had already tested 133 projects, with 40 going into stores. Fifteen hundred employees from throughout the company had also rotated through the center on short stints.[190]

Going Bold

Schultz had such a strong existential commitment that he dared to go boldly. As previously mentioned, the most notable time was at the beginning of his second run as CEO, on February 26, 2008, when he closed all 7,100 Starbucks stores for three hours. Even though he knew that it would cost the company millions of dollars in lost revenue, it was worth it to uphold the vision. In this case, it was decided that a simple video, made by Schultz himself, that demonstrated how to do a proper espresso pour was critical to maintaining his company's reputation for quality. For Schultz, quality was nonnegotiable.

Despite the backlash from the news media and some customers, and after just a few anxious days, Schultz was vindicated. Espresso sales went up, and baristas had plenty of customer success stories to share. Temporarily scaling back to address a weakness takes courage. It also takes conviction that it will improve the company, and if that conviction is strong enough, such unusual actions should not be avoided.

Likewise, Schultz was not afraid to take risks with new store locations, designs, and products. Unlike other companies that perform rigorous consumer research to determine how customers will react to a particular atmosphere or location, Starbucks is not afraid to simply open a new store and learn.

In summer 2009, Schultz spearheaded the opening of two unbranded Starbucks stores in the heart of Seattle. Intentionally "without fanfare," Schultz used the stores as blank slates, to see how customers reacted to design changes without their opinions being obscured by their conception of the brand. "We were not trying to hide anything, only to explore, and to learn. The idea to experiment with other retail concepts that would further elevate our coffee authority had actually been touched on in early transformation brainstorming sessions."[191]

What types of products and designs did the stores test? Anything that was entirely new. For companies as established as Starbucks, it's easy to fall into the trap of being constricted by your own rules, feeling the need to maintain consistency with your previous, successful products—a consistency that ultimately holds you back. With these covert launches, Schultz said that "'break the rules' was my only directive."[192]

Schultz could not predict the consumer, competitor, and media reactions to the rapid store openings and closings, but with each decision he made, he was certain that it would bring Starbucks one step closer to a better product. For a company led by courage, that certainty is enough.

Both in his refusal in 2022 to go along with many of his customers' pro-union biases, and in his insistence on quality in 2008, Schultz has resisted the usual corporate timidity. Indeed, some organizations might have learned from the backlash to the three-hour shutdown to proceed carefully. It's only natural for a large, successful, consumer-facing organization to move cautiously, aware of the higher stakes at the company's new global scale. But Schultz took the opposite conclusion: boldness paid off.

Neither the size nor the media attention should sway an organization from making a move that will ultimately increase quality, customer experience, and sales. There is a logic to temporarily scaling back to focus on a weakness. And, yes, it takes courage, but when armed with the conviction that it will improve the company, such trimmings should not be needlessly avoided.

In a statement that could apply to much of this book, Schultz described what's needed in order to succeed in disruptive times:

> There are moments in our lives when we summon the courage to make choices that go against reason, against common sense and the wise counsel of people we trust. But we lean forward nonetheless because, despite all risks and rational arguments, we believe that the path we are choosing is the right and best thing to do. We refuse to be bystanders, even if we do not know exactly where our actions will lead.

Driving Collaboration

When Schultz took over in 2008, he didn't know all of the problems he would need to solve. The company needed a drastic change, but he didn't know what form the transformation would take. He had to learn a lot. Rather than hire consultants, he went directly to the employees. Besides visiting stores around the world, he invited employees to email him directly, and got five thousand messages of concerns, ideas, and thoughts. He also called store managers directly to see how their operations were going, what worked, and what did not.[193]

These conversations were critical in helping Schultz evaluate the genuine needs of the organization. Without understanding how the business currently operated, from those actually overseeing the operations, he couldn't identify levers of change and plan the transformation. By truly listening to these colleagues, he also made them more likely to go along with plans from headquarters.

Oftentimes, employees are the best supporters for a CEO's transformation, rather than other senior leaders. They are on the front lines and can understand in concrete terms what the organization needs now.

In 2008, most of them came on board and supported the transformation. The situation was very different in 2022, on his third run as CEO. Schultz moved over to board chairman in 2016, and then left the company entirely in 2018. When growth slowed during the pandemic, the board asked him to return as interim CEO. Before turning the reins over to a permanent leader, Schultz worked again to transform the giant retailer into a purpose-driven innovator.

By then, however, the thousands of baristas and other frontline employees had a different perspective. Beaten down by what Schultz called the larger ills of current society, especially rising homeless and disorderly conduct, they were less inclined to embrace the grand vision of a "third place."

In 2012, Schultz wrote, "I was convinced that under my leadership, employees would come to realize that I would listen to their concerns. If they had faith in me and my motives, they wouldn't need a union." But more and more employees saw the giant company in transactional terms. They agitated for higher pay and benefits, and hundreds of shops have won union certification, though so far the company has refused to negotiate with the union.[194]

Schultz handed over the reins to new CEO Laxman Narasimhan in early 2023, after only a year as interim leader, and without resolving the unionization question, so it's hard to see how collaboration will play out now. But his success in his first two returns speaks for itself.

Putting It All Together

Starbucks isn't as flashy as some of the companies we've highlighted, especially game changers such as Apple and Tesla. In many ways it's utterly similar to most large companies, especially when not overseen by Howard Schultz. It's too early to assess his third attempted transformation of the company, which in fairness he led only as interim CEO until the board could replace the previous leader who had suddenly resigned.

His multiple returns do suggest some difficulties with the Pygmalion challenge of sustaining his existential purpose for the company. It's not enough for the leader and his or her senior team to embrace a distinct vision. That vision has to penetrate so deeply that it overwhelms the usual dampening pressures as companies grow and routinize their offerings. It's a challenge for every company that succeeds beyond expectations. Nevertheless, if the eight characteristics described in previous chapters are done well and preserved, there is less likelihood of the need for an organization to go through a major transformation.

A Path Forward

The rest of this chapter lays out a path to innovation, with five building blocks to promote the eight elements described in the book. If the eight elements are like an operating system of a perpetually innovative organization, these next steps will help you adopt them and transform your organization into a perpetual innovator.[195]

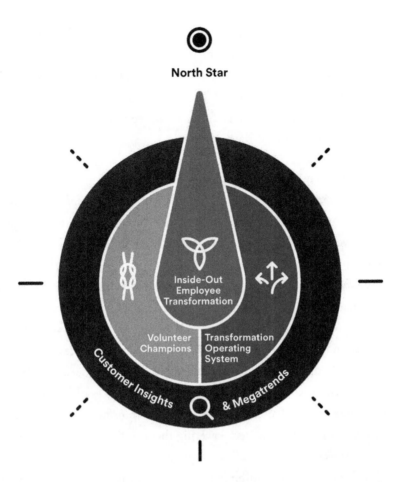

1. **Setting a North Star:** A crisp, inspiring articulation of the vision and strategic objectives for the transformation.
2. **Customer Insights and Megatrends:** Embedding a deep understanding of customers in every change you make, and in every employee—the customer you have today and the ones you want tomorrow, as well as the megatrends affecting them.
3. **Inside-Out Employee Transformation:** Tools to make the transformation personal for your employees—to connect their aspirations to the North Star and to your customers.
4. **The Transformation Operating System:** This is a flat, adaptable, and cross-functional organizational structure that enables

sustainable change. This structure promotes the elements other than existential commitment and customer obsession, with the help and scaling of leadership and volunteer champions.

5. **Volunteer Champions:** A mechanism to harness many influencers and thought leaders from across your organization to drive transformation.

Along the way are key principles to remember:

Transformations fail because we fail to transform our people. Done well, transformations help companies achieve their financial and strategic goals *and* improve the working lives of employees. Too often we underemphasize the human aspects of transformation.

Transformation must start from the inside. Too often this work is the domain of armies of external consultants. Better for it to be driven by internal talent—led by your organization's leaders, and executed by your leaders, managers, and employees. If handled by outsiders, employees at all levels lack ownership of the transformation effort, leading to reduced morale, hesitation in incorporating and adjusting to changed processes, and even outright sabotage of change efforts. Better to put transformation capabilities in the hands of your people, empowering them to find and implement the changes needed to deliver your transformation strategy.

Motivation matters. Your employees—from your executives and leaders to your mid-level managers to the staff working on the front line—want their work to matter. They want to make a difference. They want their organization to succeed. They want to do the right thing for their careers and their personal development. Successful transformations connect this inside-out approach to a deep customer-centric and trend-aware approach that gives you an outside-in view.

Sustainable results and permanent benefits. When done well, transformations bring a sustainable quantum leap in business performance and agility—improving top and bottom lines in short and long terms. By bringing people together on the transformation journey, you will also develop your talent and identify future leaders, as well as embed a transformation skill set to eliminate your dependency on external rescuers. You'll also launch a cultural transformation—engaging and shifting the mindset within your workforce across all levels to focus on customers and become aware of the wider ecosystem.

Let's delve into each building block.

① The North Star

The North Star is the vision for transformation and the long-term test for all actions. But even before laying it out, leaders need open conversations with employees across the organization. As with Howard Schultz in 2008, effective leaders commence their transformation efforts with listening. Leaders can't implement institutional change without understanding customers' needs, the businesses' current problems, and the levers of change in the organization. While executives can see the big picture, the people on the front lines often grasp these dynamics better than anyone.

That's why Satya Nadella devoted most of his first year as Microsoft CEO to listening to employees at every level—anonymously, individually, and in groups. He already knew much of the company well, having risen in the technology and cloud computing divisions. But he wanted to have an open mind. And people saw him as a good listener. He told employees he wanted to renew the company's culture and needed to hear how they saw the situation.[196] Those conversations led to an action plan informed by, rather than simply delegated to, his employees.

Leaders can't transform an organization without support from employees, and that support won't go to a leader disconnected from the company. Leaders need to understand why the status quo is unsustainable and what areas can drive future success. Yet listening is also essential to laying the foundation for ongoing collaboration because it shows respect for colleagues.

From there, leaders can articulate the strategic vision for transformation in a crisp and inspiring way so employees are motivated and excited to work outside the bounds of their day-to-day responsibilities. For example, a global Asian supply chain leader recently aimed to "build a world-class organization that enables long-term sustainable growth while developing the next generation of leaders." We've mentioned several such statements in the book, such as Amazon's ("Our vision is to be Earth's most customer-centric company; to build a place where people can come to find and discover anything they might want to buy online") and Santa Clara Valley Medical Center ("Build a world-class patient flow process that patients and families love and makes staff proud").

Next, generate three to seven strategic priorities as brief bullet points. This will act as your checklist for the change. These are typically less inspiring but more concrete. This gives your employees a clear direction for where to hunt for opportunities and how to select and prioritize them.

These priorities often lead to abandoning ideas and initiatives you've already invested in. To pay for your (likely expensive) priorities, you need to free up capital, time, energy, and talent. Cutting the good but not compelling projects—including pet projects of your top talent—will give you space to transform.

Companies seeking transformation are often strapped for cash. As described earlier, when Steve Jobs returned to Apple in 1997, the company was nearing its end. It was a few months from going broke. But Jobs had the clarity of his existential vision: "We believe that we are on the face of the earth to make great products and that's not changing." So he axed more than 70 percent of Apple's hardware and software products, including the Newton personal organizer, a project that sucked $100 million out of the failing company, despite the product's innovation and potential. Instead of focusing on dozens of mediocre products, Jobs shifted Apple's focus to a few high-potential products.

Similarly, when Howard Schultz returned as CEO of Starbucks in 2008, he permanently closed six hundred stores, which made up 7 percent of the global workforce. The company also scaled back its CD and book sales. All these measures freed up close to a billion dollars in cash.

Schultz drew on Starbucks's North Star in setting priorities for senior executives, as follows:

- Improve the US business by refocusing on the customer experience in the stores
- Slow the pace of US store openings and closing underperforming locations
- Reignite customers' emotional attachment with Starbucks coffee, brand, people, and stores
- Realign the organization and streamline management to better support customer-focused initiatives
- Outside the US, accelerate expansion while increasing the profitability of stores, partly by redeploying some of the capital earmarked for US store growth

With these priorities, everyone knew what they were working toward. Employees had a guide to navigating a world with too many things to do. Bolstered by a clear vision and priorities, people are more willing to make sacrifices and take risks.

2 Customer Insights and Megatrends

Here the challenge is to synthesize deep empathy with customers and an understanding of the megatrends in the ecosystem. Cocreate with customers—a term that can include all relevant stakeholders such as regulators, suppliers, consumers, and employees. It is helpful to identify needs you may choose to target, but also to understand how any changes you make are impacted by the broader ecosystem of competitors, new entrants, and players upstream and downstream.

For example, a hospital catering to disadvantaged sections of society made a point of broadening its understanding of customers. It now watched for shifts in public funding levels, increases in the number of patients due to the Affordable Care Act coming into effect, and new venture-funded business models in insurance, diagnosis, and health-care delivery.

Then, it focused on bringing in the megatrends in their ecosystem, such as:

1. Technology: What are your customers' expectations in your domains, and what is driving those expectations? E.g., expecting your services to be as easy as Uber.
2. Culture: What is happening in the customer ecosystem, and how does this affect their needs, wants, and behaviors?
3. Behaviors: What are the "moments of truth" in their experience with you?

For example, an automotive distributor's customer research uncovered that the test drive, so often the focus for optimization, actually was not a critical decision point for most car purchasers. Many more made their decision based on the first sight of the car or on the first review they read.

The key step is to empathize with customers at the company-wide level and at every initiative in the transformation program. Ask yourself, who is the "customer" that we are optimizing for? Go beyond traditional definitions to include stakeholders and dream customers. And what are their unmet or latent needs? Do we understand these at the planning and execution levels?

For example, a wealth management firm believes it is satisfying its clients by helping them achieve healthy returns on their investments. Yet their customers feel the firm is not meeting their need to help them plan for major life milestones such as marriage, having children, and retirement.

Finally, how can we cocreate with customers? It is not enough to understand customers; we also need to involve them in every step of the transformation.

Building empathy with customers is not an easy exercise, and rarely does one approach fit all situations (though experts in each approach will try to convince you otherwise). The pool of techniques includes ethnographic analysis, through embedding a researcher into customers' daily life as they interact with your offerings or those of your competitors. This is invasive, expensive, and time-consuming but historically has proven to be one of the most effective ways of uncovering latent needs.

Behavior diaries are a lighter-weight approach to ethnographic analysis, where customers make notes after interacting with your offerings. The goal is to elicit their aims when they approach your product, their emotions while using it, their level of satisfaction, and the level to which you met their needs.

Interviews and focus groups are the most common approach, where researchers bring in customers and potential customers and ask them questions. This approach is much easier than the others, though it can still prove expensive. Understanding how to structure and frame your questions to elicit customers' needs, rather than what you want to hear, requires a new skill set. Surveys are another common approach, enabling companies to extract information from a broad pool of customers to gain a quantitative understanding.

Data analytics is getting increased attention as companies ingest data on interactions with customers. If you have a mobile application, for example, what times of day do customers typically open the application? What context can you infer from that information? How often do they engage with you, and what tasks do they typically do regularly?

As for cocreation with customers, I can recommend using sprints—working quickly through five distinct steps: empathize, ideate, prototype, test, and refine.

Throughout this process, keep these principles in mind:

Involve real customers. This is easier than you think. There are time and availability limitations, but many customers enjoy being part of the transformation process. The resistance is more likely to be internal, from account managers or sales executives who feel (incorrectly usually) that they completely understand the user or have to protect them from being exposed to new ideas. In the rare situations where you must use a proxy for a real user, look for external proxies (such as executive assistants), rather than internal proxies.

Find leading customers. In every customer base, there will be those that are looking for the next great thing and those that are happy with following the crowd. You are more likely to find sources of inspiration from the first group than the second.

Conduct the research yourself. There is a widespread belief that only external design agencies or your marketing teams should be able to speak to customers. But to drive innovation, it's important that at some point during the process, *every* member of the transformation team have direct exposure to a real customer.

③ Inside-Out Employee Transformation

Individual transformation of employees is (at least) as important as your organizational transformation. That's how the Pygmalion effect works. Without it, the chances of your transformation succeeding are low.

Employees tend to view transformations in one of three ways—as a threat, as a burden, or as an opportunity. Too often leaders fail to recognize the fear of being replaced or minimized due to transformation, or actually stoke those fears through opaque or limited communication. To help people see the opportunity mindset, companies need to promote the transformation at a personal level, for the leadership, for the volunteer champions, and eventually for employees across the organization.

That happens best through an inside-out process. Employees can start by focusing on their personal strengths and unique contributions, and connect these to the vision of the organization after transformation. They need to understand how they can contribute to the effort and how the transformation will help their progression and growth.

It starts with them defining their aspiration for where they want to be—creating a personal vision statement with the SEE framework (see p. 36). Then they must develop an understanding of themselves. Here they can work with any of multiple tools, such as the Myers-Briggs, Enneagrams, the GC Index, or StrengthsFinder. Then they have to develop a personal transformation plan and share it with colleagues as a method of making, and getting, a public commitment.

During the transformation process, on a regular basis (at least monthly), they should revisit their plan and evaluate whether they are contributing to the transformation in the manner they had committed and whether they are getting the growth opportunities committed to them. A key aspect of leading a transformation is instituting and responding appropriately to these reflections.

4 The Transformation Operating System

Most organizations are not structured for the rapid and fluid decision-making that will make your transformation a success, hence the need for a new nonhierarchical structure that applies a "Silicon-Valley culture" of bold, fast, devolved decision-making; experimentation; and continuous testing and learning.

This will best come from flat cross-functional teams for each key area, staffed from throughout the organization. I call these "rapid response teams," each led by a "pilot." These teams need both senior and junior members of your staff to operate effectively, but operate with an open process for ideation, discussion, and (ideally) bold decision-making. They need to encourage the recent digital-native graduate to contribute equally with the experienced senior manager. Team members do not report to these pilots. It is important that these teams not be limited to "line-of-business" or "front-office" employees, but include a true cross section of capabilities, including members from human resources, finance, IT, and other functions as full team members.

Well-executed governance is critical in any project setting; however, too often governance ends up as a burden rather than a supporting mechanism. Supporting the rapid response teams should be a central team of executives in the organization led by a committed transformation leader—the person responsible for the effort's success, typically a divisional general manager, general manager, or president. All of these teams are generally supported by a program manager, the chief orchestrator for the transformation who helps to set and guide the cadence.

That support should focus on inspiring the rapid response teams, challenging them to be visionary, and removing organizational impediments—free from extensive paperwork. The program manager can lightly coordinate the teams and promote synergies between overlapping initiatives.

Transformation requires a different risk tolerance than business as usual, so companies must take on a greater, more collaborative risk appetite. Teams must be prepared to take controlled risks, make bold decisions, and be adaptable and flexible to drive the effort forward when making design and execution changes. While not dropping risk management, companies must streamline these processes and focus on the real risks involved in an initiative. Better yet, they should embed risk management capabilities, including legal, compliance, and vendor management, into each rapid response team as full members, not as gatekeepers or support functions.

Without clear metrics, it is impossible to judge the success of any transformation effort. So every rapid response team must operate from baselines agreed upon with the central team, with measurable targets that are achievable but not easy to attain. To avoid double counting of benefits, the teams need clarity with the central organization on the levers they can pull to achieve the targets.

Finally, transformation requires investment, whether for new tools, training, or resources. Many transformation approaches have seen massive investments up front resulting in disappointing and delayed payoffs. The rapid response teams should not get a blank check, but neither should they be required to write the extensive creative fiction exercises that we currently call "business cases" either. Rather, they should follow a venture capitalist-style approach. Each initiative starts with a small amount of money to meet the initial milestones and proof points. Those that prove their impact can gain a "series A" level of funding. Those that cannot must stop, freeing the rapid response team to move on to their next initiative—while learning from what has failed.

5 Volunteer Champions

Essential to the rapid response team is an army of volunteers eager to drive your strategy forward while continuing their day-to-day jobs. They come from all levels of the organization, but companies must motivate them to join the transformation. Their involvement gives all employees a sense of ownership over and a commitment to the transformation. They prevent the knowledge gaps and misunderstandings so many transformations face as they move from planning to implementation. Most importantly, they increase the likelihood that the work will be truly transformative, developing your people at the same time as your organization develops.

Most companies already have thought leaders or influencers in their domains. Yet many of them are among the 85 percent of employees who surveys suggest are not engaged in their work—because the organization typically has not valued or empowered them. Identify the people with good ideas, who are unhappy with the status quo and motivated to make a difference. Find, coach, and encourage those people, as they are the cogs to make the transformation machinery run smoothly.

Recruiting these champions depends on open, honest communication throughout the process. This is especially true in the articulation of your strategy. If you recruit volunteers under false pretenses, they won't be able to define the transformation you need, nor will they be committed to the organizational shifts you choose to institute.

There's no simple formula that HR departments can run to find potential champions, but performance reviews and manager recommendations can help. Often the best volunteers self-select based on encouraging communications at the beginning of the transformation.

Recruiting these individuals relies on two legs—the inspirational capability of your North Star, and the company's commitment to personal transformation, so they can see the benefits in career and personal growth. They in turn will be motivated by the flat structure of a rapid response team, making decisions that shape the future of the organization. They will have special attention from and direct access to senior leaders in your organization.

As the transformation moves into execution, the volunteer champions will leave the teams and return fully to the organization. By shifting them into key influencing points, companies can make sure the transformation takes hold. They will evangelize the transformation.

The process looks smooth on paper, but even with volunteer champions, the rapid response teams often find it hard to work together effectively. It helps to give them digital solutions for collaboration and cocreation, such as messaging, file-sharing, and modern project-management software. A formal cadence, especially early on, can help with intra- and inter-team coordination.

It is tempting to move members of these teams entirely out of their day-to-day jobs, but people need to retain business-as-usual roles to maintain a link to the challenges of ordinary operations. Members will learn the balancing and prioritization skills important if, as is hoped, they move into management roles. They can also informally spread the transformation message (and successes) through the hierarchy. If selected correctly, in developing these champions, companies are also identifying, retaining, and developing their next generation of leaders.

Remember the Key Elements

The building blocks draw directly on existentialism and customer obsession, but the other six elements described in the book also drive their work: promoting the Pygmalion effect, a start-up mindset, varying tempo, bimodal thinking, bold moves, and radical collaboration. Companies must emphasize the passionate work of doing better for the world, overcoming the individual wants and insecurities that prevent transformation.

Fundamental to perpetual innovation is the underlying emotional commitment to something bigger than profits or revenues. Once you get people to embrace a clear purpose and strategy, and apply the principles of this book, they'll break out of the conventional corporate bureaucratic mindset and become perpetual innovators. Best wishes on your transformational journey.

About the Author

Behnam Tabrizi is a world-renowned expert in organizational and leadership transformation, a bestselling author, and an award-winning teacher, scholar, and global advisor. He has served as a faculty member of Stanford University and its executive program for the past 25 years, over which time he's written ten books on leading innovation and change. His latest book, *The Inside-Out Effect: A Practical Guide to Transformational Leadership*, is an international bestseller and was featured by the *Washington Post* as its best book on leadership. Another book by Dr. Tabrizi, *Rapid Transformation*, was chosen by *Business Insider* and getAbstract, which covers over 25,000 business books, as their No. 1 book on leadership.

Dr. Tabrizi has advised over one thousand global CEOs and leaders in a wide range of industries—including high-tech (Apple, Google, Amazon, Microsoft, Intel, Netflix, Facebook, IBM, and HP), banking and finance, retail, health care, and government—on how to plan, mobilize, and implement transformational initiatives that have lifted leaders' aspirations and created over $27 billion in revenue and over $2.8 billion in savings for the world's most well-known companies. He's also had the privilege of advising the president of the United States, his cabinet, the top leadership team at the European Union, and the Vatican.

Dr. Tabrizi's doctoral thesis, a global study of more than 100 companies conducted with McKinsey & Co., received the prestigious ASQ award in organization studies. The study demonstrated that faster, more dedicated prototyping—versus more planning—results in a more agile culture capable of rapid product development. His research, touted as "pioneering work" in *the Chicago Tribune, Washington Post,* and the *San Jose Mercury News,* laid the research foundation behind design thinking and agile development. His work has also been featured in the *Harvard Business Review, Financial Times, The Economist, Strategy+Business, Fast Company, BusinessWeek,* and *Fortune.* Dr. Tabrizi has also been interviewed regarding his work on transformation by the BBC, CNN, and C-SPAN.

Dr. Tabrizi has served on the boards of Clever Sense (sold to Google), WebMBO (merged with Realm Corp.), Catapult Ventures, and has served as the faculty on the Doctoral Program at the Harvard Business School. He received a BS in computer science summa cum laude and then earned a master's degree in computer science at the University of Illinois Urbana. He earned an MS degree in engineering management as well as a doctorate in strategy, organizations, and digital transformation from Stanford University.

ENDNOTES

Preface
1   Karen Christensen, "Thought Leader Interview: Behnam Tabrizi," *Rotman Management Magazine*, May 2022. https://store.hbr.org/product/thought-leader-interview-behnam-tabrizi/ROT455

Chapter 1
2   "Most Big Tech Companies Have Become Places Where Talent Goes to Die," *Webinar Stores*, October 21, 2021. https://webinarstores.net/site/news/news_details/420/most-big-tech-companies-have-become-places-where-talent-goes-to-die-musk

3   Rahul Gupta, "Nokia CEO's Speech," LinkedIn, May 8, 2016. https://www.linkedin.com/pulse/nokia-ceo-ended-his-speech-saying-we-didnt-do-anything-rahul-gupta/

4   Steve Denning, "Why Agile Needs To Take Over Management Itself," *Forbes*, December 4, 2022. https://www.forbes.com/sites/stevedenning/2022/12/04/why-agile-needs-to-take-over-management-itself/?sh=360d27575b28

5   European Research Initiative Consortia ("ERIC") forum.

6   Matthew Kish, "Wild 1977 Nike Memo," *Business Insider*, January 27, 2023. https://www.businessinsider.com/wild-1970s-rob-strasser-memo-shows-origins-nike-competitive-culture-2023-1?op=1

7   Rosabeth Moss Kanter, "Managing Yourself: Zoom In, Zoom Out," *Harvard Business Review*, March 2011. https://hbr.org/2011/03/managing-yourself-zoom-in-zoom-out

8   James Clear, "First Principles: Elon Musk on the Power of Thinking for Yourself," *JC Newsletter*, undated. https://jamesclear.com/first-principles

9   Mark Bonchek, "Unlearning Mental Models," *Causeit Guide to Digital Fluency*, 2021. https://www.digitalfluency.guide/thinking-for-a-digital-era/unlearning-mental-models

10   E. Kumar Sharma, "Companies Need to Think of Continuous Reconfiguration," *Business Today*, February 15, 2014. https://www.

businesstoday.in/opinion/interviews/story/rita-gunther-mcgrath-on-companies-competition-133987-2014-02-15

11 Andrea Schneider, "Chocolate Cake vs. Fruit – Or Why Get Emotional During 'Rational' Negotiations," *Indisputably*, January 26, 2010. http://indisputably.org/2010/01/chocolate-cake-v-fruit-or-why-get-emotional-during-rational-negotiations/

12 Marc Andreesen's interview of Ken Griffin on Clubhouse, December 1, 2021. https://www.clubhouse.com/room/PGEX9zzd?s=09

13 Mark Schwartz, "Guts, Part Three: Having Backbone – Disagreeing and Committing," *AWS Cloud Strategy Blog*, July 28, 2020. https://aws.amazon.com/blogs/enterprise-strategy/guts-part-three-having-backbone-disagreeing-and-committing/

14 Amy Edmondson, *The Fearless Organization: Creating Psychological Safety in the Workplace for Learning, Innovation and Growth*, Wiley, 2018. https://www.hbs.edu/faculty/Pages/item.aspx?num=54851

15 Jeff Bezos tweet, Twitter.com, October 10, 2021. https://twitter.com/JeffBezos/status/1447403828505088011

Chapter 2

16 For Microsoft's current market capitalization, go to https://companiesmarketcap.com/microsoft/marketcap/

17 Details on Microsoft come from Satya Nadella et al., *Hit Refresh: The Quest to Rediscover Microsoft's Soul and Imagine a Better Future for Everyone*, Harper Business, 2017; and Steve Denning, "How Microsoft's Transformation Created a Billion-Dollar Gain," *Forbes.com*, June 20, 2021. https://www.forbes.com/sites/stevedenning/2021/06/20/how-microsofts-digital-transformation-created-a-trillion-dollar-gain/?sh=3536aa0d625b

18 "Who we are," Amazon. https://www.aboutamazon.com/about-us

19 "Haier ranks first in volume sales of major appliances brands in the world in 2018," Haier, January 10, 2019. https://www.haier.com/my/about-haier/news/20190604_74036.shtml

20 "Company Overview," Haier. https://www.haier.com/global/about-haier/intro/

21 Luke Lango, "Tesla Is the Next Trillion-Dollar Company," *Investor Place*, October 20, 2010. https://www.nasdaq.com/articles/tesla-is-the-next-trillion-dollar-company-2020-10-20

22 Dana Hull, "Tesla Is Plugging a Secret Mega Battery into the Texas Grid," *Bloomberg.com*, March 8, 2021. https://www.bloomberg.com/news/features/2021-03-08/tesla-is-plugging-a-secret-mega-battery-into-the-texas-grid

23 Carmine Gallo, "Steve Jobs Asked One Profound Question that Took Apple from Near Bankruptcy to $1 Trillion," *Forbes.com*, August 5, 2018. https://www-forbes-com.cdn.ampproject.org/c/s/www.forbes.com/sites/carminegallo/2018/08/05/steve-jobs-asked-one-pro-

found-question-that-took-apple-from-near-bankruptcy-to-1-trillion/amp/

24 "Market capitalization of Apple (AAPL)," Apple. https://companiesmarket-cap.com/apple/marketcap/

25 "Steve Jobs talks about Core Values at D8 2010," video, *YouTube.com*. https://www.youtube.com/watch?v=5mKxekNhMqY

26 In reminiscing about Jobs in 2022, Cook said, "I think he would be happy that we're living up to the values that he talked about so much like privacy, like protecting the environment. These were core to him, while we're keeping up innovation, and trying to give people something that enables them to do something they couldn't do otherwise." He added that Jobs would be unimpressed with Apple's soaring stock price. Tim Higgins, "Tim Cook Advises Man Concerned About Green Text Bubbles," *Wall Street Journal*, September 8, 2022. https://www.wsj.com/articles/tim-cook-advises-man-concerned-about-green-text-bubbles-buy-your-mom-an-iphone-11662614342?mod=-Searchresults_pos1&page=1

27 Eric Engleman, "Amazon.com's 1-Click Patent Confirmed Following Re-exam," *Puget Sound Business Journal*, March 10, 2010. https://www.bizjournals.com/seattle/blog/techflash/2010/03/amazons_1-click_patent_confirmed_following_re-exam.html?page=all

28 Mike Masnick, "Jeff Bezos on Innovation: Stubborn on Vision, Flexible on Details," *Techdirt.com*, June 17, 2011. https://www.techdirt.com/2011/06/17/jeff-bezos-innovation-stubborn-vision-flexible-details/

29 I discussed personal callings in detail in *The Inside-Out Effect* (Evolve, 2013), which I coauthored with Michael Terrell.

30 "The Brightline Transformation Compass," Brightline Project Management Institute, October 24, 2019. https://www.brightline.org/resources/transformation-compass/#download

31 For in-depth discussion, please see *The Inside-Out Effect*.

32 Catherine Moore, "What Is Positive Psychology?" *Positive Psychology.com*, January 8, 2019. https://positivepsychology.com/what-is-flow/

33 John Herman, "Inside Facebook's Political-Media Machine," *New York Times Magazine*, August 24, 2016. https://www.nytimes.com/2016/08/28/magazine/inside-facebooks-totally-insane-unintentionally-gigantic-hyperpartisan-political-media-machine.html

34 Siladitya Ray, "Rohingya Refugees Sue Facebook for $150 Billion," *Forbes.com*, December 7, 2021. https://www.forbes.com/sites/siladityaray/2021/12/07/rohingya-refugees-sue-facebook-for-150-billion-alleging-platform-failed-to-curb-hate-speech-that-was-followed-by-violence/?sh=24a-352dae713

35 "FTC Settles with Facebook for $5 Billion," *Business Insider*, July 2019. https://www.businessinsider.com/facebook-settlement-ftc-billion-privacy-2019-7

36 Alexandra Ma, "Facebook and Cambridge Analytica," *Business Insider*, August 23, 2019. https://www.businessinsider.com/cambridge-analytica-a-guide-to-the-trump-linked-data-firm-that-harvested-50-million-facebook-profiles-2018-3

37 Kari Paul, "Facebook's Very Bad Year," *The Guardian*, December 29, 2021. https://www.theguardian.com/technology/2021/dec/29/facebook-capitol-riot-frances-haugen-sophia-zhang-apple

Chapter 3

38 Brad Stone, *Amazon Unbounded: Jeff Bezos and the Invention of a Global Empire*, Simon & Schuster, 2021.

39 Gary Hamel and Michelle Zanini, "The End of Bureaucracy," *Harvard Business Review*, November–December, 2018. https://hbr.org/2018/11/the-end-of-bureaucracy

40 Eugenia Battaglia, "Beyond the Mechanics of Haier," *Medium.com*, October 5, 2020. https://stories.platformdesigntoolkit.com/beyond-the-mechanics-of-haier-leading-40-years-of-entrepreneurial-transformation-with-bill-fischer-2e791677b6e

41 "Shattering the status quo: A conversation with Haier's Zhang Ruimin," *McKinsey Quarterly*, July 27, 2021. https://www.mckinsey.com/capabilities/people-and-organizational-performance/our-insights/shattering-the-status-quo-a-conversation-with-haiers-zhang-ruimin

42 Hamel, "The End of Bureaucracy."

43 Covandongo O'Shea, *The Man From Zara: The Story of the Genius Behind the Inditex Group*, LID Publishing, 2012. Unless otherwise noted in this chapter, this book is my source for Zara.

44 "Lessons Learned from Working with Steve Jobs: Interview with Ken Segall," *Speaking.com*, n.d. https://speaking.com/blog-post/simplicity-and-other-lessons-from-working-with-steve-jobs-by-ken-segall/

45 Steve Denning, "How an Obsession with Customers Made Microsoft a $2 Trillion Company," *Forbes.com*, June 6, 2021. https://www.forbes.com/sites/stevedenning/2021/06/25/how-customers-made-microsoft-a-two-trillion-dollar-company/?sh=d80d7b62cc02

46 Ashley Lobo, "A Case Study of Tesla: The World's Most Exciting Automobile Company," *Medium.com*, March 24, 2020. https://medium.com/@ashley-lobo98/a-case-study-on-tesla-the-worlds-most-exciting-automobile-company-535fe9dafd30

47 Carmine Gallo, "How the Apple Store Creates Irresistible Customer Experiences," *Forbes.com*, April 10, 2015. https://www.forbes.com/sites/carminegallo/2015/04/10/how-the-apple-store-creates-irresistible-customer-experiences/?sh=5accd26a17a8

48 Bezos, *2001 Letter to Shareholders, in Invent and Wander: The Collected Writings of Jeff Bezos*, HBR Press, 2020.

49 Stone, *Amazon Unbound.*

50 Rebecca Brown, "What You Need to Know About Amazon Prime: 2005-Today," *pattern blog*, August 20, 2020. https://pattern.com/blog/amazon-prime-a-timeline-from-2005-to-2020/

51 Annie Palmer, "Jeff Bezos Says Amazon Needs to Do a Better Job for Employees in His Final Shareholder Letter as CEO," *CNBC.com*, April 15, 2004. https://www.cnbc.com/2021/04/15/jeff-bezos-releases-final-letter-to-amazon-shareholders.html

52 Stone, *Amazon Unbound.*

53 Richard Halkett, "Using Customer Obsession to Drive Rapid Innovation," *Forbes.com* sponsored, November 7, 2022; and Colin Bryar and Bill Carr, *Working Backwards: Insights, Stories and Secrets from Inside Amazon*, St. Martin's Press, 2021.

54 Rebecca Brown, "What You Need to Know About Amazon Prime: 2005-Today," *pattern blog*, August 20, 2020. https://pattern.com/blog/amazon-prime-a-timeline-from-2005-to-2020/

55 Author's interview with an ex-manager from an Amazon Fulfillment Center, January 2022.

56 David Segal, "Apple's Retail Army, Long on Loyalty but Short on Pay," *New York Times*, June 23, 2012. https://www.nytimes.com/2012/06/24/business/apple-store-workers-loyal-but-short-on-pay.html?_r=1&hp&pagewanted=all

57 Henry Blodget, "Check Out How Apple Brainwashes Its Store Employees, Turning Them into Clapping, Smiling Zealots," *Business Insider*, June 24, 2012. https://www.businessinsider.com/how-apple-trains-store-employees-2012-6

58 Author's interview with ex-Amazon Fulfillment Center manager, January 2022.

59 Jeff Bezos, 2012 letter to shareholders.

60 Author interview with ex-Tesla manager, January 2022.

61 Author's interview with Cyrus Afkhami, 2022.

62 Interview with Afkhami; and Halkett, "Using Customer Obsession."

63 Ravneet Uberoi, "Zara: Achieving the 'Fast' in Fast Fashion through Analytics," HBS Digital Initiative, April 5, 2017. https://digital.hbs.edu/platform-digit/submission/zara-achieving-the-fast-in-fast-fashion-through-analytics/

Chapter 4

64 Charles O'Reilly et al., "The Promise and Problems of Organizational Culture: CEO Personality, Culture, and Firm Performance," *Group & Organization Management*, 2014, 39:595–625.

65 Jeff Bezos, *Invent and Wander: The Collected Writings of Jeff Bezos*, Harvard Business Review Press, November 17, 2020.

66 Aine Cain, "A Former Tesla Recruiter Explains Why All the Candidates Had to Go through Elon Musk at the End of the Hiring Process,"

Business Insider, December 1, 2017. https://www.businessinsider.com/
tesla-how-to-get-hired-2017-12

67   Lydia Dishman, "How this CEO Avoided the Glass Cliff and Turned Around
     an 'Uninvestable' Company," *Fast Company*, September 11, 2018. https://
     www.fastcompany.com/90229663/how-amds-ceo-lisa-su-managed-to-turn-
     the-tech-company-around. Clare Duffy, "From the Brink of Bankruptcy
     to a 1,300% Gain," *CNN Business*, March 27, 2020. https://www.cnn.
     com/2020/03/27/tech/lisa-su-amd-risk-takers/index.html

68   Amy Kristof-Brown et al., "Consequences of Individuals' Fit at Work,"
     Personnel Psychology, 2005, 58:281–342; and Lauren Rivera, "Guess Who
     Doesn't Fit In at Work," *New York Times*, May 30, 2015. https://www.
     nytimes.com/2015/05/31/opinion/sunday/guess-who-doesnt-fit-in-at-work.
     html#:~:text=One%20recent%20survey%20found%20that,nebulous%20
     and%20potentially%20dangerous%20concept

69   Matthew DeBord, "The Model S is Still Tesla's Best Car – Here's Why,"
     Business Insider, September 9, 2017. https://www.businessinsider.com/why-
     tesla-model-s-best-electric-car-2017-9. "Tesla Motors Hires Senior Google
     Recruiter," Tesla Press Release, April 20, 2010. https://www.tesla.com/blog/
     tesla-motors-hires-senior-google-recruiter-world's-leading-electric-vehicle-man

70   Bretton Potter, "Netflix's Company Culture is not for Everybody and That's
     Exactly How It Should Be," *Forbes.com*, December 4, 2018. https://www.
     forbes.com/sites/brettonputter/2018/12/04/netflixs-company-culture-is-not-
     for-everybody-and-thats-exactly-how-it-should-be/?sh=29fcbc4b1880

71   Justin Bariso, "Steve Jobs Made a Brilliant Change When He Returned to
     Apple," *Inc.com*, April 28, 2021. https://www.inc.com/justin-bariso/steve-
     jobs-made-a-brilliant-change-when-he-returned-to-apple-it-changed-compa-
     ny-forever.html

72   Podolny and Hansen, "How Apple is Organized for Innovation," *Harvard
     Business Review*, November–December, 2020. https://hbr.org/2020/11/
     how-apple-is-organized-for-innovation

73   Deborah Petersen, "Ron Johnson: It's not about Speed. It's about Doing Your
     Best," *Insights by Stanford Business*, July 3, 2014. https://www.gsb.stanford.
     edu/insights/ron-johnson-its-not-about-speed-its-about-doing-your-best

74   "AMD Named to the 2022 Bloomberg Gender-Equality Index," AMD Press
     Release, February 8, 2022. https://finance.yahoo.com/news/amd-named-
     2022-bloomberg-gender-130014537.html?

75   Erin Sairam, "Women Thrive at the Bumble Hive," *Forbes.com*, July
     3, 2018. https://www.forbes.com/sites/erinspencer1/2018/07/03/
     women-thrive-at-the-bumble-hive/?sh=bc67eeb5741a

76   Steve Glaveski, "Leadership Lessons from Bill Campbell,"
     Medium.com, May 5, 2019. https://medium.com/steveglaveski/
     leadership-lessons-from-bill-campbell-the-trillion-dollar-coach-37d5494c8be2

77 "Performance Management at Tesla: What We Know," *PerformYard*, August 28, 2021. https://www.performyard.com/articles/performance-management-at-tesla-what-we-know#:~:text=In%20an%20email%20statement%20submitted,compensation%2C%20equity%20awards%20or%20promotions

78 Gary Hamel and Michelle Zanini, "The End of Bureaucracy," *Harvard Business Review*, Nov.-Dec. 2018. https://hbr.org/2018/11/the-end-of-bureaucracy; and https://www.haier.com/global/about-haier/intro/

79 Patty McCord, "How Netflix Reinvented HBR," *Harvard Business Review*, January–February 2014. https://hbr.org/2014/01/how-netflix-reinvented-hr

80 Callum Bouchers, "Your Boss Still Thinks You're Faking It When You're Working from Home," *Wall Street Journal*, October 20, 2022. https://www.wsj.com/articles/your-boss-still-thinks-youre-faking-it-whenyoureworking-from-home-11666216953?mod=hp_featst_pos3

81 Brad Johnson and David Smith, "Real Mentorship Starts with Company Culture, Not Formal Programs," *Harvard Business Review*, December 30, 2019. https://hbr.org/2019/12/real-mentorship-starts-with-company-culture-not-formal-programs

82 Rachel Ranosa, "How Was Steve Jobs as a Mentor," *People Matters*, October 7, 2021. https://anz.peoplemattersglobal.com/article/leadership/how-was-steve-jobs-as-mentor-tim-cook-remembers-the-icon-31184

83 Bruce Pfau, "How an Accounting Firm Convinced Its Employees They Could Change the World," *Harvard Business Review*, October 6, 2015. https://hbr.org/2015/10/how-an-accounting-firm-convinced-its-employees-they-could-change-the-world

84 Kindra Cooper, "Inside the FAANG Performance Review Process," *Candor*, May 18, 2022. https://candor.co/articles/career-paths/inside-the-faang-performance-review-process

85 Robert Sutton and Ben Wigert, "More Harm Than Good: The Truth About Performance Reviews," *Gallup*, May 6, 2019. https://www.gallup.com/workplace/249332/harm-good-truth-performance-reviews.aspx

86 Kevin Crowley, "Exxon's Exodus," *Bloomberg Businessweek*, October 13, 2022. https://www.bloomberg.com/news/features/2022-10-13/exxon-xom-jobs-exodus-brings-scrutiny-to-corporate-culture?

Chapter 5

87 Daniel Slater, "Elements of Amazon's Day 1 Culture," AWS Executive Insights. https://aws.amazon.com/executive-insights/content/how-amazon-defines-and-operationalizes-a-day-1-culture/

88 Gary Hamel, "Waking Up IBM: How a Gang of Unlikely Rebels Transformed Big Blue," *Harvard Business Review*, July–August 2000. https://hbr.org/2000/07/waking-up-ibm-how-a-gang-of-unlikely-rebels-transformed-big-blue

89 Daniel Slater, "Elements of Amazon's Day 1 Culture," AWS Executive Insights. https://aws.amazon.com/executive-insights/content/how-amazon-defines-and-operationalizes-a-day-1-culture/

90 Ram Charan and Julia Yang, *The Amazon Management System: The Ultimate Business Empire That Creates Extraordinary Value for Both Customers and Shareholders*, Ideapress, 2019.

91 Andy Ash, "The Rise and Fall of Blockbuster," *Business Insider*, August 12, 2020. https://www.businessinsider.com/the-rise-and-fall-of-blockbuster-video-streaming-2020-1

92 Luca Piacentini, "The Real Reason Blockbuster Failed," *1851Franchise.com*, March 23, 2021. https://1851franchise.com/the-real-reason-blockbuster-failed-hint-its-not-netflix-2715316#stories

93 Bidyut Durma, "Transforming DBS Banks into a Tech Company," *Banking Innovation*, December 3, 2000. https://bankinginnovation.qorusglobal.com/content/articles/transforming-dbs-bank-tech-company

94 Jim Harter, "U.S. Employee Engagement Data Holds Steady," *Gallup.com*, July 29, 2021. https://www.gallup.com/workplace/352949/employee-engagement-holds-steady-first-half-2021.aspx

95 Frank Koe, "Is Intrapreneurship the Solution?" *Entrepreneur.com*, October 7, 2021. https://www.entrepreneur.com/article/387402

96 Andy Ash, "The Rise and Fall of Pan-Am," *Business Insider*, February 21, 2021. https://www.businessinsider.com/how-pan-am-went-from-pioneering-air-travel-to-bankruptcy-2020-2

97 O'Shea, *The Man from Zara*, p. 36.

98 Jeff Bezos, *Invent and Wander*, p. 5.

99 Jeff Bezos, *Invent and Wander*, p. 330.

100 O'Shea, *The Man from Zara*, p. 36.

101 "Steve Jobs brainstorms with the NeXT team 1985," Jobs Official, *YouTube.com*, https://www.youtube.com/watch?v=Udi0rk3jZYM

102 O'Shea, *The Man from Zara*, pp. 66–73.

103 Jeff Bezos, *Invent and Wander*, p. 15.

104 O'Shea, *The Man from Zara*, pp. 66–73.

105 Jeff Bezos, *Invent and Wander*, pp. 14–15.

106 *Amazon Unbound*, pp. 167–171.

107 *Amazon Unbound*, pp. 247–257.

108 O'Shea, *The Man from Zara*, pp. 66–73.

109 Zook and Allen, *The Founder's Mentality: How to Overcome the Predictable Crises of Growth*, Harvard Business Review Press, 2016.

110 Paul Lukas, "3M, A Mining Company Built on a Mistake," *Fortune*, April 1, 2003. https://money.cnn.com/magazines/fsb/fsb_archive/2003/04/01/341016/; and 3M Canada, "The History of Masking Tape," *3M Science Centre*, March 29, 2016. https://sciencecentre.3mcanada.ca/articles/an-industrial-evolution-3m-industrial-masking-tape

111 Jacob Morgan, "Five Uncommon Internal Innovation Examples," *Forbes.com*, April 8, 2015. https://www.forbes.com/sites/jacobmorgan/2015/04/08/five-uncommon-internal-innovation-examples/?sh=4caa9bcb3a19

112 JD Rapp, "Inside Whirlpool's Innovation Machine," *Management Innovation Exchange*, January 23, 2016. https://www.managementexchange.com/story/inside-whirlpools-innovation-machine

113 Author's unpublished interview with Drew Bennett, 2022.

Chapter 6

114 Scott Gleeson, "How Did #1 Seed Virginia Lose?" *USA Today*, March 17, 2018. https://www.usatoday.com/story/sports/ncaab/2018/03/17/how-did-top-overall-no-1-seed-virginia-lose-greatest-upset-all-time-umbc/434472002/

115 Patrick Guggenberger, "The Age of Speed," *McKinsey Quarterly,* March 25, 2019. https://www.mckinsey.com/capabilities/people-and-organizational-performance/our-insights/the-organization-blog/the-age-of-speed-how-to-raise-your-organizations-metabolism

116 Robert Sutton, *Scaling Up Excellence: Getting to More without Settling for Less*, Currency, 2014. https://www.amazon.com/Scaling-Up-Excellence-Getting-Settling/dp/0385347022

117 "Discover the evolution of the domesticated cat," *Cats Protection blog*, July 29, 2019. https://www.cats.org.uk/cats-blog/how-are-domestic-cats-related-to-big-cats#:~:text=The%20oldest%20cat%20lineage%20is,leo

118 Kathleen Eisenhardt, "Making Fast Strategic Decisions in High-Velocity Environments," *Academy of Management Journal*, 1989, 32:543–576.

119 Isabela Sa Glaister, "How to Use Sprints to Work Smart and Upskill," *Ideo U blog*, n.d. https://www.ideou.com/blogs/inspiration/how-to-use-sprints-to-work-smart-and-upskill

120 "Lionel Messi: Why Does the Barcelona Icon and FSG Star Walk So Much During Games?" *GiveMeSport.com*, August 25, 2021. https://www.givemesport.com/1742726-lionel-messi-why-does-psg-star-and-barcelona-icon-walk-so-much-during-games

121 Cornelius Chang, "Slowing Down to Speed Up," *McKinsey Organizational Blog*, March 23, 2018. https://www.mckinsey.com/business-functions/people-and-organizational-performance/our-insights/the-organization-blog/slowing-down-to-speed-up and Jocelyn Davis and Tom Atkinson, "Need Speed? Slow Down," *Harvard Business Review*, May 2010. https://hbr.org/2010/05/need-speed-slow-down

122 *Amazon Unbound*, ch. 9.

123 Andrew S. Grove, *Only the Paranoid Survive: How to Exploit the Crisis Points That Challenge Every Company*, Currency, 1996.

124 Ash, "The Rise and Fall of Blockbuster."

125 Beth Galetti, John Golden III, and Stephen Brozovich, "Inside Day 1: How Amazon Uses Agile Team Structures and Adaptive Practices to Innovate on Behalf of Customers," *SHRM*, Spring 2019. https://www.shrm.org/executive/resources/people-strategy-journal/spring2019/pages/galetti-golden.aspx

126 Philippe Chain with Frederic Filloux, "How Tesla cracked the code of auto-mobile innovation," *Monday Note*, July 12, 2020. https://mondaynote.com/how-the-tesla-way-keeps-it-ahead-of-the-pack-358db5d52add

127 Justin Ferber, "Ten Years Later, Evidence is Clear," *Cavs Corner*, April 11, 2019. https://virginia.rivals.com/news/ten-years-later-evidence-is-clear-that-bennett-s-plan-works-for-uva

128 O'Shea, *The Man from Zara*.

129 Pauline Meyer, "Tesla Inc.'s Organizational Culture & Its Characteristics (Analysis)," *Panmore Institute*, updated February 22, 2019. https://panmore.com/tesla-motors-inc-organizational-culture-characteristics-analysis

130 Daniel Maiorca, "The Three Reasons BlackBerry Failed Spectacularly," *Make Use Of.com*, August 18, 2021. https://www.makeuseof.com/the-reasons-blackberry-failed-spectacularlyand-why-they-might-rise-again/

131 "2018-19 Virginia Cavaliers Men's Roster and Stats," *Sports Reference*, n.d. https://www.sports-reference.com/cbb/schools/virginia/men/2019.html

132 O'Shea, *The Man from Zara*

133 Beril Kocadereli, "Culture at Netflix," *Medium.com*, April 13, 2020. https://medium.com/swlh/culture-at-netflix-16a37deb6b75

134 Author's interview with Cyrus Afkhami, 2022.

135 Kif Leswing, "Apple is Breaking a 15-Year Partnership with Intel on Its Macs," *Business Insider*, November 10, 2020. https://www.cnbc.com/2020/11/10/why-apple-is-breaking-a-15-year-partnership-with-intel-on-its-macs-.html

136 "Cadence: Defining the Heartbeat of Your Organization," *System & Soul*, September 17, 2021. https://www.systemandsoul.com/blog/cadence-defining-the-heartbeat-of-your-organization

137 *Amazon Unbound*; and Beth Galetti et al., "Inside Day 1: How Amazon Uses Agile Team Structures," *SHRM*, Spring 2019. https://www.shrm.org/executive/resources/people-strategy-journal/spring2019/pages/galetti-golden.aspx

138 Beril Kocadereli, "Culture at Netflix," *Medium.com*, April 13, 2020. https://medium.com/swlh/culture-at-netflix-16a37deb6b75

139 Sarah Krause, "Netflix Hunts for Cost Cuts," *Wall Street Journal*, September 7, 2022. https://www.wsj.com/articles/netflix-hunts-for-cost-cuts-from-cloud-computing-to-corporate-swag-11662565220

140 Carr and Bryar, *Working Backward*.

141 Bernadine Dykes et al., "Responding to Crises with Speed and Agility," *Sloan Management Review*, October 15, 2020.

Chapter 7

142 Kevin Cool, "Gwynne Shotwell on Aiming High and Taking Big Risks," *Stanford Business Insights*, July 19, 2022. https://www.gsb.stanford.edu/insights/gwynne-shotwell-aiming-high-taking-big-risks

143 Tabrizi and Rick Walleigh, "Defining Next-Generation Products: An Inside Look," *Harvard Business Review*, November–December 1997. https://hbr. org/1997/11/defining-next-generation-products-an-inside-look

144 Sarah Kessler, "This Company Built One of the World's Most Efficient Warehouses by Embracing Chaos," *Quartz*, 2020. https://classic.qz.com/ perfect-company-2/1172282/this-company-built-one-of-the-worlds-most-ef- ficient-warehouses-by-embracing-chaos/

145 "How Algorithms Run Amazon's Warehouses," *BBC.com*, August 18, 2018; Matt Day, "In Amazon's Flagship Fulfillment Center, the Machines Run the Show," *Bloomsbury Business Week*, September 21, 2021; interview with former Amazon executive.

146 Paul Alcorn, "AMD's Market Cap Surpasses Intel for the First Time in History," *Tom's Hardware*, updated February 16, 2022. https://www.toms- hardware.com/news/amds-market-cap-surpasses-intel

147 "Apple iPhone 13 Review," *New York Times*, September 21, 2021.

148 "Dear Apple and Google, It's Time to Stop Releasing a New Phone Every Year," *Fast Company*, 2019.

149 O'Shea, *The Man from Zara*.

150 Scoop Jackson, "Impact of Jordan Brand Reaches Far Beyond Basketball," *Espn.com*, February 12, 2016; and "Michael Jordan Earns $5 Royalty on Every Air Jordan Shoe Sold," *TheSportsRush.com*, February 28, 2021. https:// thesportsrush.com/nba-news-michael-jordan-earns-5-royalty-on-every-air-jor- dan-shoe-sold-how-the-bulls-legend-amassed-a-rumored-2-1-billion-fortune- over-the-years/

151 "Defining Next Generation Products."

152 "Defining Next Generation Products."

153 Samuel Gibbs, "Facebook is not Backing Down from Its 'Innovative' Secret Experiment on Users," *The Guardian*, July 3, 2014; and Andrea Huspeni, "Why Mark Zuckerberg Runs 10,000 Facebook Versions a Day," *Entrepreneur. com*, May 24, 2017. https://www.entrepreneur.com/science-technology/ why-mark-zuckerberg-runs-10000-facebook-versions-a-day/294242

154 "Jeff Bezos: Why You Can't Feel Bad About Failure," *CNBC.com*, May 22, 2020; and Chris Velasco, "Amazon's Flop of a Phone Made Newer Better Hardware Possible," *Engadget*, January 13, 2018.

155 "Defining Next Generation Products."

156 This section draws mainly from Kathleen Eisenhardt and Behnam Tabrizi, "Accelerating Adaptive Processes: Product Innovation in the Global Computer Industry," *Administrative Science Quarterly*, 40:84–110, 1995.

157 Eisenhardt and Tabrizi, "Accelerating Adaptive Processes."

Chapter 8

158 Ron Miller, "How AWS Came to Be," *Tech Crunch*, July 2, 2016. https://techcrunch.com/2016/07/02/andy-jassys-brief-history-of-the-genesis-of-aws/?guccounter=1

159 Brandon Butler, "The Myth About How Amazon's Web Service Started Just Won't Die," *Network World*, March 2, 2015. https://www.networkworld.com/article/2891297/the-myth-about-how-amazon-s-web-service-started-just-won-t-die.html

160 Andy Wu and Goran Calic, "Does Elon Musk Have a Strategy?" *Harvard Business Review*, July 15, 2022. https://hbr.org/2022/07/does-elon-musk-have-a-strategy?ab=hero-main-text

161 Mariella Moon, "John Carmack Leaves Meta with a Memo Criticizing the Company's Efficiency," *Yahoo! Finance*, December 16, 2022. https://finance.yahoo.com/news/john-carmack-leaves-meta-043202664.html

162 *Amazon Unbound*, p. 81.

163 Gary Hamel and Michele Zanini, "How to lead with courage and build a business with heart," *Fast Company*, March 4, 2022. https://www.fastcompany.com/90727231/how-to-lead-with-courage-and-build-a-business-with-heart

164 "You Can't Be a Wimp: Make the Tough Calls," *Harvard Business Review*, November 2013.

165 Arthur Brooks, "Go Ahead and Fail," *Atlantic*, February 2021.

166 Kathleen Reardon, "Courage as a Skill," *Harvard Business Review*, January 2007.

167 Deborah Petersen, "Ron Johnson: It's not about Speed. It's about Doing Your Best," *Insights by Stanford Business*, July 3, 2014. https://www.gsb.stanford.edu/insights/ron-johnson-its-not-about-speed-its-about-doing-your-best

168 Charlotte Alter, "How Whitney Wolfe Herd Turned a Vision of a Better Internet into a Billon-Dollar Brand," *Time*, March 19, 2021.

169 Author's interview with a former Tesla executive, February 2022.

Chapter 9

170 Ian Leslie, "Before You Answer, Consider the Opposite Possibility," *Atlantic*, April 2021.

171 Rob Cross and Inga Carboni, "When Collaboration Fails and How to Fix It," *Sloan Management Review*, December 8, 2020.

172 Jeff Haden, "When Jeff Bezos's Two-Pizza Teams Fell Short," *Inc.*, February 10, 2021.

173 Rob Cross et al., "Collaborative Overload," *Harvard Business Review*, January–February 2016.

174 Michael Hyatt, "Don't Hire People Unless the Batteries Are Included," *Full Focus*, n.d. https://fullfocus.co/batteries-included/

175 Candace Whitney-Morris, "The World's Largest Private Hackathon," *Microsoft.com*, July 23, 2018.

https://news.microsoft.com/life/hackathon/

176 "Radical Collaboration in Enterprises: How Does It Work," *Techtarget. com*, February 24, 2022. https://www.techtarget.com/searchcio/feature/ Radical-collaboration-in-enterprises-How-does-it-work

Chapter 10

177 Carmine Gallo, "How Starbucks CEO Inspired Us to Dream Bigger," *Forbes.com*, December 2, 2016. https://www.forbes.com/sites/carmine-gallo/2016/12/02/how-starbucks-ceo-howard-schultz-inspired-us-to-dream-bigger/?sh=32184913e858

178 "Our Mission," Starbucks. https://archive.starbucks.com/record/our-mission

179 Nathaniel Meyerson, "Three Times Howard Schultz Saved Starbucks," *CNN Money*, June 5, 2018. https://money.cnn.com/2018/06/05/news/companies/ starbucks-howard-schultz-coffee/index.html

180 Julia Hanna, "Starbucks Reinvented," *Forbes.com*, August 25, 2017. https://www.forbes.com/sites/hbsworkingknowledge/2014/08/25/ starbucks-reinvented/?sh=c2226c730d0c

181 "Our Mission," Starbucks. https://archive.starbucks.com/record/our-mission

182 "Net revenue of Starbucks worldwide from 2003 to 2022," *Statista*. https:// www.statista.com/statistics/266466/net-revenue-of-the-starbucks-corporation-worldwide/

183 Max Pakapol, "The Perfect Blend: Starbucks and Data Analytics," *HBS Digital Initiative*, March 23, 2021; and Bernard Marr, "Starbucks: Using Big Data, Analytics and AI to Boost Performance," *Forbes.com*, May 28, 2018.

184 "Our Mission," Starbucks. https://archive.starbucks.com/record/our-mission

185 Jim Ewel, "The Transformation Agenda," *Agile Marketing*, June 3, 2013. https://agilemarketing.net/transformation-agenda/

186 "Net revenue of Starbucks worldwide from 2003 to 2022," *Statista*. https:// www.statista.com/statistics/266466/net-revenue-of-the-starbucks-corporation-worldwide/

187 Hanna, "Starbucks Reinvented."

188 Howard Schultz, Onward: *How Starbucks Fought for Its Life Without Losing Its Soul*, Rodale, 2012, p. 278.

189 Alberto Onetti, posting on LinkedIn.com, September 2022. https:// www.linkedin.com/posts/aonetti_startbucks-fintech-banking-activi-ty-6971732990083104768-u_kV/?utm_source=share&utm_medium=mem-ber_ios

190 "Starbucks is speeding up innovation at its Seattle research hub," *CNBC.com*, May 2, 2019. https://www.cnbc.com/2019/05/02/starbucks-is-speeding-up-innovation-at-its-seattle-research-hub.html

191 Schultz, *Onward*

192 Schultz, *Onward*, p. 278

193 Aimee Groth, "19 Amazing Ways CEO Howard Schultz Saved Starbucks," *Business Insider*, June 19, 2011. https://www.businessinsider.com/howard-schultz-turned-starbucks-around-2011-6

194 "Interim Starbucks CEO Howard Schultz on Labor Unions," *Reuters*, March 16, 2022. https://www.reuters.com/business/retail-consumer/interim-starbucks-ceo-howard-schultz-labor-unions-2022-03-16/

195 This section draws closely on two of my previous books, *Rapid Transformation* and *The Inside-Out Effect*, and in particular a methodology, the Brightline Transformation Compass, that I developed with help from the Project Management Institute, for carrying out major corporate change. Copyright Project Management Institute. https://www.brightline.org/resources/transformation-compass/

196 "Satya Nadella Employed a Growth Mindset," *Business Insider*, March 7, 2020. https://www.businessinsider.com/microsoft-ceo-satya-nadella-company-culture-shift-growth-mindset-2020-3

INDEX

Note: Endnote information is denoted by n and note number following the page number

A

Activision Blizzard, 155

Advanced Micro Devices (AMD)
  boldness of, 159–160, 166
  compression at, 130–131
  performance requirements at, 72
  Pygmalion effect at, 64–65, 69–70,
    72
  radical collaboration at, 185–186
  recruitment at, 64–65

Affordable Care Act, 205

Afkhami, Cyrus, 72

agile innovation
  bimodal operations including, 9,
    15–16, 123–144, 196
  boldness for, 9, 16, 147–166,
    197–198
  building blocks for path to,
    200–212
  challenges of, 1–3, 7
  controlled chaos driving, 12–13,
    119–120
  customer obsession driving, 8, 14,
    43–60, 162–163, 192,
    201–202, 205–208
  definition of, 2
  disagree and commit supporting, 13
  existential purpose driving (*see*
    existential purpose)
  failure to achieve, 1–2, 6, 21–22,
    87–90, 110, 112–113, 120
    (*see also specific companies*)
  first principles challenging assump-
    tions impeding, 10–11,
    164
  key elements and characteristics of,
    8–13, 212
  meta-agility for, 10
  Pygmalion effect creating culture of,
    8–9, 14–15, 61–79, 193,
    200, 208
  radical collaboration for, 9, 16,
    167–187, 199–200
  requirements for, 3–7
  research methodology on, 7–8
  Starbucks case study of, 16,
    189–200, 203, 204–205
  start-up mindset driving, 9, 15, 51,
    83–102, 193–194
  subtraction to empower, 11–12, 94
  tempo management for, 9, 15,
    103–121, 124, 126,
    194–196
  unlearning and reconfiguring men-
    tal models for, 11

Air Cube, 44

Alexa, 75, 110–111, 117, 139, 148,
    152–153
Alibaba, 118–119
Allen, James, 98
Altman, Jack, 176
Amazon. *See also* Bezos, Jeff
    agile innovation of, 18, 189
    Alexa by, 75, 110–111, 117, 139,
        148, 152–153
    anticipated failure of, 17–18
    boldness of, 16, 147–148, 149,
        151, 152, 166
    compression at, 128–130
    customer obsession and innovation
        of, 33, 51–55, 57–59
    data collection by, 58–59
    disagree and commit at, 13
    Echo by, 110, 139, 148, 153
    existential purpose of, 27, 28, 32,
        33–34, 38, 41, 204
    experiential development at,
        138–139
    Fire Phone by, 138–139, 148, 151,
        152
    Kindle by, 22, 53–54, 57, 148, 151
    Microsoft and, 21, 22, 24, 155
    performance requirements at,
        71–72
    performance reviews at, 79
    Prime by, 34, 52–54, 57
    Pygmalion effect at, 63, 64, 71, 72,
        75, 79
    radical collaboration at, 174–175,
        186
    recruitment at, 64
    single-threaded leaders at, 117–118,
        175
    start-up mindset of, 51, 83, 89,
        95–96, 108

    tempo management of, 108–109,
        110–111, 114, 115,
        117–118
Amazon Web Services (AWS), 16,
    52–54, 57–59, 148, 153, 155
AMD. *See* Advanced Micro Devices
Andersen Consulting, 83
Anderson, Brad, 49
Aphrodite, 62–63
Apple. *See also* Jobs, Steve
    agile innovation of, 6–7, 189, 200
    Blackberry and, 112
    boldness of, 157–159, 166
    compression at, 131
    customer obsession and innovation
        of, 14, 47–48, 49, 50–51,
        55–56
    existential purpose of, 27, 32–33,
        34, 41, 204, 217n26
    experiential development at,
        135–136
    experts as managers at, 67–69,
        172–173
    Facebook (Meta) and, 40
    IBM and, 98
    iPads by, 32, 33, 172, 177
    iPhones by, 14, 32, 131, 135–136,
        158, 172, 177
    iPods by, 32, 136, 158, 194
    Macintosh computers by, 136, 157,
        172
    Microsoft and, 21, 23, 49, 177–178
    Nokia and, 2, 161–162
    performance reviews at, 78
    Pygmalion effect at, 61–62, 63, 64,
        67–69, 73, 75, 78
    radical collaboration at, 171–173,
        176, 178, 187
    recruitment at, 61–62, 64
    start-up mindset of, 89, 93

tempo management of, 114,
115–116, 194
Apple TV+, 1
artificial intelligence, 2, 23, 29,
154–155
Audi, 111
Audible, 53–54
automation, 129–130
AWS (Amazon Web Services), 16,
52–54, 57–59, 148, 153, 155
Azure, 155

B
Bain, 98
Ballmer, Steve, 22
Barron's, 17
behavior diaries, 206–207
belonging, sense of, 69–71
Bennett, Tony, 103, 111–112
Bezos, Jeff
boldness of, 148, 149, 151,
152–153, 166
on customer obsession, 43, 45,
51–55, 57
existential purpose driven by, 33–34
experiential development under,
138–139
mentoring by, 75
mentor to, 71
origin story of, 91–92
Pygmalion effect of, 63, 64, 75
on start-up vs. established mindset,
83, 86–87, 91–92, 93,
95–96, 98
on success, 17–18
on tempo management, 105–106,
111
Bickert, Monika, 137
bimodal operations, 123–144
advantages of, 124–127

CAD use in, 131, 140, 143–144
compression for efficiency in,
124–134, 143–144
delegation and outsourcing in, 124,
130–131, 141
derivative opportunities in, 141
example of value of, 123–124
experiential development in, 124,
125–127, 128, 134–144
frequent milestones in, 137–138
mixed modes in, 143–144
multifunctional teams in, 142, 143
multiple options in, 134–136
for new product development, 128
overplanning in, 139–140
overview of, 9, 15–16, 124–127,
144
planning and monitoring in,
128–130, 133, 139–140,
143
powerful project leadership in,
138–139
schedule-based incentive avoidance
in, 142–143
shortening design stages in,
131–132
simplicity of innovation in,
132–134
of Starbucks, 196
tempo management vs., 124, 126
testing in, 136–137
Bing, 21
Black, Benjamin, 148, 149
BlackBerry, 112–113
Blockbuster, 54, 87–89, 110, 161–162,
166
boldness, 147–166
for agile innovation, 9, 16
clarity with, 164–166

conformity vs., 150–151, 152,
    161–162, 166
creating bold organizations,
    150–151
development of, 155–156
emotions driving, 9, 156
employee engagement with, 150,
    162–164, 165, 166
example of value of, 147–148
for failing project discontinuance,
    151, 154, 159–160
fear of failure hampering, 156
leaders embodying, 151–153, 166
organizational, 151–155
overview of, 9, 16, 166
pulling back with, 157–161, 166
risk aversion, risk reduction, and,
    155–156, 161–162
simplified organizational structure
    for, 155, 166
of Starbucks, 197–198
strategic benefits of, 149–150
sunk cost fallacy resistance with,
    153–155, 159, 166
Bonchek, Mark, 11
Boring Company, 149–150
Brightline Transformation Compass,
    228n195
Brooks, Arthur, 156
Bumble, 16, 70, 109, 160–161, 186
bureaucracy
    agile innovation vs., 2–3, 6, 189
    existential purpose lost in, 191
    start-up mindset vs., 86–90, 101,
        194
    subtraction to avoid load of, 11–12
Businessweek, 78

C

CAD (computer-aided design), 131,
    140, 143–144
Cambridge Analytica, 39
Campbell, Bill, 71
Campbell, Joseph, 85
Casey, Tom, 88, 161
Causeit, Inc., 11
change. *See also* transformation
    resistance to, 3, 24, 26
    tempo management of, 9, 15, 103–
        121, 124, 126, 194–196
Charan, Ram, 156
Citadel, 12
Clark, Dave, 108
Clear, James, 11
cocreation, 45–47, 51–52, 58–59,
    162–163, 205–208
collaboration
    difficulty of, 168–170
    existential purpose supporting, 23,
        27
    Pygmalion effect encouraging, 15,
        69–70
    radical, 9, 16, 167–187, 199–200
Columbia Business School, 11
Compaq, 75
compression
    advantages of, 124–127
    in bimodal operations, 124–134,
        143–144
    delegation and outsourcing in, 124,
        130–131
    experiential development combined
        with, 143–144
    for new product development, 128
    planning and monitoring in,
        128–130, 133
    shortening design stages in,
        131–132

simplicity of innovation in, 132–134
computer-aided design (CAD), 131, 140, 143–144
conformity
  boldness vs., 150–151, 152, 161–162, 166
  controlled chaos vs., 12
controlled chaos, 12–13, 119–120
Cook, Tim, 33, 75, 114, 217n26
core values. *See* values, core
Cornell University, 83
COVID-19 pandemic, effects of, 3–4, 7, 10, 90, 120, 180
crowdsourced judgments, 167–168
culture
  of belonging, 69–71
  of boldness, 162, 166 (*see also* boldness)
  of collaboration, 170, 176, 178–179, 186–187 (*see also* collaboration)
  of customer obsession, 60 (*see also* customer obsession)
  of employees' voices being heard, 76
  existential purpose changing, 27
  of feedback, 77–79
  fit tied to organizational, 65–67
  identity and, 66–67
  of learning, 67–69
  megatrends reflecting, 205–206
  mentoring as reinforcement of, 74–75
  performance requirements in, 71–72, 163, 164–165
  Pygmalion effect on, 8–9, 14–15, 61–79, 193, 200, 208
  start-up (*see* start-up mindset)
  of trust and autonomy, 73–74, 114, 163, 179

Cuomo, Margaret, 167
customer insights, 201, 205–208
customer obsession, 43–60
  cocreation and, 45–47, 51–52, 58–59, 162–163, 205–208
  customer service and, 50, 56–58
  data for, 47, 49, 52, 54, 58–59, 192, 201, 205–208
  definition of, 45
  empathetic imagination and, 46, 47–48, 49, 51, 52–55, 206–207
  employee engagement in, 44–45, 50, 54, 55–56, 59, 60
  entire experience and, 49–51
  error response and complaint avoidance with, 56–58
  example of value of, 43–45
  existential purpose and, 43, 45, 55
  as innovation driver, 8, 43, 49–55, 60
  internal enforcement of, 55–56
  overview of, 8, 14, 45–46, 60
  at Starbucks, 192
  use of product and, 49
  zero-distance policy with, 44

D

data analytics, 207. *See also under* customer obsession
DBS (originally Development Bank of Singapore), 88–89
decision-making
  collaborative, 175, 178–180
  decentralized, 95–97, 117–118
  disagree and commit process of, 13
  subtraction improving, 12
  tempo of, 105–106, 108, 117–118
  transformation operating system for rapid and fluid, 209–210

type-one and type-two, 105–106,
    108
Denning, Steve, 2
Digital Equipment, 84
disagree and commit, 13
diversity, equity, and inclusion, 69–70
Donne, John, 181
Drew, Richard, 98–99
Dumra, Bidyut, 88–89
Dunkin' Donuts, 191

E

Echo, 110, 139, 148, 153
EDS, 83
Eisenhardt, Kathleen, 8, 106
Elop, Stephen, 1–2
emotions
    agile innovation and, 5–7, 9, 53,
        212
    boldness driven by, 9, 156
    customer obsession and, 43, 45, 58
        (*see also* empathetic imagi-
        nation)
    existential purpose aligned with, 36
empathetic imagination, 46, 47–48,
    49, 51, 52–55, 206–207
ESPN, 133
ethnographic analysis, 206–207
Etsy, 120
Evi, 152
existential goals, 28–30, 35, 38
existential purpose/vision, 21–41. *See
    also* North Star
    absence or derailment of, 39–40
    alignment with personal visions
        of staff, 34–38, 41, 79,
        208–209
    boldness clarifying, 164, 197
    changes and refinement of, 28–30,
        40, 41

customer obsession and, 43, 45, 55
    determination of, 31–34
    employees voicing contributions to,
        76
    example of value of, 21–23
    as innovation driver, 8, 26–27, 31,
        34, 41
    internalization of, 34–38, 41, 79,
        208–209
    motivation from, 26–27, 41
    operationalization of, 27–30, 35,
        38, 203–205
    overview of, 8, 14, 23–25, 41
    philosophy and psychology on,
        24–25
    scale/scope of, 31–32, 41
    of Starbucks, 190–192, 193–194,
        197, 200, 205
    start-up mindset and, 85–86, 92–
        93, 100–101, 193–194
experiential development
    advantages of, 124, 125–127
    in bimodal operations, 124,
        125–127, 128, 134–144
    CAD overuse in, 140
    caveats and dangers for, 139–141
    compression combined with,
        143–144
    derivative products during, 141
    frequent milestones in, 137–138
    multifunctional teams for, 142, 143
    multiple options in, 134–136
    for new product development, 128
    overplanning for, 139–140
    powerful project leadership in,
        138–139
    schedule-based incentive avoidance
        in, 142–143
    supplier reliance concerns for, 141
    testing in, 136–137

experts, as management, 67–69,
    172–173
ExxonMobil, 78
EyeGaze, 180

F

Facebook (now Meta), 1, 39–40, 89,
    136–137, 150–151, 183
Federal Trade Commission, US, 39
FedEx, 108
Fire Phone, 138–139, 148, 151, 152
first principles, 10–11, 164
focus groups, 207
Ford, Henry, 11, 14, 46
Ford Motor Company, 129
Frankl, Viktor, 25

G

Galatea, 62–63
Gallup, 77, 89
Galton, Francis, 167
Gambit Energy Storage, 32
Gandhi, Mohandas, 165–166
Gartner, 123
Gateway, 51
General Electric, 12
General Motors, 149
Gerstner, Lou, 83–84
Geshuri, Arnnon, 65–66
GitHub, 177
Gleeson, Scott, 103–104, 111–112
Goethe, Johann Wolfgang von, 147
Google
    Amazon and, 111
    innovation decline at, 1
    Microsoft and, 21, 154, 177
    Myspace and, 183
    recruitment from, 65
    start-up mindset of, 89, 99
Great Resignation, 4

Griffin, Ken, 12
Grossman, David, 83–85, 90
Grove, Andrew, 109–110
Guy, Kyle, 103

H

Haier
    Air Cube by, 44
    customer obsession of, 43–45, 55
    decentralized microenterprises of,
        30, 43–44, 55, 73, 96,
        171, 173
    employee autonomy at, 73,
        171–172
    existential purpose and goals of,
        29–30, 41
    Pygmalion effect at, 73
    radical collaboration at, 171–172,
        173, 178, 187
    start-up mindset of, 96
Hansen, Morten, 68
Hart, Greg, 75, 152
Harvard Business Review, 7, 10
Harvard Business School, 194
Hastings, Reed, 66, 163
Haugen, Frances, 40
Heidegger, Martin, 25
hero's journey, 85–86, 91, 100
Hero with a Thousand Faces, The
    (Campbell), 85
Hsieh, Tony, 183
Hunter, De'Andre, 103

I

IBM, 75, 83–85, 98, 185
Inditex, 46, 113. *See also* Zara
innovation. *See* agile innovation
Inside-Out Effect, The (Tabrizi), 36,
    228n195

inside-out employee transformation, 201, 208–209
Intel
    AMD and, 65, 130, 159–160
    Apple and, 114
    disagree and commit at, 13
    IBM and, 83
    tempo management of, 109–110
interviews, customer, 207
intrapreneurship, 98–100
iPads, 32, 33, 172, 177
iPhones, 14, 32, 131, 135–136, 158, 172, 177
iPods, 32, 136, 158, 194
Isaacson, Walter, 6
Ive, Jony, 48

J
Jackson, Scoop, 133
Jassy, Andy, 51, 59, 148, 154
Jerome, Ty, 103
Jobs, Steve
    boldness of, 157–159
    on empathetic imagination, 47–48
    on employee autonomy, 73–74
    existential purpose driven by, 31–32, 204, 217n26
    experiential development driven by, 135–136
    mentoring by, 75
    personality and passions of, 6–7, 61, 71
    Pygmalion effect of, 61–62, 63, 64, 67–69, 73–74, 75
    radical collaboration supported by, 172–173
    start-up mindset of, 92–93, 94
    on subtraction, 94
Johnson, Kevin, 196
Johnson, Ron, 68–69, 158–159

Jones, Tom, 194
Jope, Alan, 155
Joyo, 52

K
Kamangar, Salar, 99
Kanter, Rosabeth Moss, 10
KBank, 38
Kierkegaard, Søren, 24
Kindle, 22, 53–54, 57, 148, 151
King, Martin Luther, Jr., 166
Kiva Systems, 129
Koehn, Nancy, 194
KPMG, 76
Kurani, Sanjay, 35

L
Lattice, 176
leadership and management. *See also specific leaders*
    agile innovation by (*see* agile innovation)
    boldness embodied by, 151–153, 166
    as coaches, 71, 72
    collaboration of, 168–169, 174–175, 180–182, 184–185
    command-and-control structure of, 3
    of experiential development projects, 138–139
    experts as, 67–69, 172–173
    meta-agility of, 10
    Pygmalion effect of, 63–64 (*see also* Pygmalion effect)
Learning Tools for OneNote, 180
Limp, Dave, 117
LinkedIn, 89, 155
Linux, 23
lions, tempo management by, 104–106,

108–111, 195
listening, 14, 25, 43–45, 50, 95,
    199–200, 203

M
Macintosh computers, 136, 157, 172
management. *See* leadership and man-
    agement
May, Rollo, 25
McCord, Patty, 78
McDonald's, 191
McGrath, Rita Gunther, 11
McKinsey, 175
McKnight, William, 98–99
megatrends, 201, 205–208
mentoring, 15, 71, 74–75
Messi, Lionel, 107
Meta (formerly Facebook), 1, 39–40,
    89, 136–137, 150–151, 183
meta-agility, 10
Metamorphoses (Ovid), 62
Microsoft. *See also* Nadella, Satya
    acquisitions by, 1, 154–155
    agile innovation of, 189
    Apple and, 21, 23, 49, 177
    boldness of, 153–155, 166
    customer obsession of, 49
    existential purpose of, 22–23, 24,
        26–27, 28–29, 34, 38, 41
    Facebook (Meta) and, 39
    IBM and, 83, 84–85, 98
    innovation decline at, 21–22,
        23–24, 26
    listening to employees at, 203
    Office by, 21–22, 154, 177
    Partner [Cloud Partner] Program,
        177–178
    performance reviews at, 77, 179
    radical collaboration at, 177–182,
        186–187

Starbucks and, 191
    tempo management of, 116
    Windows by, 21–22, 154, 177
    Windows Phone by, 21–22, 177
Minnesota Mining and Manufacturing
    (3M), 98–99
monitoring, 74, 128–130
multi-case theory building, 8
Musk, Elon
    bimodal operations of, 123
    boldness of, 149–150, 151, 153,
        164–165, 166
    customer obsession of, 58
    existential purpose driven by, 31
    first principles applied by, 11, 164
    performance requirements of, 71
    Pygmalion effect of, 63, 64, 65–66,
        71
    radical collaboration supported by,
        170
    start-up mindset of, 97, 100–102
    on tech company innovation de-
        cline, 1
    tempo management of, 111, 112,
        119
Myspace, 183–184

N
Nadella, Satya
    boldness of, 154–155
    existential purpose driven by,
        22–23, 24, 27, 38
    listening of, 203
    on organizational structures, 116
    radical collaboration under,
        177–182
    transformation under, 190
    on usability, 49
Narasimhan, Laxman, 200
NATO, 165

Neal, Jessica, 72, 78, 116–117
Netflix
  boldness of, 161–162, 163–164
  cultural fit at, 66–67
  employee trust at, 73–74
  performance requirements at, 72,
    163–164
  performance reviews at, 78
  Pygmalion effect at, 66–67, 72,
    73–74, 78
  start-up mindset of, 87–88, 89
  tempo management of, 113,
    116–117
Neumann, Adam, 184–185
Neuralink, 149
Next, 6, 93
Nietzsche, Friedrich, 21, 24
Nike, 4–5, 132–134
Nokia, 1–2, 90, 154, 161
North Star, 8, 27–28, 33, 34–38, 201,
    203–205. See also existential
    purpose/vision

O

Office (Microsoft), 21–22, 154, 177
Onward (Schultz), 194
Opendoor, 1
organizational structure. See also bu-
    reaucracy; teams
  boldness with simplified, 155, 166
  Haier's decentralized, 30, 43–44,
    55, 73, 96, 171, 173
  radical collaboration affected by, 16,
    168–176, 178, 178–180,
    182–184, 187
  startup mindset and, 96 (see also
    under bureaucracy)
  tempo management supported by,
    115, 116–119

Ortega, Amancio
  on cocreation, 46–47, 162–163
  Pygmalion effect of, 75
  start-up mindset of, 91, 92, 94, 98
outsourcing, 114, 124, 130–131, 141,
    147
Ovid, 62

P

Pan Am, 90
Patrick, John, 84–85
Paulus, Diane, 103
Peloton, 120
Pepsi, 67
Peretz, Marissa, 64
performance requirements, 71–72,
    163, 164
performance reviews, 15, 38, 77–79,
    179
perpetual innovation. See agile inno-
    vation
Pixar, 159
Podolny, Joel, 68
Polman, Paul, 155
Prime, 34, 52–54, 57
Project Management Institute,
    228n195
purpose. See existential purpose/vision;
    North Star
Pygmalion (sculptor), 9, 14, 62–63
Pygmalion effect, 61–79
  on crafting sense of belonging,
    69–71
  on cultural fit, 65–67
  example of value of, 61–62
  on experts as managers, 67–69
  on giving employees a voice, 76
  as innovation driver, 8–9, 79
  on inside-out employee transforma-
    tion, 208

on mentoring, 71, 74–75
overview of, 8–9, 14–15, 62–64, 79
on performance requirements,
71–72
on performance reviews, 77–79
on recruitment of talent, 61–62,
64–65
scale of, 62–64
at Starbucks, 193, 200
on trust and autonomy, 73–74

Q
Qingdao Refrigerator Company, 29
quiet quitting, 4, 87

R
radical collaboration, 167–187
for agile innovation, 9, 170, 173,
187
with competitors and suppliers,
177–178, 186
crowdsourced judgments and,
167–168
cultivating culture of, 170, 176,
178–179, 187
definition of, 169
difficulty of, 168–170
employee autonomy and, 171–172,
174–175
employees with energy for, 176–
177
failure to achieve, 183–185
leadership for, 168–169, 174–175,
180–182, 184–185
limits of, 182–183
organizational structure effects
on, 16, 168–176, 178,
178–180, 182–184, 187
outside organization, 177–178, 186
overview of, 9, 16, 186–187

principles of, 186–187
promotion and implementation of,
185–186
readiness for, 169–170
at Starbucks, 199–200
teams for, 174–176
Randolph, Marc, 66
rapid response teams, 209–210
Rapid Transformation (Tabrizi),
228n195
Reardon, Kathleen, 156
recruitment
for cultural fit, 65–67
diversity, equity, and inclusion in,
69–70
of experts as managers, 67–69
Pygmalion effect on, 61–62, 64–65
of volunteer champions, 210–212
Renault, 111
"Rendanheyi" philosophy, 44
Rilke, Rainer Maria, 23
robotics, 129–130
Ross, JD, 1

S
Sagan, Carl, 21
Salesforce, 177, 178
Samsung, 177
Santa Clara Valley Medical Center
(SCVMC), 27, 35–38, 204
Sartre, Jean-Paul, 25
Schmidt, Eric, 71
Schultz, Howard
bimodal operations of, 196
boldness of, 197–198
customer obsession of, 192
existential purpose driven by,
190–192, 193–194, 197,
200, 205

Pygmalion effect of, 193, 200
radical collaboration under,
    199–200
Starbucks transformation under,
    189–200, 203, 204–205
start-up mindset of, 193–194
tempo management of, 194–196
Schwartz, Mark, 13
ScienceSoft, 178
Sculley, John, 67, 157–158
SCVMC (Santa Clara Valley Medical
    Center), 27, 35–38, 204
See (television series), 1
SEE (Strengths-Evokes-Elates) frame-
    work, 36, 208
Seeing AI, 180
Segall, Ken, 48
Selipsky, Adam, 59
Shiv, Baba, 12
Shotwell, Gwynne, 123
Shu, Patty, 61–62
single-threaded leaders, 117–118, 175
Sondergaard, Peter, 123
SpaceX, 11, 64, 123–124, 149, 153
Stanford University, 7, 12
Starbucks
    bimodal operations of, 196
    boldness of, 197–198
    case study of, 16, 189–200, 203,
        204–205
    customer obsession at, 192
    existential purpose of, 190–192,
        193–194, 197, 200, 205
    Pygmalion effect at, 193, 200
    radical collaboration at, 199–200
    start-up mindset of, 193–194
    tempo management of, 194–196
    unionization at, 198, 199–200
start-up mindset, 83–102
    beginner's mind for, 97

customer obsession and, 51
Day 1 mindset as, 93–94, 108
Day 2 mindset vs., 86–90, 108
decentralized decisions with, 95–97
employee engagement with, 86,
    89–90, 95–96, 98–101
example of value of, 83–85
existential purpose and, 85–86,
    92–93, 100–101, 193–194
hero's journey and, 85–86, 91, 100
lean and simple approach with, 94
as missionary mindset, 92–93
origin stories for, 91–92
overview of, 9, 15, 85–86, 102
pivoting back to, 93–94
spreading of, 98–100
of Starbucks, 193–194
subtraction and, 94
of Tesla, 100–102
Strasser, Rob, 4–5
Su, Lisa, 64–65, 72, 159–160, 185–
    186
subtraction, 11–12, 94
sunk costs, 3, 6, 153–155, 159, 166,
    204
Sun Microsystems, 83–84
surveys, customer, 45, 47, 207
Sutton, Bob, 104

T
teams
    collaborative, 174–176 (*see also*
        collaboration)
    multifunctional, in bimodal opera-
        tions, 142, 143
    rapid response, 209–210
tempo management, 103–121
    for agile innovation, 9, 15, 111–
        113, 124

alertness importance to, 108–109
barrier elimination for, 116–117
bimodal operations vs., 124, 126
breadth of vision and, 110–111
cadence of, 115–116
controlled chaos and, 119–120
control of, 111–113, 114, 121
employee management and, 109,
    110, 113–114, 115–119
example of value of, 103–104
frequent check-ins supporting, 119
goal clarity influencing, 118–119
importance of, 104–105
inefficiencies purged for, 117–118
internal control and integration for,
    114
lion analogy of, 104–106, 108–111,
    195
organizational structure and pro-
    cesses supporting, 115,
    116–119
overview of, 9, 15, 121
paranoia importance to, 109–110
resource allocation and, 113–114,
    195
for sprint readiness, 107–108
of Starbucks, 194–196
star focus and, 113–114
Tesla. *See also* Musk, Elon
agile innovation of, 189, 200
boldness of, 149–150, 153,
    164–165
cultural fit at, 65–67
customer obsession of, 49–50, 51,
    58
existential purpose of, 31–32, 41,
    100–101
performance requirements at, 71,
    72, 164–165
performance reviews at, 77

Pygmalion effect at, 64, 65–67, 71,
    72, 77
radical collaboration at, 170, 179,
    187
recruitment at, 64, 65–67
start-up mindset of, 100–102
tempo management of, 111, 112,
    114, 119
3M, 98–99
Toyota, 97
transformation
to agile innovation (*see* agile innova-
    tion)
bimodal operations driving, 9,
    15–16, 123–144, 196
boldness driving, 9, 16, 147–166,
    197–198
building blocks for path to,
    200–212
customer obsession driving, 8, 14,
    43–60, 162–163, 192,
    201, 205–208
existential purpose driving (*see*
    existential purpose)
key principles for, 202–203
Pygmalion effect driving, 8–9,
    14–15, 61–79, 193, 200,
    208
radical collaboration driving, 9, 16,
    167–187, 199–200
Starbucks case study of, 16,
    189–200, 203, 204–205
start-up mindset driving, 9, 15, 51,
    83–102, 193–194
tempo management driving, 9,
    15, 103–121, 124, 126,
    194–196
transformation operating system,
    201–202, 209–210
trust, culture of, 73–74, 114, 163, 179

Tryer Center, 196
Twitter, 151

U

Unilever, 155
United States Postal Service (USPS),
    108–109
University of Maryland at Baltimore
    County Retrievers, 103–104
University of Virginia Cavaliers,
    103–104, 108, 110, 111–112,
    113, 114, 119–121
unlearning and reconfiguring mental
    models, 11
UPS, 108
usability data, 49
USA Today, 103

V

values, core
    existential purpose and, 28–29, 35,
        38, 40, 191–192
    Pygmalion effect reflecting, 63–64,
        79, 193
vertical integration, 114
Virginia Cavaliers, 103–104, 108, 110,
    111–112, 113, 114, 119–121
virtual reality, 23, 40, 150
vision. *See* existential purpose/vision;
    North Star
volunteer champions, 202, 210–212

W

Walker, Daniel, 61–62, 78
Wang, Cliff, 35
Welch, Jack, 12–13
WeWork, 184–185
Whirlpool, 99–100
Whitwam, David, 99
Whole Foods, 34, 53–54

Williams-Sonoma, 61
Windows (Microsoft), 21–22, 154, 177
Winterson, Jeanette, 61
wisdom of crowds, 167–168
Wolfe Herd, Whitney, 70, 109,
    160–161, 186
World Trade Organization, 30
Wozniak, Steve, 157

X

Xerox, 90
Xilinx, 130–131

Y

Yahoo, 183
Yalom, Irvin, 25

Z

Zappos, 183
Zara. *See also* Ortega, Amancio
    compression at, 131–132
    customer obsession and cocreation
        at, 46–47, 59, 162–163
    employee engagement and boldness
        of, 162–163
    Pygmalion effect at, 75
    start-up mindset of, 91, 94, 95
    tempo management of, 112, 113
Zelensky, Volodymyr, 165
ZeniMax, 155
zero-distance policy, 44
Zhang, Sophie, 40
Zhang Ruimin, 29
Zook, Chris, 98
Zuckerberg, Mark, 40, 136–137